THE DEUTERONOMIC HISTORY AND
THE BOOK OF CHRONICLES

Society of Biblical Literature

Ancient Israel and Its Literature

Number 6

THE DEUTERONOMIC HISTORY AND
THE BOOK OF CHRONICLES
Scribal Works in an Oral World

Volume Editor
Steven L. McKenzie

THE DEUTERONOMIC HISTORY AND THE BOOK OF CHRONICLES

Scribal Works in an Oral World

by

Raymond F. Person Jr.

Society of Biblical Literature
Atlanta

THE DEUTERONOMIC HISTORY AND THE BOOK OF CHRONICLES
Scribal Works in an Oral World

Copyright © 2010 by the Society of Biblical Literature

Library of Congress Cataloging-in-Publication Data

Person, Raymond F.
  The deuteronomic history and the book of Chronicles : scribal works in an oral world / by Raymond F. Person, Jr.
      p. cm. — (Society of Biblical Literature ancient Israel and its literature ; v. 6)
    Includes bibliographical references and index.
    ISBN 978-1-58983-517-7 (paper binding : alk. paper) — ISBN 978-1-58983-518-4 (electronic : alk. paper)
    1. Bible. O.T. Former Prophets—Criticism, interpretation, etc. 2. Bible. O.T. Chronicles—Criticism, interpretation, etc. I. Title.
  BS1286.5.P47   2010
  222'.606—dc22

                          2010028281

          17 16 15 14 13 12 11 10   5 4 3 2 1

CONTENTS

ABBREVIATIONS

AB	Anchor Bible
ABD	*Anchor Bible Dictionary.* Edited by David Noel Freedman. 6 vols. New York: Doubleday, 1992.
AOAT	Alter Orient und Altes Testament
BEATAJ	Beiträge zur Erforschung des Alten Testaments und des antiken Judentum
BETL	Bibliotheca ephemeridum theologicarum lovaniensium
BibInt	*Biblical Interpretation*
BIOSCS	*Bulletin of the International Organization for Septuagint and Cognate Studies*
BZ	*Biblische Zeitschrift*
BZAW	Beihefte zur Zeitschrift für die alttestamentliche Wissenschaft
CahRB	Cahiers de la Revue biblique
CBQ	*Catholic Biblical Quarterly*
FAT	Forschungen zum Alten Testament
FRLANT	Forschungen zur Religion und Literatur des Alten und Neuen Testaments
HAR	*Hebrew Annual Review*
HS	*Hebrew Studies*
HSM	Harvard Semitic Monographs
HTR	*Harvard Theological Review*
IDBSup	*The Interpreter's Dictionary of the Bible: Supplementary Volume.* Edited by Keith Crim. Nashville: Abingdon, 1976.
JBL	*Journal of Biblical Literature*
JNSL	*Journal of Northwest Semitic Languages*
JQR	*Jewish Quarterly Review*
JSOT	*Journal for the Study of the Old Testament*
JSOTSup	Journal for the Study of the Old Testament: Supplement Series
NCB	New Century Bible Commentary
OBO	Orbis biblicus et orientalis
OTL	Old Testament Library
SBLMS	Society of Biblical Literature Monograph Series
SBLSCS	Society of Biblical Literature Septuagint and Cognate Studies
SemeiaSt	Semeia Studies
SJOT	*Scandinavian Journal of the Old Testament*

SSN	Studia semitica neerlandica
STDJ	Studies on the Texts of the Desert of Judah
VT	*Vetus Testamentum*
VTSup	Vetus Testamentum Supplements
WUNT	Wissenschaftliche Untersuchungen zum Neuen Testament
ZAW	*Zeitschrift für die alttestamentliche Wissenschaft*

PREFACE

As any author is fully aware, a large project like this book is the result of the influence of many previous authors, teachers, colleagues, friends, and family. This project continues research interests I cultivated while a doctoral student at Duke University. In my dissertation I drew significantly from text-critical studies and their impact on redactional issues, including the work of Graeme Auld and Julio Trebolle.[1] Auld's and Trebolle's publications continue their influence here. I first encountered the work of Milman Parry and Albert Lord while a doctoral student and then had the opportunity to attend the National Endowment of the Humanities Summer Seminar on Oral Tradition in Literature directed by John Miles Foley in 1991. The influence of the Parry-Lord-Foley approach to oral traditions and orally derived literature also continues its influence here.

This project, however, also breaks some new ground. The response to my earlier monograph, *The Deuteronomic School: History, Social Setting, and Literature*, both positive and negative, seemed to beg for this project.[2] The negative evaluations required a response, especially in terms of the consensus model of historical linguistics. The positive evaluations required a response, especially in terms of how a later dating of the Deuteronomic History affected the question of its relationship to other works, especially the book of Chronicles. Robert Rezetko provided me with the initial opportunity to explore these questions in an essay for a Festschrift for Graeme Auld.[3] In my final stages of writing this essay I had the opportunity to present the work as a guest lecture to the Korean Old Testament Society meeting at Yonsei University, Seoul, South Korea, on July 18, 2006. Yoon Jong Yoo of Pyeongtaek University reproduced the text of my lecture in two columns, my English text with his Korean translation,

---

1. Raymond F. Person Jr., *Second Zechariah and the Deuteronomic School* (JSOTSup 167; Sheffield: Sheffield Academic Press, 1993).

2. Raymond F. Person Jr., *The Deuteronomic School: History, Social Setting, and Literature* (Studies in Biblical Literature 2; Atlanta: Society of Biblical Literature, 2002).

3. Raymond F. Person Jr., "The Deuteronomic History and the Books of Chronicles: Contemporary Competing Historiographies," in *Reflection and Refraction: Studies in Biblical Historiography in Honour of A. Graeme Auld* (ed. Robert Rezetko, Timothy H. Lim, and W. Brian Aucker; VTSup 133; Leiden: Brill, 2006), 315–36.

to facilitate my lecture. He then translated during the following hour-long question-and-answer session. My interaction with the society members was invigorating and rewarding. I am especially thankful for the translating that Yoon Jong Yoo did to help my lecture be such a success as well as the hospitality that the society members granted me, my wife, and my friends, the family of Moon Ki Choi, who attended the meeting with me.

Although Rezetko's own work had provided me with a helpful perspective concerning criticisms of my thesis from the perspective of historical linguistics, this project has been especially reinvigorated by the recent publication of the two-volume work *Linguistic Dating of Biblical Texts* by Ian Young, Robert Rezetko, and Martin Ehrensvärd.[4] I am confident that this work will bring a much-needed reexamination of how we approach the diachronic study of Biblical Hebrew, and I have profited from various conversations with the authors, especially Rezetko and Young. Although I devote an entire chapter to their work and its bearing on my topic, I am nevertheless aware that my summary does not nuance their arguments as well as their own writing. Therefore, I encourage readers to become familiar with *Linguistic Dating of Biblical Texts*.

Although we continue to disagree with each other in print, Steven McKenzie has supported me in my research as a friend and colleague. I am especially thankful that he is acting as the editor of this series, so that he is directly related to the publication of this work. His insights and challenges have helped me sharpen my arguments as he and I continue respectfully to disagree.

The topic of this work can be difficult, especially if readers do not have a good synopsis of Samuel–Kings and Chronicles before them. Unfortunately most synopses do not include the parallels from LXX Samuel–Kings. Although I provide some sample synopses in English translation, I think readers will profit by having a thorough synopsis available to them as they read my work. For my own work I used Accordance Bible Software, which provided me with various helpful synopses in Hebrew, Greek, and English. For readers who are limited to English, I recommend the synopsis edited by John Endres et al. for the comparison of MT Samuel–Kings and MT Chronicles with consultation of *A New English Translation of the Septuagint* for LXX Samuel–Kings (= 1–4 Reigns).[5] In this work I consistently use the English versification. The English translations are my own unless otherwise noted.

---

4. Ian Young, Robert Rezetko, and Martin Ehrensvärd, *Linguistic Dating of Biblical Texts* (2 vols.; London/Oakville, Conn.: Equinox, 2008).

5. John C. Endres et al., *Chronicles and Its Synoptic Parallels in Samuel, Kings, and Related Biblical Texts* (Collegeville, Minn.: Liturgical Press, 1998); Albert Pietersma and Benjamin G. Wright, *A New English Translation of the Septuagint* (Oxford: Oxford University Press, 2009; also at http://ccat.sas.upenn.edu/nets/edition/).

I have chosen not to spend a lot of time with extensive reviews of secondary literature, especially concerning text criticism. One possible unfortunate consequence could be an impression that the text-critical evidence is more univocal than it is. I am certainly aware that not all text critics will agree with the text-critical works on which I based my arguments, and occasionally I refer to contrary studies. However, I urge readers who are interested in the text-critical issues to explore the secondary sources I use more thoroughly. In these works readers will find further references to various opinions concerning the text-critical evidence.

As readers will become aware, I am skeptical about our ability to discern various sources behind these works and the different redactional layers, especially when text-critical evidence is lacking. One consequence of this skepticism is my decision to avoid in this work recent discussions of the diachronic development of the Deuteronom(ist)ic History and its parts (especially Deuteronomy) in relation to the other pentateuchal sources in Genesis–Numbers. This is not because I am unaware of these issues, but primarily because it is far beyond the scope of the present work.[6]

I want to thank various individuals who contributed directly in one way or another to this project. Leigh Andersen of the Society of Biblical Literature encouraged me to submit this project for consideration, and she and her staff have been helpful in its development. Other SBL members have helped me clarify my position when they responded to related papers I have presented in various sections of the annual meeting, including the Deuteronomistic History section, the Chronicles–Ezra–Nehemiah section, and the Orality, Textuality, and the Formation of the Hebrew Bible section. The following have read earlier drafts of my manuscript and provided beneficial feedback: Steven McKenzie, Thomas Römer, and Robert Rezetko. The following have provided me with prepublication copies of forthcoming works that proved insightful: Robert Rezetko, Ian Young, Julio Trebolle, David Carr, Ehud Ben Zvi, and Donald Polaski. Brian Holman, one of my students at Ohio Northern University, has capably acted as my copyeditor.

I also want to thank Koninklijke Brill NV and Eisenbrauns for permission to use portions of earlier works in this book as follows.

Portions of the introduction are revisions of Raymond F. Person Jr., "The Deuteronomic History and the Books of Chronicles: Contemporary Competing Historiographies," in *Reflection and Refraction: Studies in Biblical Historiography in Honour of A. Graeme Auld* (ed. Robert Rezetko, Timothy H. Lim,

---

6. For a variety of recent views concerning these issues, see Raymond F. Person Jr. and Konrad Schmid, eds. *Deuteronomy in the Pentateuch, Hexateuch, and the Deuteronomistic History* (FAT; Stuttgart: Mohr Siebeck, forthcoming in 2012).

and W. Brian Aucker; VTSup 113; Leiden: Brill, 2006), 315–36. Permission granted by Koninklijke Brill NV.

Portions of chapter 2 are revisions of sections of Raymond F. Person Jr., *The Deuteronomic School: History, Social Setting, and Literature* (Studies in Biblical Literature 2; Atlanta: Society of Biblical Literature, 2002), chapters 3–4.

Portions of chapter 3 are revisions of Raymond F. Person Jr., "The Story of David and Goliath from the Perspective of the Study of Oral Traditions," in *Celebrate Her for the Fruit of Her Hands: Studies in Honor of Carol L. Meyers* (ed. Charles C. Carter and Karla G. Bolmbach; Winona Lake, Ind.: Eisenbrauns, 2010); and Raymond F. Person Jr., "The Deuteronomic History and the Book of Chronicles: Scribal Works in an Oral World," in *Raising Up a Faithful Exegete: Essays in Honor of Richard D. Nelson* (ed. Kurt L. Noll and Brooks Schramm; Winona Lake, Ind.: Eisenbrauns, 2010), 113–21. Permission granted by Eisenbrauns.

Introduction

The work of Martin Noth has had a significant influence on the scholarship of Deuteronomy through Kings and Chronicles–Ezra–Nehemiah, including the relationship between these collections.[1] One consequence of this influence has been the generally accepted conclusion that the Deuteronomistic History is exilic, the work of the Chronicler is postexilic, and the Chronicler used the Deuteronomistic History as one of its sources. This conclusion has further led to a model that explains the linguistic difference between the Deuteronomistic History and the Chronicler's History as Early Biblical Hebrew and Late Biblical Hebrew, respectively.[2] For example, Isaac Kalimi wrote:

> Since the books of Samuel–Kings were largely composed during the First Temple Period and certainly no later than the Babylonian Exile, the text of Chronicles and its earlier parallels provide an extensive and enlightening example of a later biblical author's editing and adaptation of earlier literary-historiographical sources available to him. The parallel texts thus offer a wealth of material for diachronic research in various fields: linguistic (vocabulary, syntax, morphology, and orthography), textual, and theological-ideological.[3]

Recently, however, these conclusions have been challenged from various perspectives, requiring a thorough reevaluation of the Deuteronomistic History, the Chronicler's History, and their relationship. I will explore

---

1. Martin Noth, *Überlieferungsgeschichtliche Studien* (Tübingen: Niemeyer, 1943). See the excellent discussions of Noth's influence in Steven L. McKenzie and M. Patrick Graham, eds., *The History of Israel's Traditions: The Heritage of Martin Noth* (JSOTSup 182; Sheffield: Sheffield Academic Press, 1994) and in the introductions to the English translations of *Überlieferungsgeschichtliche Studien*: Martin Noth, *The Deuteronomistic History* (trans. E. W. Nicholson; JSOTSup 15; Sheffield: JSOT Press, 1981), vii–x; and Martin Noth, *The Chronicler's History* (trans. H. G. M. Williamson; JSOTSup 50; Sheffield: Sheffield Academic Press, 2001), 11–26.

2. For a brief discussion of the history of the development of this linguistic model and additional bibliographical information, see Ian Young, "Introduction: The Origin of the Problem," in *Biblical Hebrew: Studies in Chronology and Typology* (ed. Ian Young; JSOTSup 369; London: T&T Clark, 2003), 1–6.

3. Isaac Kalimi, *The Reshaping of Ancient Israelite History in Chronicles* (Winona Lake, Ind.: Eisenbrauns, 2005), 1–2.

these challenges and propose that the Deuteronomic History and the book of Chronicles are historiographies from different competing, contemporary scribal groups.

The Deuteronomic History

Until recently Noth's thesis of the Deuteronomistic History has been so widely accepted that its justification was rarely necessary, even though his thesis has undergone various revisions, especially related to the number of Deuteronomistic redactions. Some scholars are now directly challenging Noth's thesis, thereby requiring a reassessment of the influence of Noth upon the study of Deuteronomy through Kings. In this section, I will reexamine Noth's arguments, focusing on two questions. First, can we still speak of a literary unity called the Deuteronom(ist)ic History? Second, when should this work be dated? I will conclude that (1) Deuteronomy through Kings is a literary unity and there is no compelling reason to abandon the label "Deuteronom(ist)ic History" and (2) the redactional work of the Deuteronomic school spanned the exilic and postexilic periods.

Is There a Deuteronom(ist)ic History?

Noth's thesis of the Deuteronomistic History strove to explain both the literary unity and the diversity he saw in Deuteronomy through Kings. Noth's understanding of the literary unity of Deuteronomy through Kings was based on linguistic evidence, literary style, a chronological framework spanning Joshua through Kings, and smooth transitions between the books. The "linguistic uniformity" that Noth perceived in "a 'Deuteronomistic' stratum" of Deuteronomy through Kings included "vocabulary, diction and sentence structure," making the Deuteronomistic style "the simplest Hebrew in the Old Testament."[4] The most important features of the literary style to which Noth refers are the "speeches of anticipation and retrospection" (Josh 1, Josh 23, 1 Sam 12, 1 Kgs 8:14–21), speeches in which there are clear allusions to earlier and/or later events narrated in the Deuteronomistic History.[5] A chronological framework that spans Deuteronomy to Kings is also evident. In Josh 14:10, Joshua refers to the present as "forty-five years since the LORD spoke this word to Moses" and in 1 Kgs 6:1 the date for the building of the temple—"in the four hundred eightieth year after the Israelites came out of the land of Egypt"—connects Kings with Deuteronomy. Noth also noted the smooth transitions between the individual books. In Deut 3:28 Moses refers to Joshua as his suc-

---

4. Noth, *Deuteronomistic History*, 5.
5. Ibid., 5–6, 9.

cessor and in Deut 34:9 Moses lays hands on Joshua. The book of Joshua then begins "After the death of Moses" (Josh 1:1) and the book of Judges, "After the death of Joshua" (Judg 1:1), concluding with "In those days there was no king in Israel; each did what was right in his own eyes" (Judg 21:25). Moreover, Samuel acts as a transitional figure from the judges to the kings.

Although Noth argued for a literary unity of Deuteronomy through Kings, he did not ignore their diversity. He observed that there were, in fact, obvious differences between Deuteronomy and Joshua. Therefore, Noth's thesis allowed for both literary unity and diversity in Deuteronomy through Kings, and, as far as I can tell, his insights on these matters still have tremendous influence even on those who have recently challenged his thesis. These challenges and the revisions that followed Noth's work are not direct challenges of his observation of the literary unity of Deuteronomy through Kings, but of his explanation of how this literary unity was produced. Noth's conclusion was that this unity was the result of the work of one individual, his Deuteronomist. The obvious diversity among the books thus stems from the various sources that the Deuteronomist used in order to construct his history. In this way, Noth not only explicated the literary unity of Deuteronomy through Kings but provided an explanation for how this unity with the continuing diversity came to be—that is, the Deuteronomist brought diverse sources together into one unified literary work.

The two major revisions of Noth's thesis—that is, the dual-redaction school of Frank Moore Cross and others (mostly Americans) and the trito-redaction school of Rudolf Smend, Walter Dietrich, and others (mostly Europeans)—are attempts to explain further the diversity within the Deuteronomistic History.[6] Both schools accept the literary unity of Deuteronomy through Kings and also suggest that this unity is the result of an initial redactor who brought together diverse sources into one literary unity (Dtr^1 or DtrG/DtrH) as well as at least one later redactor who reworked the entire Deuteronomistic History in a similar style (Dtr^2 or DtrP and DtrN). Both schools can therefore provide an additional explanation for the diversity in the Deuteronomistic History. The diversity in each of the redactional levels, especially the earliest, can still be explained by the use of diverse sources, but both schools now can explain the diversity as due additionally to the theological interests or historical circumstances of the different redactors (preexilic, pro-monarchical versus exilic, anti-monarchical; historical versus prophetic versus nomistic). In fact, separating out the redactors according to such diverse interests creates a more unified initial redaction (Dtr^1 and DtrG/DtrH), with each successive redaction

---

6. For a fuller discussion of these schools, see Person, *Deuteronomic School*, 2–4, 31–34.

having its own literary unity based on the redactional interests of the later redactor(s).

Much of the energy in scholarly discussions has been devoted to discerning the different Deuteronomistic redactional layers and issues related to this process (for example, dating the preexilic redaction or how many nomistic redactors there were). However, additional support for the literary unity of Deuteronomy through Kings has been gathered. The best example of such additional support is in the work of Moshe Weinfeld, who has provided an excellent resource on the "linguistic uniformity" that Noth observed in his appendix on "Deuteronomic Phraseology."[7] Weinfeld's appendix spans forty-five pages and includes over one hundred phrases that are found in more than one of the books of the Deuteronomic History. For example, the phrase "to do that which is evil in the sight of the LORD" occurs numerous times in Deuteronomy, Judges, Samuel, Kings, and the prose sermons in Jeremiah but occurs rarely elsewhere. Even a casual look at Weinfeld's appendix reveals significant phraseological similarities among the books of the Deuteronomic History, thereby highlighting their literary connections.

If Noth's thesis was an attempt to explain both the literary unity and diversity in Deuteronomy through Kings, then this has also been the case with those scholars who have recently challenged his thesis. As we will see, all of these challenges acknowledge (even if only implicitly) the literary unity of Deuteronomy through Kings but emphasize the diversity of the books. They also all arrive at different conclusions from Noth concerning the process that produced this literary unity. I will selectively discuss three scholars who recently have challenged Noth's thesis of the Deuteronomistic History, taking them in order of what I see as moving farther and farther from Noth's original thesis.[8]

In his 1994 sketch introducing the collection of his work on the Deuteronomistic History,[9] Ernst Würthwein questioned some basic elements of Noth's thesis. Würthwein argued that the direction of influence ran the opposite way—that is, from Kings to Samuel to Judges to Joshua. Since each book was added in front of the other book(s), each book had a certain independence from the others; however, Joshua through Kings still has a literary unity in that

---

7. Moshe Weinfeld, *Deuteronomy and the Deuteronomic School* (Oxford: Clarendon, 1972), 320–65.

8. See also Thomas Römer's discussion of recent challenges (*The So-Called Deuteronomistic History: A Sociological, Historical and Literary Introduction* [London/New York: T&T Clark, 2007], 35–41). Römer also concludes that the thesis of a Deuteronomistic History remains valid, even though revisions to Noth's original idea are necessary (41).

9. Ernst Würthwein, "Erwägungen zum sog. Deuteronomistischen Geschichtswerk: Eine Skizze," in *Studien zum Deuteronomistischen Geschichtswerk* (BZAW 227; Berlin: Walter de Gruyter, 1994), 1–11.

each book was written to precede the other(s). Even with this revision Würthwein remained within the Göttingen school in his discussion of later revisions
of DtrH by DtrP and DtrN. He basically accepted Noth's understanding of a
literary unity of Joshua through Kings, but explained the origins of this unity
differently (1) by reversing the direction of influence among the books (Kings
to Joshua), (2) by explaining the diversity by giving each book a more independent development, and (3) by drawing on the revision of Noth's thesis by the
Göttingen school of Smend, Dietrich, and Timo Veijola. He did not reject the
literary unity of the Deuteronomistic History, even though he did not explicitly discuss the relationship of Deuteronomy to Joshua through Kings; he simply had a different explanation for how this unity came to be.

     In ways quite similar to Würthwein, Graeme Auld critiqued Noth's thesis
of the Deuteronomistic History.[10] Auld also privileged Kings so that he saw
the literary influence running from Kings to Deuteronomy as each book was
added to the following book(s). In this way (like Würthwein), Auld accepted
the literary unity of Deuteronomy through Kings but rejected Noth's explanation of the origins of this unity (1) by reversing the direction of influence
among the books (Kings to Deuteronomy) and (2) by explaining the diversity
by giving each book a more independent development. Because of his understanding of the origin of this literary unity, Auld rejected the term "Deuteronomistic" to refer to this literary work, noting that Noth's use of the term was
based on his argument that the influence began with Deuteronomy. However,
Auld's rejection of the term "Deuteronomistic" was not a rejection of the literary unity of Deuteronomy through Kings based on linguistic and thematic
similarities. For example, Auld wrote recently "Deuteronomy is intimately
connected to Joshua to Kings; but to call these books Deuteronomistic may be
to misread the direction of influence."[11]

     The recent challenge that has most directly questioned the validity of
Noth's original thesis is that of Ernst Axel Knauf.[12] Knauf did not challenge the

---

10. A. Graeme Auld, "The Deuteronomists and the Former Prophets, Or What Makes
the Former Prophets Deuteronomistic?" in *Those Elusive Deuteronomists: The Phenomenon
of Pan-Deuteronomism* (ed. Linda S. Schearing and Steven L. McKenzie; JSOTSup 268;
Sheffield: Sheffield Academic Press, 1999), 116–26. See also A. Graeme Auld, "The Deuteronomists between History and Theology," in *Congress Volume: Oslo 1998* (ed. A. Lemaire
and M. Sæbø; VTSup 80; Leiden: Brill, 2000), 353–67 (358).
     In ways similar to Würthwein and Auld, Claus Westermann argues for independent
development of each of the books of Joshua through Kings. However, he also allows that
a Deuteronomistic redactor may have worked through these individual books. See Claus
Westermann, *Die Geschichtsbücher des Alten Testaments: Gab es ein deuteronomistisches
Geschichtswerk?* (Theologische Bücherei 87; Gütersloh: Chr. Kaiser, 1994).
     11. Auld, "Deuteronomists between History and Theology," 362–63.
     12. Ernst Axel Knauf, "Does 'Deuteronomistic Historiography' (DH) Exist?" in *Israel*

observation that there is a linguistic similarity between the books of Deuteronomy through Kings. Instead he offered a different explanation for it.

> "Dtr" designates a literary style . . . as well as a group of theological notions such as those of the "conquest of the promised land" and of the "covenant" (that is to say the *b^{e}rit*, which means "vassal treaty"). This style and this theology are both derived from Assyrian imperialism. . . . Since the Dtr texts have been produced over a long period—from the court of Josiah up to the final addition to the book of Jeremiah in the second century BCE—Dtr style conceals a vast multiplicity of theological positions.[13]

If "Dtr style" applies to literature that spans three hundred or more years, then Knauf correctly noted that one individual cannot be the author of this material. Another possible explanation—"a homogeneous group" (that is, the "Dtr school")—Knauf believed to be unlikely. Rather, he argued that this literary style was more widespread based on Assyrian influence on the culture, and he could therefore conclude that there must have been "several 'Dtr schools' with their own texts."[14] Thus, Knauf could account for the unity of this literature based on linguistic similarities by positing that the style was a common one deriving from Assyrian influence and used by various scribal schools. Further, he could account for the diversity among the writings as due to the various individuals or groups in different historical periods who produced the literature using this common style.

In *The Deuteronomic School: History, Social Setting, and Literature*, I revised Noth's thesis of the Deuteronomistic History, drawing from four different perspectives to advance the conversation concerning this literature: (1) the use of text-critical controls for redactional arguments, (2) the contribution of the study of oral tradition to understanding the composition and transmission of biblical texts in ancient Israel, (3) arguments for a postexilic setting for the Deuteronomic History, and (4) the use of comparative material (especially Udjahorresnet and Qumran) to understand scribal guilds in ancient Israel. I argued that, although the Deuteronomic school had its roots in the preexilic bureaucracy of the monarchy, the redaction history of the Deuteronomic History began during the Babylonian exile and continued into the Persian period. Since my understanding of the Deuteronomic History has not changed significantly since the publication of that monograph, below I will simply respond directly to Würthwein, Auld, and Knauf on the issue as a way of providing further clarification of my understanding of the Deuteronomic History.

Constructs Its History: Deuteronomistic Historiography in Recent Research (ed. Albert de Pury, Thomas Römer, and Jean-Daniel Macchi; JSOTSup 306; Sheffield: Sheffield Academic Press, 2000), 388–98.

13. Ibid., 389.

14. Ibid., 393.

Würthwein, Auld, and Knauf all accepted that there is a stylistic similarity in Deuteronomy through Kings. Würthwein accepted the label "Deuteronomistic" for the redaction process that produced this similarity; Auld rejected the term "Deuteronomistic" but nevertheless maintained that Deuteronomy through Kings has a literary unity based on a common redactional history; and Knauf argued that the similarities are strictly due to the cultural norms of the various individuals or schools that produced these works, such that they share no redactional history.

With Würthwein and Auld, I argue that the literary unity of Deuteronomy through Kings is due to a common redactional history. I agree with Auld that, *if* "Deuteronomistic" *requires* Noth's understanding of the literary influence moving from Deuteronomy to Kings, then the term should be rejected. However, I do not think that the term requires this understanding; the term already means in the current literature more than what Noth originally meant by the term. Although I am well aware of the difficulty of translating one scholar's use of "Deuteronomistic" versus another scholar's use,[15] I nevertheless think that the term remains useful, *even though* one must carefully devote significant energy, on the one hand, to explicating what one means by the term and, on the other hand, to understanding what others mean by it. The term does give preference to the book of Deuteronomy when discussing the books of Deuteronomy through Kings, but I think that this choice can be defended synchronically from the perspective of the present canonical work, even if the literary history of the work did not begin with an early form of Deuteronomy. Therefore, although I may have preferred a different term if I had had some say from the beginning, I nevertheless do not have difficulty justifying the continued use of "Deuteronomistic" or "Deuteronomic," when referring to this literature and the group that produced it. However, since I do not share Noth's clear distinction between "Deuteronomic" and "Deuteronomistic," I prefer to use "Deuteronomic" as the simpler of the two terms to refer to all of the literature and its various redactional layers.

Like both Würthwein and Auld, I am not convinced that the influence among the books ran unilinearly from Deuteronomy to Kings, as Noth suggested. Although one may want to give theological privilege to the Mosaic law as presented in Deuteronomy from a synchronic perspective of the present text, this theological privilege certainly does not require an understanding of the redactional history of the written literary work as having begun with an early version of the law. The law may have been primarily in oral tradition or the Deuteronomic version of the law may have come later. It is certainly

---

15. On this problem, see especially Richard Coggins, "What Does 'Deuteronomistic' Mean?" in *Words Remembered, Texts Renewed: Essays in Honor of John F. A. Sawyer* (ed. J. Davies, G. Harvey, and W. G. E. Watson; JSOTSup 195; Sheffield: Sheffield Academic Press, 1995), 135–48.

possible that, as Würthwein and Auld argue, the literary history began with the material most recent to the authors/redactors, who worked backwards from Kings to Joshua and then prefaced this with their understanding of the law in Deuteronomy. My own position, however, is not to give preference to either direction. The redaction history of the Deuteronomic History spanned such a long period of time that I cannot reach an informed opinion about the issue of which of the books was written first. As found in all of the extant texts, the Deuteronomic History betrays such a complex intertextuality among the various books that I suspect that the influence ran in multiple directions over the redaction history of the text such that it is probably impossible to conclude which book was written first. This is also the case at the level of phraseology. For example, the phrase "to do that which is evil in the sight of the LORD" is found numerous times in Deuteronomy, Judges, Samuel, Kings, and the prose sermons in Jeremiah. All of the occurrences of this phrase could not have been written at the same time, so certainly one occurrence of this phrase must have been the first occurrence. However, whenever one reads this phrase wherever it might occur, all of the other occurrences are referenced to some extent, thereby negating any significance of which of these phrases was written first from the perspective of the literature itself. Therefore, even though I would like to know which book or which occurrence of a particular phrase was written first, this is a modern question that is unanswerable unless clear text-critical evidence is available and can provide some limited assistance with a relative chronology for particular occurrences of phrases. We must, therefore, be content with the acknowledgment that the literature betrays significant intertextual influences, which may run in various directions.

I agree with Knauf that the redaction history of the material associated with what he calls the "Dtr style" spans a long period of time. I agree also that the literature betrays a diversity of theological positions. These two observations together certainly suggest that no one individual was responsible for this material, greatly calling into question Noth's idea of the Deuteronomistic Historian and, in my opinion, even the Harvard school's notion of two individuals (Dtr[1] and Dtr[2]). Interestingly, the current understanding of many scholars in the Göttingen school has so many different redactional layers, especially in DtrN, that Knauf's criticism seems not to apply as much to the Göttingen school. Although I agree with Knauf on these points, I think he too easily rejected the idea of the Deuteronomic school. In fact, his entire argument against this possibility is as follows: "it is besides rather unlikely that there would have been just one Dtr school."[16] Why is this so unlikely? And what exactly does he mean by "just one Dtr school"?

---

16. Knauf, "Does 'Deuteronomistic Historiography' (DH) Exist?" 391.

If "just one Dtr school" means only one group of scribes, each one of whom was active when all of the redactional work was done on the Deuteronomic literature, then I would agree that this is unlikely for the same reasons that it is unlikely that one individual in one historical period produced this literature. However, if Knauf means that it is unlikely that some specific group of scribes was organized in such a way as to perpetuate their own basic theological concerns expressed with a certain amount of linguistic uniformity over a long span of time, then I must disagree. It seems to me that very few of the ancients could write, so that there would rarely be more than one scribal school active in one specific location, especially within one specific institution in that location.[17] Since the society required the service of this scribal group for purposes of record keeping as well as for the transmission of whatever authoritative texts there may have been, the school would continue for quite some time by protecting its craft and knowledge from those outside the guild through a careful and regimented training routine. Therefore, significant changes in scribal groups or schools would occur in the context of significant societal change. This certainly differs significantly from Knauf's notion that there were "several 'Dtr schools,'" if by this he means that there were several scribal schools working contemporaneously over a long period of time in the same location.

Würthwein, Auld, and Knauf have correctly identified some problems with Noth's thesis of the Deuteronomistic History; however, none of these problems necessarily requires a full rejection of the core of Noth's thesis—that is, that Deuteronomy through Kings is a literary unity produced by a common redactional process that can be labeled as the Deuteronom(ist)ic History. Therefore, I answer the question "Is there a Deuteronom(ist)ic History?" with an affirmative reply qualified by significant revisions to Noth's original thesis.

WHEN WAS THE DEUTERONOMIC HISTORY REDACTED?

Martin Noth dated his Deuteronomistic Historian to the exilic period:

> He wrote in the middle of the 6th century BCE when the history of the Israelite people was at an end; for the later history of the post-exilic community was a completely different matter—both its internal and external conditions were

---

17. See further, Person, *Deuteronomic School*, 60–63, 98–101. See also Römer, *So-Called Deuteronomistic History*, 45–49; and idem, "Response to Richard Nelson, Steven McKenzie, Eckart Otto, and Yairah Amit," in "In Conversation with Thomas Römer, *The So-Called Deuteronomistic History: A Sociological, Historical, and Literary Introduction*," *Journal of Hebrew Scriptures* 9 (2009): Article 17, 44–45.

different—and it was the Chronicler who first thought of explaining it as a linear continuation of the earlier history of the nation.[18]

Noth's dating—based solely on the assumption that the work was written shortly after the last mentioned event (about 560 B.C.E.)—has been widely accepted, even though few scholars today accept his idea that Deuteronomy through Kings as a literary unity is primarily the redactional work of one individual.[19] Those who argue for two redactions (Dtr^1 and Dtr^2) have accepted Noth's dating and applied it to their last redaction. Those who argue for three (or more) redactions (DtrG, DtrP, DtrN) have generally accepted his dating and applied it to their first two redactions. In other words, both schools' revisions accepted Noth's dating but differ in that one revision postulates a redaction earlier than Noth's exilic work, while the other postulates two (or more) later redactions.

Clearly Noth's argument for dating the Deuteronomistic History to the exile is inadequate, but few scholars have directly questioned his dating. Two exceptions are Robert P. Carroll and Auld. Carroll wrote:

> it should not be assumed that Deuteronomistic circles operated for a brief period and then disappeared; nor should the possibility of a much later (i.e., fifth-century) date for Deuteronomistic activity be ruled out a priori. . . . The termination of the history with an episode from c. 560 (II Kings 25.27–30; cf. Jer. 52.31–34) does not necessarily date the history to the mid-sixth century. It may simply represent a positive ending of the story of the kings of Israel and Judah with a detail from the life of the last living Judean king.[20]

Auld, in his characteristically sardonic style, wrote: "The fact that Kings ends with the fate of Judah's last king tells us no more about the date of composition (generally believed exilic) than the fact that the Pentateuch ends with the death of Moses."[21]

In my own work I have presented various arguments for dating the Deuteronomic school's redactional activity not only to the exilic period,

---

18. Noth, *Deuteronomistic History*, 79.

19. However, see Steven L. McKenzie, "Trouble with Kingship," in *Israel Constructs Its History: Deuteronomistic Historiography in Recent Research* (ed. Albert de Pury, Thomas Römer, and Jean-Daniel Macchi; JSOTSup 306; Sheffield: Sheffield Academic Press, 2000), 286–314. McKenzie argued for the Deuteronomistic Historian as the primary author of the Deuteronomistic History and the only Deuteronomist; however, he allowed for post-Deuteronomistic additions.

20. Robert P. Carroll, *Jeremiah: A Commentary* (OTL; Philadelphia: Westminster, 1986), 67.

21. A. Graeme Auld, "Prophets through the Looking Glass: A Response to Robert Carroll and Hugh Williamson," *JSOT* 27 (1983): 41–44 (44).

but extending into the postexilic period.[22] My redactional arguments make extensive use of text-critical evidence, including post-LXX additions to the MT of various passages in the Deuteronomic History that contain both Deuteronomic phraseology and evidence of postexilic origins.[23] A brief summary of my reconstruction of the Deuteronomic school is as follows: The destruction of Jerusalem and the Babylonian exile produced significant social changes that dramatically impacted earlier institutions, including the scribal guilds. The Deuteronomic school grew out of this social restructuring in Babylon based on the remnants of the preexilic scribal guilds and their existing literature and began to produce Deuteronomic literature based on these preexilic sources. The Deuteronomic school later returned to Jerusalem, probably under Zerubbabel, to provide scribal support for the rebuilding of the temple and in this context continued its redactional activity. In both the exilic period and the early restoration period, the Deuteronomic school thrived with the support of the exiled Judean bureaucracy and the Persian-supported restoration administrations. However, the hopes of the Deuteronomic school relating to the restoration of Israel symbolized by the idealized past glory under David and Solomon went unfulfilled, and increasingly the Deuteronomic school's theology became eschatological.[24] As the Deuteronomic school became increasingly critical of the Persian-supported administration in Jerusalem, the Persian empire needed to respond. The response came in the form of the missions of Ezra and Nehemiah, leading to an undercutting of the social support of the Deuteronomic school and eventually to the school's demise. Ezra and the scribes who accompanied him certainly would have had a different theological perspective, even though they may have had the same beginnings as the Deuteronomic school. In short, the Deuteronomic school began in the Babylonian exilic community, returned to Jerusalem under Zerubbabel, and declined significantly as a result of Ezra's imposition of a different authoritative literature, especially relating to the law of Moses.

This complicated and varied history of the Deuteronomic school over a long period of time would certainly explain the diverse theological perspectives in the literature—that is, this diversity is due to the use of a variety of sources from the preexilic period and beyond as well as the school's changing theology

---

22. See Raymond F. Person Jr., "II Kings 24,18–25,30 and Jeremiah 52: A Text-Critical Case Study in the Redaction History of the Deuteronomistic History," *ZAW* 105 (1993): 174–205; idem, *Second Zechariah and the Deuteronomic School*; idem, *The Kings–Isaiah and Kings–Jeremiah Recensions* (BZAW 252; Berlin: Walter de Gruyter, 1997); and, most importantly, idem, *Deuteronomic School*.

23. See esp. Person, *Deuteronomic School*, chapters 1–2.

24. For my discussion of eschatology in Deuteronomic literature, see Person, *Second Zechariah and the Deuteronomic School*, 177–81.

in light of dramatic historical and social events, such as the Babylonian exile, the restoration of the Jerusalem temple, and the school's displacement by Ezra and his scribes. At the same time, the idea that this same school had a long history explains how Deuteronomic language that betrays what Noth saw as a "linguistic uniformity" is used to express these diverse theological perspectives. That is, even though scribes may continue to use the Deuteronomic phraseology that they were taught by their predecessors, these same scribes must respond theologically to their own times, thereby producing theological perspectives that may differ somewhat from their predecessors. In this way, I strive to explain both the literary unity of Deuteronomy through Kings and the theological and literary diversity in these same books.

Admittedly, the details of my reconstruction of the Deuteronomic school have not been widely accepted; however, my argument that the Deuteronomic school's redactional activity continued over a long period of time and into the Persian period has been described as "highly plausible."[25] Some recent treatments of the Deuteronomic History include discussions of the Deuteronomic school's redactional activity in the Persian period. In *The So-Called Deuteronomistic History*, Thomas Römer devotes an entire chapter to "Editing the Deuteronomistic History during the Persian Period," using my work as the starting point in his discussion.[26] In a recent essay, Jon Berquist accepts the Persian period as a setting for the final redaction of the Deuteronomistic History, referring to Römer's monograph.[27] Both Römer and Berquist argue that the Deuteronomic school used preexilic sources and that its redactional activity spanned the exilic and postexilic periods. They then reconstruct the ideology

---

25. Michael H. Floyd, review of Raymond F. Person Jr., *Second Zechariah and the Deuteronomic School, JBL* 114 (1995): 726. See also Norbert Lohfink, "Gab es eine deuteronomistische Bewegung?" in *Jeremia und die "deuteronomistische Bewegung"* (ed. Walter Groß; Bonner Biblische Beiträge 98. Weinheim: BELTZ Athenäum, 1995), 360, 364; Robert Rezetko, *Source and Revision in the Narratives of David's Transfer of the Ark: Text, Language, and Story in 2 Samuel 6 and 1 Chronicles 13; 15–16* (Library of Biblical Studies 470; London: T&T Clark, 2007), 12, 62–63; Ehud Ben Zvi, "Are There Any Bridges Out There? How Wide Was the Conceptual Gap between the Deuteronomistic History and Chronicles?" in *Community Identity in Judean Historiography: Biblical and Comparative Perspectives* (ed. Gary N. Knoppers and Kenneth A. Ristau; Winona Lake, Ind.: Eisenbrauns, 2009), 84; and Mark A. Christian, "Priestly Power that Empowers: Michel Foucault, Middle-tier Levites, and the Sociology of 'Popular Religious Groups' in Israel," *Journal of Hebrew Scriptures* 9 (2009): Article 1, 30 n. 96.

26. Römer, *So-Called Deuteronomistic History*, 165–83.

27. Jon L. Berquist, "Identities and Empire: Historiographic Questions for the Deuteronomistic History in the Persian Period," in *Historiography and Identity: (Re)formulation in Second Temple Historiographical Literature* (ed. Louis C. Jonker; Library of Hebrew Bible/ Old Testament Studies 534; London: T&T Clark, 2010), 3–13.

of the Deuteronomic school during the Persian period. Although subtle differences remain between our works, Römer and Berquist agree with my general conclusions concerning the Deuteronomic History in the Persian period.[28]

THE CHRONICLER'S HISTORY

Similar to his understanding of the Deuteronomistic History, Noth viewed the books of Chronicles, Ezra, and Nehemiah as a literary unity, the result of the work of a single individual, the Chronicler. The major difference between the Deuteronomistic History and the Chronicler's History was temporal—Noth's exilic Deuteronomistic History ended with the mention of Jehoiachin in exile and his Hellenistic Chronicler's History ended with mention of the missions of Ezra and Nehemiah.[29] In this section, I will reexamine Noth's arguments, focusing on two questions. First, can we speak of a literary unity called the Chronicler's History? [30] Second, when should this work be dated? Drawing on the work of other scholars, I will conclude that (1) Chronicles–Ezra–Nehemiah exhibit a degree of literary unity because of their production within the same scribal school and (2) that Chronicles likely predates Ezra and Nehemiah.

IS THERE A CHRONICLER'S HISTORY?

Noth's thesis of the literary unity of the Chronicler's History (Chronicles–Ezra–Nehemiah) being based on authorship by one individual is still accepted by some scholars;[31] however, his thesis has been revised in various ways, including postulating different Chronistic redactors[32] and understanding Chronicles

---

28. For my discussion of the differences, see Raymond F. Person Jr., review of Thomas Römer, *The So-Called Deuteronomistic History*, CBQ 69 (2007): 561–62; and idem, "Identity (Re)Formation as the Historical Circumstances Required," in *Historiography and Identity: (Re)formulation in Second Temple Historiographical Literature* (ed. Louis C. Jonker; Library of Hebrew Bible/Old Testament Studies 534; London: T&T Clark, 2010), 113–21.

29. Noth, *Chronicler's History*, 69–73.

30. For a recent survey of research on Chronicles, see Rodney K. Duke, "Recent Research in Chronicles," *Currents in Biblical Research* 8 (2009): 10–50.

31. For example, see Klaus Koch, "Weltordnung und Reichsidee im alten Iran und ihre Auswirkungen auf die Province Jehud," in *Reichsidee und Reichsorganisation im Perserreich* (ed. Peter Frei and Klaus Koch; 2nd ed.; OBO 55; Göttingen: Vandenhoeck & Ruprecht, 1996), 133–337.

32. For a review of scholarship on multiple redactions of Chronicles, see Steven L. McKenzie, "The Chronicler as Redactor," *The Chronicler as Author: Studies in Text and Texture* (ed. M. Patrick Graham and Steven L. McKenzie; JSOTSup 263; Sheffield: Sheffield Academic Press, 1999), 71–80.

as independent of Ezra–Nehemiah.[33] Although there are different understandings of how many authors are responsible for the books of Chronicles,
Ezra, and Nehemiah, there remains agreement that there is a certain degree
of literary unity among the books.[34] Therefore, although I cannot agree with
Noth's thesis that one author was responsible for "the Chronicler's History,"
I nevertheless think that discussing Chronicles–Ezra–Nehemiah as coming
from a similar school of thought continues to have credence.[35] In fact, I readily
agree with Rainer Albertz on Chronicles and Jacob Wright on Ezra–Nehemiah. Concerning Chronicles, Albertz wrote that "the literary evidence is best
explained by the assumption of several authors in a closed group of tradents
who were active over a lengthy period."[36] Concerning Ezra–Nehemiah, Wright
concluded that

> the history of the rebuilding of Jerusalem and the consolidation of the province in
> the book of [Ezra–Nehemiah] represents how generations of authors, beginning
> in the mid-Persian period and continuing into the Hasmonean period—long
> after the fourth century—struggled to define the political and ethnic boundaries
> between Judah and its neighbors. [37]

---

33. For an excellent summary of this issue, see Ralph W. Klein, "Chronicles, Books
of 1–2," *ABD* 1:992–1002 (993). In addition, some now argue for different authors for Ezra
and Nehemiah. See James C. VanderKam, "Ezra–Nehemiah or Ezra and Nehemiah?" in
*Priest, Prophets and Scribes: Essays on the Formation and Heritage of Second Temple Judaism
in Honour of Joseph Blenkinsopp* (ed. Eugene Ulrich et al.; JSOTSup 149; Sheffield: Sheffield
Academic Press, 1992), 55–75. For an excellent collection of essays on this issue, see Mark J.
Boda and Paul L. Redditt, eds., *Unity and Disunity in Ezra–Nehemiah: Redaction, Rhetoric,
and Reader* (Sheffield: Sheffield Phoenix, 2008). Although in this work I continue referring to Ezra–Nehemiah as a literary unity, my argument primarily concerns the relationship of Samuel–Kings and Chronicles and, therefore, is not adversely affected even if Ezra
and Nehemiah are separate literary works from the same Chronistic school as the book of
Chronicles.

34. For a recent example, see John W. Wright, "The Fabula of the Book of Chronicles,"
in *The Chronicler as Author: Studies in Text and Texture* (ed. M. Patrick Graham and Steven
L. McKenzie; JSOTSup 263; Sheffield: Sheffield Academic Press, 1999), 136–55; and Paul L.
Redditt, "The Dependence of Ezra–Nehemiah on 1 and 2 Chronicles," in *Unity and Disunity
in Ezra–Nehemiah: Redaction, Rhetoric, and Reader* (ed. Mark J. Boda and Paul L. Redditt;
Sheffield: Sheffield Phoenix, 2008), 216–40.

35. See also Gary N. Knoppers, *I Chronicles 1–9: A New Translation with Introduction
and Commentary* (AB 12; New York: Doubleday, 2003), 80–89.

36. Rainer Albertz, *A History of Israelite Religion in the Old Testament Period* (trans.
John Bowden; 2 vols.; OTL; Louisville: John Knox, 1994), 2:654 n. 9.

37. Jacob L. Wright, "A New Model for the Composition of Ezra–Nehemiah," in *Judah
and the Judeans in the Fourth Century B.C.E.* (ed. Oded Lipschits, Gary N. Knoppers, and
Rainer Albertz; Winona Lake, Ind.: Eisenbrauns, 2007), 334.

Because of the close connections between Chronicles and Ezra–Nehemiah, I apply the combined insights of Albertz and Wright to all of Chronicles–Ezra–Nehemiah, postulating a scribal school (the Chronistic school) that produced these different works over an extended period of time. In this way, I can account for their similarities, but can also allow for arguments that, on the basis of certain dissimilarities, suggest different authors for the books and/or different redactors within the same book.[38]

WHEN WERE THE BOOKS OF CHRONICLES, EZRA,
AND NEHEMIAH WRITTEN?

Noth's dating to the Hellenistic period was based on his argument for the literary unity of the Chronicler's History and what he understood as a somewhat confused use of source materials relating to the mission of Ezra and Nehemiah—that is, the Chronicler was removed far enough from the events described in the source materials that he made certain errors in his combination of the source materials.[39] Many of those scholars who have argued that Chronicles and Ezra–Nehemiah have different authors have also argued for an earlier date for Chronicles, preferring the late Persian period. When the later historical references to the missions of Ezra and Nehemiah are no longer considered, Chronicles can be dated earlier. In their excellent summaries of the issue of dating Chronicles both Ralph Klein and Kai Peltonen reach the conclusion that the late Persian period is the probable date, but neither is willing to state this with much certainty, allowing reasonable dates to span the late Persian period and the early Hellenistic period.[40]

My own understanding of the dating of Chronicles–Ezra–Nehemiah will be discussed in more detail below, but for the moment I state simply that, because of my view of the literary relationship between Chronicles and the Deuteronomic History, Chronicles should be dated to the late Persian period, with Ezra–Nehemiah produced by later authors/redactors in the same scribal tradition probably in the early Hellenistic period.

---

38. My argument here is analogous to my argument for the Deuteronomic school's redactional activity over a lengthy period of time; therefore, readers may want to consult the arguments I made there especially concerning analogous scribal schools in the ancient Near East. See Person, *Deuteronomic School*, esp. chapters 3–4. I will also take this issue up again in chapter 2 below.

39. Noth, *Chronicler's History*, 69–73.

40. Klein, "Chronicles," 995–96; and Kai Peltonen, "A Jigsaw with a Model? The Date of Chronicles," in *Did Moses Speak Attic? Jewish Historiography and Scripture in the Hellenistic Period* (ed. Lester L. Grabbe; JSOTSup 317; Sheffield: Sheffield Academic Press, 2001), 225–71.

The Relationship between the Deuteronomic History and the Book of Chronicles

Noth's understandings of the Deuteronomistic History and the Chronicler's History were very similar. He thought that both historiographic works were primarily the product of one individual, whose work could be dated not too long after the last historical events reported. The primary difference between these works was the time period in which they were written; the Deuteronomistic History was exilic and the Chronicler's History was postexilic. Since the Chronicler's History came later, the Chronicler could use the Deuteronomistic History as his primary source for Chronicles.[41] With an exilic date for the Deuteronomistic History and the lapse of time between the Deuteronomistic Historian and the Chronicler, Noth argued that the Chronicler used the MT of the Deuteronomistic History, "the traditional books of Samuel and Kings in the form that we now know them."[42]

Many parts of Noth's understanding have been challenged and revised. Few scholars think that the Deuteronomic History was produced primarily by one individual, and increasingly scholars are dating some Deuteronomic redaction to the postexilic period. Many scholars now question whether Ezra–Nehemiah was written by the same individual as Chronicles. Furthermore, taking account of evidence from the Dead Sea Scrolls and a resulting reassessment of the value of the LXX, few scholars would agree with Noth's assumption that the Chronicler used a proto-MT of the Deuteronomistic History.[43] Together these different perspectives require a careful reexamination of Noth's understanding of the relationship of these two historiographies.

Yet few scholars have seen the necessity of such a thorough reevaluation, continuing to interpret Chronicles on the basis of its reinterpretation of the Deuteronomic History as one of its major sources. One exception has been Graeme Auld, who has proposed that Samuel–Kings and Chronicles have a common source, what he called "the Shared Text" and later "the Book of Two Houses."[44] Auld built significantly on text-critical work, especially that of Julio Trebolle and Steven McKenzie, that suggests that MT Samuel–Kings

---

41. See esp. Noth, *Chronicler's History*, 51–61.

42. Noth, *Chronicler's History*, 52.

43. See the summary of this issue in Klein, "Chronicles," 995–96.

44. Auld first proposed this thesis in A. Graeme Auld, "Prophets through the Looking Glass: Between Writings and Moses," *JSOT* 27 (1983): 3–23 (7–8). His fullest development of the thesis is in A. Graeme Auld, *Kings without Privilege: David and Moses in the Story of the Bible's Kings* (Edinburgh: T&T Clark, 1994). For an excellent bibliographic summary of others who have proposed a common source, Auld's thesis, and Auld's response to his critics, see Rezetko, *Source and Revision*, 6–7 n. 11.

has undergone independent expansive revisions so much so that MT Samuel–Kings could not be the source for Chronicles.[45] This allowed him to make the argument that the Chronicler did not omit significant sections of text, because the nonsynoptic sections in Samuel–Kings can be explained as additions to the common source. When he reconstructed this Shared Text, he found a historiographical narrative concerning the monarchy in Judah that is, in his judgment, "coherent and self-sufficient."[46]

The idea of Samuel–Kings and Chronicles having a common source itself is not that controversial, for the consensus understanding that MT Samuel–Kings and MT Chronicles are both descended from an earlier redactional form of Samuel–Kings is really also an argument for a common source. For example, George Brooke concluded that "4QSam^a indicates that Chronicles preserves evidence for a Hebrew text of Samuel that is earlier than that of the MT. Thus for Samuel both MT and Chronicles rewrite earlier texts and incorporate other sources; why not for Kings too?"[47] The most controversial aspects of Auld's thesis concern his rejection of "Deuteronomistic" to apply to the common source (and, in fact, to Deuteronomy through Kings in any form). For example, Gary Knoppers has argued that even Auld's Shared Text should be understood as Deuteronomistic, because some of the synoptic texts are Deuteronomistic in character. For example, Knoppers wrote that "Solomon's visions (1 Kings 3; 9) and prayer (1 Kings 8) . . . [have a] preponderance of Deuteronomistic expressions and themes."[48] Similarly, Steven McKenzie has written, "2 Samuel 7 and 1 Kings 8, even as Auld has rendered them for his shared source, remain replete with deuteronomistic vocabulary and ideology."[49]

---

45. Auld, *Kings without Privilege*, 6–9. For recent text-critical work that explicitly lends some qualified support to Auld's thesis, see George J. Brooke, "The Books of Chronicles and the Scrolls from Qumran," in *Reflection and Refraction: Studies in Biblical Historiography in Honour of A. Graeme Auld* (ed. Robert Rezetko, Timothy H. Lim, and W. Brian Aucker; VTSup 113; Leiden: Brill, 2007), 35–48; and, in the same volume, Julio C. Trebolle, "Kings (MT/LXX) and Chronicles: The Double and Triple Textual Tradition," 483–501.

46. Auld, *Kings without Privilege*, 40.

47. Brooke, "Books of Chronicles and the Scrolls from Qumran," 47. For a selection of text-critical studies that support the notion that Chronicles generally used a form earlier than the MT of Samuel and/or Kings, see Frank Moore Cross, "A New Reconstruction of 4QSamuel^a 24:16–22," in *Studies in the Hebrew Bible, Qumran, and the Septuagint Presented to Eugene Ulrich* (ed. Peter W. Flint, Emanuel Tov, and James C. VanderKam; VTSup 101; Leiden: Brill, 2006), 77–83; Steven L. McKenzie, *The Chronicler's Use of the Deuteronomistic History* (HSM 33; Atlanta: Scholars Press, 1985); Julio C. Trebolle, "Redaction, Recension, and Midrash in the Books of Kings," *BIOSCS* 15 (1982): 12–35; and Eugene C. Ulrich, *The Qumran Texts of Samuel and Josephus* (HSM 19; Missoula, Mont.: Scholars Press, 1978).

48. Knoppers, *I Chronicles 1–9*, 67.

49. McKenzie, "Chronicler as Redactor," 86.

Although I certainly agree that the Deuteronomic school used earlier sources in its production of the Deuteronomic History and that the Chronistic school used earlier sources, including some form of what became Samuel–Kings, I remain skeptical that we can adequately isolate redactional layers and original sources well enough to be able to establish who the authors were or were not for any particular source.[50] Therefore, my reconstruction does not rest on my source-critical evaluations so much as on what I can imagine about the historically probable process that produced these two competing contemporary historiographies.

Competing Contemporary Historiographies

My reconstruction of the history of the Deuteronomic school, especially the comparative work I have done on scribal schools and the role of literacy in a primarily oral culture,[51] have implications for the relationship of the Deuteronomic History and Chronicles. The Deuteronomic History and Chronicles certainly have a common source between them. This common source, in my opinion, is an early redaction of the Deuteronomic History that was undertaken in the Babylonian exile, something toward which the text-critical evidence of Samuel–Kings points us.[52] This would explain the similarities between the Deuteronomic History and Chronicles. The dissimilarity can be explained simply by the history of the Deuteronomic school that first produced this exilic common source—that is, this scribal guild experienced a division when the Deuteronomic school returned to Yehud probably under Zerubbabel. At this time there were two scribal communities with a common origin—the returnees in Jerusalem and those who remained in Babylon. Both scribal schools used this common source, but they continued to revise this

---

50. For an excellent discussion of the history of research and current problems in the source-critical work on Chronicles, see Kai Peltonen, "Function, Explanation and Literary Phenomena: Aspects of Source Criticism as Theory and Method in the History of Chronicles Research," in *The Chronicler as Author: Studies in Text and Texture* (ed. M. Patrick Graham and Steven L. McKenzie; JSOTSup 263; Sheffield: Sheffield Academic Press, 1999), 18–69. Peltonen shares my skepticism concerning the identification of redactional layers and sources (66). On my own skepticism, especially as it relates to the Deuteronomic History, see further Person, *Deuteronomic School*, 24–26.

51. See Person, *Deuteronomic School*, esp. chapters 3–4.

52. See ibid., 34–50, and chapters 4 and 5 below. I prefer to refer to this common source as an early redaction of the Deuteronomic History rather than simply a common source, because the Deuteronomic History preserves what was closer to the most likely type of Hebrew in this source (that is, Early Biblical Hebrew) whereas Chronicles reflects the different type of Hebrew (Late Biblical Hebrew). On this linguistic distinction, see further chapter 1 below.

source independently of each other, responding to their increasingly diverse social and theological perspectives and including additional source material.[53] Over time this produced two different historiographical works, the Deuteronomic History and the book of Chronicles.[54]

These two different works came into contact with each other when Ezra and his accompanying scribes (the Chronistic school) returned to Jerusalem to "introduce" the Mosaic law with a least some tacit Persian support.[55] Certainly this "introduction" of the law with any accompanying authoritative literature could have conflicted to some degree with the law and authoritative literature in use in Second Temple Jerusalem before Ezra's mission. Most importantly, however, because of limited resources, the introduction of a competing scribal guild would have undercut the authority of the scribal guild that had been active in the Jerusalem bureaucracy before Ezra. This circumstance provides an excellent explanation as to why the Deuteronomic school declined and eventually ceased to exist as an institution producing its own literature and why the Chronistic school continued and can also be associated with the later book of Ezra–Nehemiah.

In his work on the Shared Text, Auld "summarily answered" the expected criticism of his thesis on the basis of the consensus model of historical linguistics for Biblical Hebrew.[56] Some of his critics have used the consensus linguistic model of Samuel–Kings representing preexilic Early Biblical Hebrew and Chronicles representing postexilic Late Biblical Hebrew to reject his thesis altogether. Auld has not given a detailed response to these criticisms. Some of the critics of my work on a postexilic setting for the final redaction of the Deuteronomic History have likewise used the consensus regarding linguistic development as a basis to reject my arguments. In chapter 1, I will discuss recent work in Hebrew linguistics that undercuts these criticisms and then show how this work lends support to my thesis.

---

53. For example, MT 1 Sam 16–18 is a conflation of two stories of David and Goliath, one preserved in LXX 1 Sam 16–18 and another story. This conflation probably occurred sometime in the early postexilic period. On 1 Sam 16–18, see chapter 3 below, pp. 74–78.

54. Robert Rezetko has independently argued for a very similar understanding of a common source for the Deuteronomic History and Chronicles. See Rezetko, *Source and Revision*.

55. For excellent discussions of the Persian administration's possible intervention into local legal issues, see Joseph Blenkinsopp, "Was the Pentateuch the Civic and Religious Constitution of the Jewish Ethnos in the Persian Period?" in *Persia and Torah: The Theory of Imperial Authorization of the Pentateuch* (ed. James W. Watts; Symposium 17; Atlanta: Society of Biblical Literature, 2001), 41–62; and Tamara Cohn Eskenazi, "The Missions of Ezra and Nehemiah," in *Judah and the Judeans in the Persian Period* (ed. Oded Lipschits and Manfred Oeming; Winona Lake, Ind.: Eisenbrauns, 2006), 509–29.

56. Auld, *Kings without Privilege*, 9–10.

Scribal Activity in a Predominantly Oral Culture

Biblical scholars have long assumed that oral traditions lie behind many biblical texts; however, as was the case throughout the humanities, models of orality and oral traditions were generally imagined without reference to comparative sources. The work of Milman Parry and Albert Lord—especially the publication of Lord's dissertation, *The Singer of Tales* (1960)—sparked interest in various fields in using comparative evidence to understand better how oral traditions may have influenced many of the great literary works, especially ancient and medieval texts.[57] The application of oral traditional theory to literature in Lord's own work included the following: Homeric epic, *Beowulf*, the *Song of Roland*, and the Bible.[58] The one contemporary scholar who has contributed most to discussions of oral traditions and orally derived literature is John Miles Foley.[59] Foley's own work continues in areas in which Lord worked—that is, Serbo-Croatian, Homeric epic, and Old English—and his work as the editor of the journal he founded, *Oral Tradition*, and other projects have greatly expanded the circle of influence of the study of oral traditions on literature.

The Parry-Lord-Foley approach to oral traditions has had a significant impact on my own work, including *The Deuteronomic School*.[60] This influence continues in this monograph, especially in chapters 2–5. In chapter 2, I re-present arguments I made in *The Deuteronomic School*, setting them in the context of more recent discussions of scribal culture of the ancient Near East, and discuss how the Deuteronomic History, the book of Chronicles, and

---

57. Albert B. Lord, *The Singer of Tales* (Harvard Studies in Comparative Literature 24; Cambridge, Mass.: Harvard University Press, 1960). For an excellent discussion of the work of Parry and Lord and their continuing influence, see John Miles Foley, *The Theory of Oral Composition: History and Methodology* (Folkloristics; Bloomington: Indiana University Press, 1988). For an excellent collection of essays on the Parry-Lord-Foley approach to ancient sources, see John Miles Foley, ed., *A Companion to Ancient Epic* (Oxford: Blackwell, 2005).

58. See Foley's chapter on Lord's work in *Theory of Oral Composition*, chapter 3. See also the bibliography of Lord's work and the introduction in John Miles Foley, ed., *Oral Traditional Literature: A Festschrift for Albert Bates Lord* (Columbus: Slavica Publishers, 1981), 22–26, 27–122.

59. Foley, *Theory of Oral Composition*; idem, *Traditional Oral Epic: The Odyssey, Beowulf, and the Serbo-Croatian Return Song* (Berkeley: University of Califorina Press, 1990); idem, *Immanent Art: From Structure to Meaning in Traditional Oral Epic* (Bloomington: Indiana University Press, 1991); idem, *The Singer of Tales in Performance* (Bloomington: Indiana University Press, 1995); idem, *Homer's Traditional Art* (University Park: Pennsylvania State University Press, 1999); and idem, "Analogues: Modern Oral Epics," in *A Companion to Ancient Epic* (ed. John Miles Foley; Oxford: Blackwell, 2005), 196–212.

60. Person, *Deuteronomic School*, esp. chapter 4, which is a revision and expansion of Raymond F. Person Jr., "The Ancient Israelite Scribe as Performer," *JBL* 117 (1998): 601–9.

Ezra–Nehemiah portray the role of scribes in ancient Israel in the context of an interplay between the oral and the written. In chapter 3, I discuss the notion of multiformity in oral traditions and apply this concept to the Deuteronomic History and Chronicles. Chapter 4 contains a discussion of the multiformity between the Deuteronomic History and Chronicles in their synoptic sections, and chapter 5 in their nonsynoptic sections. This discussion of multiformity within and between the Deuteronomic History and Chronicles leads to the conclusion that, despite these works coming from competing scribal schools, the theological perspectives preserved in these two historiographies do not necessarily differ significantly from each other. Rather, these two historiographies can be understood as faithfully preserving and re-presenting a shared theology from the broader tradition that each of them only selectively re-presents. The role of multiformity in the broader tradition allowed for much greater theological breadth and fluidity than generally imagined, so much so that the apparent differences both between the synoptic sections of Samuel–Kings and Chronicles and in their unique readings are not necessarily competing re-presentations of the broader tradition but complementary performances. Therefore, on the one hand, these two historiographies exist because of an institutional struggle between competing scribal schools, but, on the other hand, both were preserved by the tradition, because theologically they do not differ that significantly when we read them from the perspective of the ancients—that is, allowing for the important role of multiformity within the primarily oral society of ancient Israel.

1

THE LINGUISTIC DIFFERENCE BETWEEN THE DEUTERONOMIC HISTORY AND THE BOOK OF CHRONICLES

The consensus model of historical linguistics divides Biblical Hebrew into three chronologically sequential stages: Archaic Biblical Hebrew, Early Biblical Hebrew (Standard Biblical Hebrew), and Late Biblical Hebrew. This model is dependent to a large extent on Martin Noth's (and his predecessors') understanding of the Deuteronomistic History and the book of Chronicles—that is, the Deuteronomistic History is an exilic work that makes extensive use of preexilic sources and the Chronicler's work is a postexilic (in fact, Hellenistic) work that updates its source material from the Deuteronomistic History and other earlier works. Once the consensus model of historical linguistics has been defined, then it is used, in a clear circular argument, to support the consensus dating of the Deuteronomistic History and the Chronicler's work as well as their interrelationship.[1]

The most influential scholar in the diachronic study of Biblical Hebrew is Avi Hurvitz.[2] Hurvitz's linguistic model is significantly influenced by the scholarly consensus of the 1970s that the Deuteronomistic History is a late preexilic/exilic work and the book of Chronicles is postexilic. Since the Chronicler used Samuel–Kings as a major source, the difference in the language between Samuel–Kings and Chronicles represents the diachronic variations between Early Biblical Hebrew and Late Biblical Hebrew. In fact, Samuel (as a part of Genesis–Kings) and Chronicles (as a part of Esther–Chronicles) most accurately represent Early Biblical Hebrew and Late Biblical Hebrew, respectively. Hurvitz and others have then bolstered these arguments with their interpretation of epigraphic sources, such as Hebrew inscriptions, and

---

1. For an example of such circular argument, see Kalimi, *Reshaping of Ancient Israelite History*, 1, 6.
2. For excellent surveys of Hurvitz's work as well as that of many others in the diachronic study of Biblical Hebrew, see Young, "Introduction"; and Young, Rezetko, and Ehrensvärd, *Linguistic Dating of Biblical Texts*.

comparative Semitic evidence, including Ugaritic, Aramaic, Qumran Hebrew, and Mishnaic Hebrew.

In *The Deuteronomic School*, I challenged the scholarly consensus concerning the dating of the Deuteronomic History that provided the foundation for the work of Hurvitz and others. In this work and others, however, I referred to diachronic studies of Biblical Hebrew (especially that of Robert Polzin) to lend support to my argument that the Deuteronomic school continued its redactional activity into the postexilic period. For example, post-LXX additions in MT 2 Kgs 24:18–25:30 (//Jer 52) include both Deuteronomic language and features associated with (postexilic) Late Biblical Hebrew, for example, the postexilic term היהודים.[3]

Written responses to my earlier work have rarely focused on my use of linguistic evidence for a postexilic setting for the final redaction of the Deuteronomic History.[4] However, especially in conversations, my work is sometimes dismissed for not taking into account the linguistic difference between the Early Biblical Hebrew of the Deuteronomic History and the Late Biblical Hebrew of the book of Chronicles. My dating of the Deuteronomic History has also been associated with the work of other scholars who date much, if not all, of the Hebrew Bible to the Persian period, *even though* I differ significantly from some, especially with regard to the existence of preexilic monarchic institutions and written sources. Therefore, although he did not include my work in his references, the following quotation from Gary Rendsburg typifies this common linguistic response to my dating of the Deuteronomic History to the postexilic period:

> In recent decades, as is well known, there has been a rush among scholars to date virtually the entire biblical canon to the Persian period. . . . In my reading of this literature—from the pens of such people as Niels Peter Lemche, Thomas L. Thompson, and Keith W. Whitelam—I have been struck as to how infrequently, if ever, these individuals invoke the evidence of language. The reasons for this are clear: the linguistic evidence . . . contradicts the effort to shift the date of clearly preexilic compositions to the post-exilic period. Accordingly, those involved in this movement simply ignore the evidence. This is true not only of the aforementioned individuals, who are the most public figures in the minimalist movement, but also of others who have followed suit.[5]

---

3. Person, *Deuteronomic School*, 40–42, 48. For my fullest discussion of these passages, see Person, *Kings–Isaiah and Kings–Jeremiah Recensions*, 80–113.

4. An exception being Young, Rezetko, and Ehrensvärd, *Linguistic Dating*, 2:23, 24, 31–33.

5. Gary A. Rendsburg, "Hurvitz Redux: On the Continued Scholarly Inattention to a Simple Principle of Hebrew Philology," in *Biblical Hebrew: Studies in Chronology and Typology* (ed. Ian Young; JSOTSup 369; London: T&T Clark, 2003), 107. Also see the summary of

Although I do not hold such "minimalist" claims—for example, my reconstruction assumes that the Deuteronomic school developed in the Babylonian exile from the remnants of the preexilic scribal bureaucracy that served both temple and palace—I argue that the Deuteronomic History (one of Rendsburg's "clearly preexilic compositions") was first redacted in the exilic period using some preexilic sources, but that the Deuteronomic school's redactional activity in this work continued into the postexilic period. Therefore, I have shifted the date of what many understand as a composition representing preexilic Early Biblical Hebrew to the postexilic period. I must acknowledge that, although I have made some brief references to the linguistic evidence in earlier works, I have not yet undertaken a thorough response to this criticism. Furthermore, the argument I am making in this work complicates the matter even more, by arguing explicitly that the Deuteronomic History and the book of Chronicles were contemporary works that used a common source. Therefore, as my response to these expected criticisms, in this chapter I draw extensively from recent linguistic work by Ian Young, Robert Rezetko, and Martin Ehrensvärd that undercuts these expected criticisms and thereby lends some support to a late dating of the Deuteronomic History and the possibility that the Deuteronomic History and the book of Chronicles were contemporary historiographies.

CHALLENGES TO THE CONSENSUS MODEL OF EARLY BIBLICAL HEBREW VERSUS LATER BIBLICAL HEBREW

ROBERT REZETKO ON SAMUEL–KINGS//CHRONICLES

In his work on the Shared Text behind Samuel–Kings and Chronicles, Graeme Auld summarily answered the expected criticism of his thesis on the basis of the consensus regarding linguistic development for Biblical Hebrew.[6] Some of his critics have used the consensus linguistic model of Samuel–Kings representing preexilic Early Biblical Hebrew (EBH) and Chronicles representing postexilic Late Biblical Hebrew (LBH) to reject his thesis altogether and Auld has not given a detailed response to these criticisms. However, Auld's former student Robert Rezetko has presented an excellent argument that responds to these linguistic objections, even though Rezetko himself does not give unqualified support to Auld's thesis.[7] Rezetko began by summarizing various arguments about the difficulty of using linguistic evidence for dating biblical texts.

---

linguistic arguments against late dating of Genesis–Kings in Young, Rezetko, and Ehrensvärd, *Linguistic Dating*, 2:6.

6. Auld, *Kings without Privilege*, 9–10.

7. Robert Rezetko, "Dating Biblical Hebrew: Evidence from Samuel–Kings and

He then carefully analyzed sixteen features of what is generally considered Late Biblical Hebrew and demonstrated that "the conventional diachronic explanation is inadequate."[8] For example, one of the sixteen features concerns the first-person pronoun. He wrote:

> it is misleading to claim that אנכי in Samuel and Kings is "systematically" replaced by אני in Chronicles "wherever" the former is found. In fact, if one considers synoptic passages, אנכי occurs in both Samuel–Kings and Chronicles on a single occasion; אני occurs in both Samuel–Kings and Chronicles on eight occasions; אנכי occurs in Samuel–Kings and אני occurs in Chronicles on *only four* occasions. Interestingly, all three situations appear in 2 Samuel 7//1 Chronicles 17. Finally, in the Bible as a whole I am aware of 14 occasions on which both forms occur side by side in the same verse. [9]

Rezetko concluded that the distribution of many so-called early and late linguistic features in Chronicles and elsewhere does not fit the chronological paradigm, and therefore the language of Chronicles cannot be used as a control for the diachronic study of Biblical Hebrew. He advocated further exploration of "non-chronological explanations such as dialect, diglossia, and editorial and scribal activities" to account for the linguistic variation in Biblical Hebrew.[10] These conclusions undercut the standard linguistic criticisms of a common source for Samuel–Kings and Chronicles.

In his essay "'Late' Common Nouns in the Book of Chronicles," Rezetko noted that Chronicles has about seven hundred unique common nouns, ninety-one of which are not found in Genesis–Kings. He showed that these nouns are a small percentage of those in the Hebrew Bible and concluded that, on the basis of common nouns, "the vocabulary of LBH Chronicles is virtually identical to the vocabulary of EBH."[11] He also concluded that "LBH is not monolithic or uniform. Chronicles' language is different than the language of Ezra–Nehemiah."[12] Concerning the relationship of Chronicles and books written in EBH, including Samuel–Kings, he concluded, "The difference between the Chronicler and his EBH counterparts was his openness to draw slightly

---

Chronicles," in *Biblical Hebrew: Studies in Chronology and Typology* (ed. Ian Young; JSOT-Sup 369; London: T&T Clark, 2003), 215–50.

8. Ibid., 222.

9. Ibid., 225–26.

10. Ibid., 249.

11. Robert Rezetko, "'Late' Common Nouns in the Book of Chronicles," in *Reflection and Refraction: Studies in Biblical Historiography in Honour of A. Graeme Auld* (ed. Robert Rezetko, Timothy H. Lim, and W. Brian Aucker; VTSup 113; Leiden: Brill, 2007), 415.

12. Ibid., 416.

more often from the broad linguistic reservoir at his *and their* disposal. Furthermore, he was not haphazard, but purposeful in his methodology."[13]

In this way, the Chronicler was not as conservative as his EBH counterparts—that is, the Chronicler was more willing to draw from "non-standard" varieties of Hebrew for his literary purposes.

In "The Recent Debate on Late Biblical Hebrew: Solid Data, Experts' Opinions, and Inconclusive Arguments," Avi Hurvitz defended the diachronic consensus model against its challengers in the volume edited by Young, *Biblical Hebrew*, especially referring to Rezetko's essay "Dating Biblical Hebrew."[14] Hurvitz used the different spellings of "Damascus" (with or without the ר) as his prime example to demonstrate that Chronicles is "late" (with ר) with reference to extrabiblical sources. However, Rezekto has responded to Hurvitz's criticism in "The Spelling of 'Damascus' and the Linguistic Dating of Biblical Texts."[15] Rezetko demonstrated that Hurvitz's discussion of "Damascus" in Biblical Hebrew is somewhat selective and that his discussion of extrabiblical materials are even more selective. After reviewing all occurrences in Biblical Hebrew and additional extrabiblical attestations, Rezetko concluded that "Damascus" with and without ר were coexisting once the with-ר form appeared. He noted that, based on the extrabiblical texts, there is no evidence for the with-ר form appearing before 150 B.C.E.; therefore, the with-ר forms in Chronicles could be scribal, as it clearly is also in 4QIsaᵃ. He demonstrated that other similar examples of dissimilation involving ר do not have a distribution in the Bible that fits the standarad chronological paradigm. Therefore, Rezetko provided additional evidence in response to Hurvitz's criticism for his conclusion that Chronicles contains a linguistic mixture of so-called early and late features that were coexisting and that chronological explanations are unhelpful when discussing the linguistic variation between Samuel–Kings and Chronicles.

Rezetko has provided qualified support to Auld's thesis of a Shared Text by undercutting the linguistic objections made by Auld's critics; however, this does not mean that his work necessarily supports Auld's thesis in its entirety.[16] Likewise, his arguments do not necessarily provide support for my arguments for postexilic redactional activity in the Deuteronomic school, but they

---

13. Ibid., 417.

14. Avi Hurvitz, "The Recent Debate on Late Biblical Hebrew: Solid Data, Experts' Opinions, and Inconclusive Arguments," *HS* 47 (2006): 191–210.

15. Robert Rezetko, "The Spelling of 'Damascus' and the Linguistic Dating of Biblical Texts," *SJOT* 24 (2010): 119–37.

16. In his monograph Rezetko discusses how his arguments relate to Auld's thesis without explicitly affirming or rejecting it. He does, however, provide some suggestions of caution, which undercut Auld's method to some degree (*Source and Redaction*, 6–7 n. 11).

nevertheless undermine arguments by those critics who have rejected my arguments because of their understanding of the historical development of Biblical Hebrew. Rezetko's arguments allow for the possibility of the Deuteronomic History and Chronicles being contemporary works by raising other possible explanations for the diverse language between the two collections (for example, dialect and diglossia). In fact, in his essay on Chronicles, Rezetko concluded the following with reference to my earlier work as well as others, including Auld's: "With respect to Chronicles and Samuel–Kings we should think in terms of different regional schools or scribal traditions of biblical composition and redaction. Several scholars have suggested that this is the path to follow. I agree."[17]

IAN YOUNG, ROBERT REZETKO, AND MARTIN EHRENSVÄRD,
LINGUISTIC DATING OF BIBLICAL TEXTS

Rezetko joined forces with two other scholars, Ian Young and Martin Ehrensvärd, whose work directly challenged the consensus model of Avi Hurvitz and others.[18] Together they produced the two-volume work *Linguistic Dating of Biblical Texts*, an impressively thorough survey of linguistic scholarship on dating Hebrew texts that provides a devastating blow to the consensus model and proposes a new model for approaching linguistic variation in Biblical Hebrew. In this section I provide a summary of their arguments; however, I encourage readers to read the volumes for themselves. Their summaries of others' work is fair and accessible to those with at least a year of Hebrew study. The linguistic data marshaled against the consensus model itself are impressive, even if many readers may not accept the conclusions based on the data.[19]

The bulk of volume 1 is the most thorough survey of scholarship on the linguistic development of Biblical Hebrew, including an excellent discussion of the assumptions behind this work, the principles guiding the research, and the methodologies used. Although the authors discuss the research of many others, I will focus my brief comments on the work of the three main scholars whom they highlight: Avi Hurvitz, Robert Polzin, and Frank Polak.

---

17. Rezetko, "'Late' Common Nouns," 417.

18. The work of Young, Rezetko, and Ehrensvärd first came together in a volume of essays edited by Young that included essays by authors defending the scholarly consensus as well as those challenging the consensus (*Biblical Hebrew: Studies in Chronology and Typology*).

19. See the similar conclusion by Ziony Zevit in review of Ian Young, ed. *Biblical Hebrew: Studies in Chronology and Typology, Review of Biblical Literature* 8 (2004), http:www.bookreviews.org/pdf/4084_3967.pdf.

Hurvitz is the one scholar who has devoted his career to advancing the diachronic understanding of Hebrew and who is most responsible for the consensus model.[20] His basic approach is sound, including the following criteria: linguistic distribution, linguistic opposition, extrabiblical attestation, and accumulation. Linguistic distribution determines whether a feature can truly be understood as located predominantly or exclusively in texts dated to a specific period—for example, a late feature is predominantly or exclusively in a postexilic text. Linguistic opposition illustrates that a particular later feature contrasts with an earlier feature that is equivalent in meaning. Extrabiblical attestation of linguistic features helps place them in a relative chronology by reference to epigraphic and/or literary data that can be more accurately dated. Linguistic accumulation requires that there be a sufficient amount of late linguistic data in a particular text as deduced from the other methodological criteria, in order to be able to assign a late date to a text. When Hurvitz applied this methodology, he reached the conclusion that the linguistic variety evident in Biblical Hebrew can be grouped into three main types that reflect successive stages: Archaic Biblical Hebrew, Early Biblical Hebrew, and Late Biblical Hebrew.

Polzin's 1971 Harvard dissertation, published as the 1976 monograph *Late Biblical Hebrew*, has been widely influential, especially among American scholars.[21] Polzin's work is based on a study of the language of Chronicles (especially the nonsynoptic passages) and the Priestly source of the Pentateuch. He concluded that the Priestly source is written in a transitional Hebrew between Early Biblical Hebrew and Late Biblical Hebrew and that one can also distinguish the language of the original Priestly source (P^g = "groundwork") and the redactional material (P^s = "secondary additions") diachronically.

While both Hurvitz and Polzin argue that Chronicles is the exemplar for Late Biblical Hebrew and Polzin accepted Hurvitz's treatment of Aramaisms, they differ on what evidence in Chronicles is most reliable. Whereas Hurvitz used all of Chronicles, Polzin criticized the use of the synoptic passages of Chronicles for linguistic analysis, emphasizing rather the nonsynoptic passages. Although the work of Hurvitz and Polzin is often viewed as complementary and mutually supportive, Young, Rezetko, and Ehrensvärd concluded that "Polzin and Hurvitz rely on different methods and arrive at different results. There are certain similarities between their conclusions, but their theories or

---

20. See the summary of Hurvitz's work and the bibliographic references in Young, Rezetko, and Ehrensvärd, *Linguistic Dating*, esp. 1:12–25, 2:242–45.

21. Robert Polzin, *Late Biblical Hebrew: Toward a Historical Typology of Biblical Hebrew Prose* (HSM 12; Missoula, Mont.: Scholars Press, 1976). See the summary of Polzin's work in Young, Rezetko, and Ehrensvärd, *Linguistic Dating*, esp. 1:25–31.

results as a whole cannot be brought into harmony."[22] That is, Young, Rezetko, and Ehrensvärd argued that the work of the two most influential scholars in the consensus model actually disagree with each other in terms of methods and conclusions.

Frank Polak brought a different approach to the diachronic study of Hebrew, in order to provide additional support for the distinction between Early Biblical Hebrew and Late Biblical Hebrew.[23] Drawing from older studies of orality versus literacy, he applied a new criterion of differing styles—the "oral" rhythmic-verbal style versus the "scribal" complex-nominal style—for the purpose of dating biblical texts. He developed four successive styles that parallel the transition from Early Biblical Hebrew to Late Biblical Hebrew: the Classical Style, the Transitional Classical Style, the Late Preexilic and Exilic Style, and the Postexilic Style.

Young, Rezetko, and Ehrensvärd made use of Hurvitz's own methodological criteria in their critique of the work of Hurvitz, Polzin, Polak, and others. They summarized the consensus model as follows:

> The Hebrew Bible's linguistic variety (heterogeneity) reflects three main types of Hebrew (typology) which are successive stages in the language's development (chronology). Furthermore, linguistic dating is possible because of this correlation between linguistic typology and chronology. [24]

They agreed with the consensus concerning the heterogeneity of the language of the Hebrew Bible, but they disagreed with the consensus explanation for the cause of this heterogeneity on the basis of combining typology and chronology. Not only did they conclude that the three types—that is, Archaic Biblical Hebrew, Early Biblical Hebrew, and Later Biblical Hebrew—coexisted during the biblical period, but other types of Hebrew existed at the same time. For example, they argued that both Mishnaic Hebrew and Qumran Hebrew provide additional evidence of language variation during the biblical period. Therefore, they rejected the threefold typology and the idea that this typology correlates to successive stages in the language's development. Rather, the various types of written Hebrew represent the various choices biblical writers made in relation to the standard literary language. For example, some authors/

---

22. Young, Rezetko, and Ehrensvärd, *Linguistic Dating*, 2:80.

23. See the summary of Polak's work and the bibliographic references in Young, Rezetko, and Ehrensvärd, *Linguistic Dating*, esp. 1:32–37, 2:260.

24. Young, Rezetko, and Ehrensvärd, *Linguistic Dating*, 14. This quotation is actually their summary of Hurvitz's work, but it serves equally well as their summary of the consensus model as a whole. Note, however, that, even in Hurvitz's work, the emphasis tends to be on the two types Early Biblical Hebrew and Late Biblical Hebrew, since Archaic Biblical Hebrew is generally limited to a few poetic passages.

scribes were conservative by adhering closely to a standard written form of language whereas others drew more freely from a pool of features not represented in the standard written language. Therefore, the dating of biblical texts on the sole basis of linguistic analysis is impossible.

Admittedly, the conclusions of Young, Rezetko, and Ehrensvärd are a radical departure from the consensus model. However, these authors support their conclusions by applying Hurvitz's own methodology to the same data that are used by those who created and defend the consensus. Below I will briefly summarize some of the arguments they make to demonstrate that what have been identified as chronologically distinguishable features occur in texts where they do not belong (for example, so-called late features in early texts). At the end of each of their chapters, they include illustrative analyses of various texts. In chapter 5, they provide a chart of "late" features in twenty-eight selected biblical and nonbiblical texts of approximately five hundred words. Below I offer a quick list of some of these illustrations from biblical texts other than Samuel–Kings//Chronicles and selected extrabiblical texts, and then I give a fuller summary of their analysis of Samuel–Kings//Chronicles.

"Early" *features in late biblical texts*: Zech 6:9–15, an undisputed postexilic text, contains more "early" features than "late" features.[25]

"Late" features in "early" biblical texts: Gen 24:1–36 (typically assigned to the preexilic Pentateuch source of the Yahwist) contains four "late" features, the same number as the Masada manuscript of Ben Sira.[26]

"Early" features in Qumran Hebrew: The Habakkuk Commentary (Pesher Habakkuk) contains "early" features.[27]

"Late" features in monarchic Hebrew inscriptions: The Arad Ostraca (late seventh/early sixth century) contains nine "late" features, more than the Habakkuk Commentary.[28]

Features of Mishnaic Hebrew in biblical texts: Esther and Song of Songs have some linguistic features that are "more typical of MH than BH in general."[29]

---

25. Young, Rezetko, Ehrensvärd, *Linguistic Dating*, 1:106–9. See also Martin Ehrensvärd, "Linguistic Dating of Biblical Texts," in *Biblical Hebrew: Studies in Chronology and Typology* (ed. Ian Young; JSOTSup 369; London: T&T Clark, 2003), 164–88; and idem, "Why Biblical Texts Cannot Be Dated Linguistically," *Hebrew Studies* 47 (2006): 177–89.

26. Young, Rezetko, Ehrensvärd, *Linguistic Dating*, 1:136.

27. Ibid., 1:255–62. See also Ian Young, "Late Biblical Hebrew and the Qumran Pesher Habakkuk," *Journal of Hebrew Scriptures* 8 (2008): Article 25.

28. Young, Rezetko, Ehrensvärd, *Linguistic Dating*, 1:134-35, 163–68. See also Ian Young, "Late Biblical Hebrew and Hebrew Inscriptions," in *Biblical Hebrew: Studies in Chronology and Typology* (ed. Ian Young; JSOTSup 369; London: T&T Clark, 2003), 276–311.

29. Young, Rezetko, Ehrensvärd, *Linguistic Dating*, 1:243 (see 242–45).

Since the parallels between Samuel–Kings and Chronicles are often the starting point for discussions of the difference between Early Biblical Hebrew and Late Biblical Hebrew, Young, Rezetko, and Ehrensvärd provided numerous examples where the chronological distinction breaks down when these synoptic texts are compared. The following selective list illustrates their conclusions concerning Samuel–Kings and Chronicles.[30]

> 2 Samuel 6:16–23: "It is remarkable that a comparison of linguistic features in synoptic 2 Samuel 6 and 1 Chronicles 13, 15–16 brings to light cases in which Samuel has LBH but Chronicles has EBH."[31]
>
> 1 Kings 22//2 Chronicles 18: "1 Kings 22.6–35 has eight LBH features, while synoptic 2 Chron. 18.5–34 has only seven. However, whereas three LBH features are shared in common, Kings had five LBH features not found in Chronicles, and Chronicles has four LBH features not found in Kings."[32]
>
> 2 Chronicles 30:1–12: "The appearance in this passage of LBH and EBH features side by side illustrates the combination of archaisms and neologisms which one generally finds in LBH texts."[33] Furthermore, none of the fifteen "late" features found in this passage is "absolutely late," since they are also found in "early" texts.[34]

The following selective list further illustrates their understanding of Samuel–Kings and Chronicles by looking at the distribution of specific linguistic features.

> *Theophoric names*: "According to some scholars, the long ending יָהוּ- is preexilic and the short ending יָה- is postexilic, the result of Aramaic influence. However, Ezra and Nehemiah unequivocally have 'late' יָה-, whereas Chronicles generally has 'early' יָהוּ-, in independent material and in synoptic parallels where Kings has ['late'] יָה-. In fact, there are many such differences in language between Ezra–Nehemiah and Chronicles. It is often difficult to determine which feature in which book would represent truly late language."[35]

---

30. See also Rezetko, "Dating Biblical Hebrew"; and Robert Rezetko, "What Happened to the Book of Samuel in the Persian Period and Beyond?" in *A Palimpsest: Rhetoric, Ideology, Stylistics and Language Relating to Persian Israel* (ed. Ehud Ben Zvi, Diana V. Edelman, and Frank Polak; Perspectives on Hebrew Scriptures and Its Contexts 5; Piscataway, NJ: Gorgias Press, 2009), 237-52.

31. Young, Rezetko, Ehrensvärd, *Linguistic Dating*, 1:105.

32. Ibid., 1:137. Also see their excellent discussion of these synoptic passages in their chapter on the impact of text-critical evidence on linguistic issues (1:353–58).

33. Ibid., 1:43.

34. Ibid., 1:80.

35. Ibid., 1:86–87.

The particle נָא-: The use of the particle נָא- is generally understood to decline in use in Late Biblical Hebrew. However, careful analysis of Samuel–Kings// Chronicles does not support this. Samuel–Kings and Chronicles have five parallel uses of נָא-. Chronicles has three pluses in nonsynoptic texts and four minuses.[36]

Paronomastic infinitive absolute: The use of the paronomastic infinitive absolute is generally understood to decline in use in Late Biblical Hebrew. However, careful analysis of the synoptic passages of Samuel–Kings//Chronicles does not support this. "Chronicles has four ParonIA minuses in synoptic material, four shared cases of ParonIA, two non-synoptic instances of ParonIA (1 Chron. 4.10; 2 Chron. 36.15), and one synoptic plus."[37]

Young, Rezetko, and Ehrensvärd drew five conclusions concerning the synoptic sections of Samuel–Kings//Chronicles:

> First, the language of Samuel–Kings on the one hand and the language of Chronicles on the other are nearly identical in their characteristics. These two sets of books have, linguistically speaking, far more similarities than differences. Second, the core postexilic books of Esther–Chronicles are set apart by an overall higher accumulation of LBH features than we find in other biblical books and especially in the books of Genesis–Kings. However, LBH imprints occur regularly in these core EBH books, and sometimes, as we saw in our analysis of 1 Kgs. 22.1–35//2 Chron. 18.1–34, there may be a greater accumulation of typical LBH features in EBH than in LBH texts. . . . Third, we observe in the MT that these synoptic passages are characterised by fluidity in their linguistic traits. . . . Fourth, it is important to observe that each chapter has its own separate list of LBH features. Some are held in parallel but others are not. This is strong evidence that significant clusterings of LBH features could be added (or substracted) to texts during the course of their scribal transmission. . . . Fifth, we have only touched the surface of the significance of a polyglot approach to the study of the language of Samuel–Kings and Chronicles. Scholarship has not yet come to grips with the interplay of literary, textual and linguistic features of these books. It is likely that more systematic research will show that most differences in language between Samuel–Kings and Chronicles have a textual rather than linguistic explanation. [38]

(I will return to the implications of their conclusions for the thesis of the book below; for the moment I continue to discuss how their evidence undercuts the consensus concerning the linguistic development of Biblical Hebrew.)

The consistent application of the same principles and methods led Young, Rezetko, and Ehrensvärd to make some stunning observations, especially

---

36. Ibid., 2:120.
37. Ibid., 2:139.
38. Ibid., 1:357–58.

when they contrasted the results of one passage with another. Below I provide two examples.

> [I]t is remarkable that when we compare the number of typical LBH features in 2 Sam. 6.16–23 and Zech. 6.9–15 we find significantly more of these in Samuel than Zechariah.[39]

> It is sobering to realise that Ben Sira and Pesher Habakkuk, *from the end of the Second Temple period*, have fewer LBH elements than the Arad Ostraca, *from the end of the First Temple period.*[40]

In fact, Young, Rezetko, and Ehrensvärd went so far as to conclude that, *if* linguistic evidence alone is used to date biblical texts as advocated as possible by Hurvitz and others, then the linguistic evidence requires a postexilic dating for all of the biblical books. However, they clearly stated that this is not their conclusion but the logical outcome of the current insistence by others that texts can be dated on linguistic grounds alone.[41] They ultimately concluded that linguistic evidence cannot be helpful for dating biblical books, especially when it is not combined with text-critical and literary methods.[42]

> The questions facing language scholars who seek to date books and sections of the Hebrew Bible on the basis of linguistic analysis alone are: (1) Can diachronic linguistic analysis work effectively with composite literature? And (2) Can diachronic linguistic analysis demonstrate that some biblical literature must have been written early? Our argument has been that both answers are negative. Consequently, attempts to date the origins of biblical literature must rely on a multifaceted approach rather than primarily or solely on linguistic analysis.[43]

If the consensus model of explaining the language variation in Biblical Hebrew on chronological grounds alone is now unconvincing, then what linguistic model can be proposed to take its place? Young, Rezetko, and Ehrensvärd proposed such a new model.

In his "Concluding Reflections" in his 2003 edited volume of essays, Young synthesized the arguments of the challengers' positions, including Rezetko and Ehrensvärd, and proposed a geographical explanation as follows:[44] Early Biblical Hebrew (EBH) and Late Biblical Hebrew (LBH) represent different dialects that coexisted during the exilic and early postexilic periods. EBH was

---

39. Ibid., 1:109.
40. Ibid., 1:274.
41. Ibid., 1:130.
42. Ibid., esp. vol. 1, chapter 13.
43. Ibid., 2:71.
44. Young, "Concluding Reflections," in *Biblical Hebrew*, 315–17.

the literary language of the monarchy, the Babylonian exiles, and the early returnees to Persian Yehud and in this sense represents the "western" dialect. LBH is connected with books that have a decidedly "eastern" emphasis—Esther and Daniel are set in the eastern Diaspora; Ezra and Nehemiah concern late returnees from the eastern Diaspora; and Chronicles may also be included. The first appearance of some form of LBH (proto-LBH) occurs in Ezekiel, set in Babylon.[45]

Young, Rezetko, and Ehrensvärd developed Young's first proposal further by drawing more fully on studies of dialect in Biblical Hebrew and text-critical studies, thereby expanding the possible explanations to include other social and literary factors in addition to geographical location.

Young, Rezetko, and Ehrensvärd devoted a chapter to surveying evidence of dialect and diglossia in Biblical Hebrew.[46] They included a discussion of biblical passages that suggest different dialects—for example, the Shibboleth incident in Judges 12. They summarized the work of other scholars, most importantly that of Gary Rendsburg. They also examined the contribution of extrabiblical epigraphic evidence—for example, the Samaria Ostraca and Gezer Calendar. They concluded:

> Rendsburg has documented a great deal of linguistic diversity in BH. We cannot conceive of ancient Hebrew, whether northern or southern, early or late, as being a monolithic entity. The existence of variant forms side by side with standard linguistic forms indicates the likelihood that beside, or under, any standard language of the biblical period there existed a diversity of other linguistic usages. . . . Since, furthermore, this linguistic diversity is mostly beneath the surface of the literary language(s) being used in various eras, the impact of this linguistic diversity is unpredictable. Thus, at one time, different scribal schools may have different evaluations of what are acceptable linguistic forms in literary works. [47]

---

45. See also Ehud Ben Zvi, "The Communicative Message of Some Linguistic Choices," in *A Palimpsest: Rhetoric, Ideology, Stylistics and Language Relating to Persian Israel* (ed. Ehud Ben Zvi, Diana V. Edelman, and Frank Polak; Perspectives on Hebrew Scriptures and Its Contexts 5; Piscataway, N.J.: Gorgias Press, 2009), 269–90. Ben Zvi argued that EBH/SBH and LBH are linguistic choices made in Persian Yehud that, when used in texts, carry with them ideological connotations concerning the origins and authoritative status of the texts.

See also Lisbeth Fried's argument that a follower of Ezekiel was the writer of Ezra–Nehemiah ("Who Wrote Ezra–Nehemiah—and Why Did They?" in *Unity and Disunity in Ezra–Nehemiah: Redaction, Rhetoric, and Reader* [ed. Mark J. Boda and Paul L. Redditt; Sheffield: Sheffield Phoenix, 2008], 75–97). Even if we do not accept all the details of her argument, she has provided another explanation for the relationship among Ezekiel and Chronicles–Ezra–Nehemiah.

46. Young, Rezetko, Ehrensvärd, *Linguistic Dating*, vol. 1, chapter 7.

47. Ibid., 1:195.

Young, Rezetko, and Ehrensvärd also devoted a chapter to the impact of text criticism on the study of Biblical Hebrew.[48] Drawing from the work of various scholars, especially that of Julio Trebolle, they illustrated the impact of text criticism on the discussion of various linguistic features, including an excellent discussion of 1 Kgs 22:1–35//2 Chr 18:1–35. They concluded:

> [S]cholars of the language of the Hebrew Bible must take seriously the text-critical dimension in their research on chronological layers in BH and in their efforts to date biblical texts on a linguistic basis. Linguistic analysis cannot afford to ignore scholarly consensuses about the Hebrew Bible's literary complexity and textual fluidity. Assigning dates to biblical *texts* on the basis of linguistic analysis stands at odds with text-critical perspectives on those *texts*. Textual stability is a fundamental premise of the linguistic dating of biblical texts, yet the extant evidence shows that ancient texts of the Bible were characterised by textual *instability*. [49]

Their conclusions concerning the impact of dialects and textual fluidity led them to expand the possible explanations for the linguistic diversity beyond the geographical model first proposed by Young. They concluded:

> We argue that a better model sees LBH as merely one style of Hebrew in the Second Temple period and quite possibly First Temple period also. "Early" BH and "Late" BH, therefore, do not represent different chronological periods in the history of BH but instead represent co-existing styles of literary Hebrew throughout the biblical period. These two general language types, EBH and LBH, are best taken as representing two tendencies among scribes of the biblical period: conservative and non-conservative. The authors and scribes who composed and transmitted works in EBH exhibit a tendency to "conservatism" in their linguistic choices, in the sense that they only rarely use forms outside a narrow core of what they considered literary forms. At the other extreme, the LBH authors and scribes exhibited a much less conservative attitude, freely adopting a variety of linguistic forms in addition to (not generally instead of) those favoured by the EBH scribes. Between extreme conservatism (e.g., Zechariah 1–8) and extreme openness to variety (e.g., Ezra), there was a continuum into which other writings may be placed (e.g., Ezekiel, the Temple Scroll).[50]

They suggested that this model has an ancient analogy in the two styles of Aramaic used in the Persian period, eastern and western. In fact, owing to evidence of both Aramaic styles in the Elephantine letters, they concluded that neither chronological nor geographical distance is necessary to explain the linguistic variety in Biblical Hebrew. Rather, scribes in the same location, like

---

48. Ibid., vol. 1, chapter 13.
49. Ibid., 1:359.
50. Ibid., 1:361.

those of Elephantine, could choose to use different styles based on literary considerations.[51]

In a recent essay, Young returned to his geographical model, only this time with more nuance.[52] He concluded:

> I would now formulate my geographical theory somewhat differently. LBH linguistic features were available to pre-exilic writers, but it was only in the eastern diaspora in the post-exilic period that a style developed fully open to their literary use. Ezekiel is not in LBH, but its eastern connections may be an explanation for its unusually high accumulation of LBH features for a prophetic book. If the last chapters of Daniel are western, then it shows that the style eventually migrated to the west. The knowledge of this style, and the influence of a book like Daniel may be one factor that helps to explain why some Qumran Hebrew documents have a somewhat higher accumulation of LBH features than EBH. However, outside Daniel, so far there is no evidence of the continuation of the LBH style proper in the west. [53]

However, Young continued to note that a chronological or geographical explanation is not necessary. The linguistic evidence of different styles of Aramaic in the Elephantine letters suggests the possibility of different styles being produced in the same location.[54]

CONCLUSION

To begin the conclusion of this chapter, I will return to the five conclusions Young, Rezetko, and Ehrensvärd made concerning Samuel–Kings//Chronicles:

> First, the language of Samuel–Kings on the one hand and the language of Chronicles on the other are nearly identical in their characteristics. These two sets of books have, linguistically speaking, far more similarities than differences. Second, the core postexilic books of Esther–Chronicles are set apart by an overall higher accumulation of LBH features than we find in other biblical books and especially in the books of Genesis–Kings. However, LBH imprints occur regularly in these core EBH books, and sometimes, as we saw in our analysis of 1 Kgs. 22.1–35//2 Chron. 18.1–34, there may be a greater accumulation of typical LBH features in EBH than in LBH texts. . . . Third, we observe in the MT that these

---

51. Ibid., 2:99.

52. Ian Young, "What Is 'Late Biblical Hebrew'?" in *A Palimpsest: Rhetoric, Ideology, Stylistics and Language Relating to Persian Israel* (ed. Ehud Ben Zvi, Diana V. Edelman, and Frank Polak; Perspectives on Hebrew Scriptures and Its Contexts 5; Piscataway, N.J.: Gorgias Press, 2009), 253–68. For his explicit discussion of the issues and how his mind changed on various issues leading him back to the geographical model, see esp. 263–68.

53. Ibid., 265–66.

54. Ibid., 266–67.

synoptic passages are characterised by fluidity in their linguistic traits. . . . Fourth, it is important to observe that each chapter has its own separate list of LBH features. Some are held in parallel but others are not. This is strong evidence that significant clusterings of LBH features could be added (or substracted) to texts during the course of their scribal transmission. . . . Fifth, we have only touched the surface of the significance of a polyglot approach to the study of the language of Samuel–Kings and Chronicles. Scholarship has not yet come to grips with the interplay of literary, textual and linguistic features of these books. It is likely that more systematic research will show that most differences in language between Samuel–Kings and Chronicles have a textual rather than linguistic explanation.[55]

A common criticism of my earlier work dating the final redaction of the Deuteronomic History to the postexilic period has been on the basis of the diachronic consensus model—that is, the Early Biblical Hebrew of the Deuteronomic History and the Late Biblical Hebrew of Chronicles–Ezra–Nehemiah require that these works come from successive time periods, with the work of the Chronicler using the Deuteronomic History as a source. However, the conclusions of Young, Rezetko, and Ehrensvärd undercut that linguistic criticism significantly and, in my view, fatally.[56] Furthermore, their conclusion that the linguistic variety is best explained not by chronological arguments but by textual or scribal phenomena lends qualified support to my present thesis of the Deuteronomic History and the book of Chronicles as competing, contemporary historiographies, in that my thesis at least falls within the broader category of explanations they favor. Young favors a geographical explanation in which an "eastern" scribal school that was more open in its use of "non-standard" linguistic features was responsible for Esther–Chronicles, which contains a high accumulation of LBH features, and a "western" scribal school that was more conservative in its use of "standard" linguistic features was responsible for much of the rest of the Hebrew Bible, especially the early versions of Genesis–Kings, written with a low accumulation of LBH features. I would associate the "eastern" school with the scribes who returned to Yehud

---

55. Young, Rezetko, Ehrensvärd, *Linguistic Dating*, 1:357–58.

56. Young, Rezetko, and Ehrensvärd do not reject the likelihood that ancient Hebrew underwent chronological developments; in fact, comparative evidence suggests that this was the case. Rather, they deny the possibility of detecting such chronological development in composite texts that are the result of long compositional processes, such as the Hebrew Bible. If we had a sufficient number of extant texts that were not composite and could be accurately dated by their epigraphy or archaeological contexts, and if we could accurately eliminate other possible explanations of linguistic diversity (for example, dialect), then we could begin to identify chronological variations in ancient Hebrew. That is, the methods of historical linguistics require a set of data that we simply do not have for ancient Hebrew— we lack biblical texts near the time of their production and have very few contemporary extrabiblical texts from the same period.

with Ezra, which I understand to be the Chronistic school, and the "western" school with the returnees under Zerubbabel, which I understand to be the Deuteronomic school. The "eastern" school produced Esther–Chronicles and the "western" school produced the Deuteronomic History.[57] Furthermore, since the languages of Samuel–Kings and Chronicles are "nearly identical in their characteristics," this is consistent with my contention that Samuel–Kings and Chronicles have a common source, which was an exilic version of Samuel–Kings. The "eastern" and "western" schools had a common ancestry—that is, the exilic Deuteronomic school. However, this scribal guild split into two groups, "eastern" and "western," when the Deuteronomic school returned to Yehud under Zerubbabel. Each group continued its redactional activity on this common source, thereby producing the two works, the Deuteronomic History and the book of Chronicles (with the later addition of Ezra–Nehemiah).

The arguments in my present work may also help Young, Rezetko, and Ehrensvärd in response to some of their critics. Although few responses to their most recent work are available, we can predict what some criticisms may be by looking at some of the critiques of Young's earlier collection of essays, *Biblical Hebrew*. Here I refer specifically to some questions posed by Ziony Zevit in his review of this earlier volume.[58] Zevit concluded that, while the challengers of the consensus model in this volume, especially Young and Rezetko, pointed out serious weaknesses in the consensus model, he was unconvinced that the diachronic model could not be salvaged. He was also critical of their proposal of a new model:

> The major arguments of the challengers . . . are very problematic at the theoretical level at which they are expressed. They assume either (1) that in Yehud there were people writing texts in both a living language and an archaic form of the same language, though they provide no reason for such an odd construct, or (2) that there were two communities in Yehud speaking and writing two different dialects, that literati in one community wrote of contemporary concerns while those in the other made up things about the past.[59]

---

57. Ben Zvi considered and then rejected the theoretical possibility of "an originally diasporic, separate social group settled in Jerusalem that shaped and communicated to others (embodied as it were) its own separate character within its society by selecting LBH as the language of their writing" ("Communicative Message," 288). He rejected this possibility because he thinks that Jerusalem in the Persian period was too small to support separate competing sectarian groups (288). Although I argue that such competing groups did exist in Persian Jerusalem—that is, the Deuteronomic school and the Chronistic school—I agree with Ben Zvi that the society simply could not support two competing scribal guilds. This is why I think that the arrival of Ezra and his scribes displaced the Deuteronomic school, leading to its demise as an institution.

58. Zevit, review of Young, ed., *Biblical Hebrew*.

59. Ibid., [13].

First, concerning Zevit's second criticism, his dichotomy between, on the one hand, a scribal community and its "contemporary concerns" and, on the other hand, a scribal community that "made up things about the past" is not a fair summary of the work of Young and Rezetko. Any historiographical work, including both the Deuteronomic History and the book of Chronicles, was created out of a combination of both antiquarian and contemporary interests. In addition, Young, Rezetko, and Ehrensvärd provide an analogy to such regional dialects by referring to the "eastern" and "western" styles of Imperial Aramaic. The Ezra material certainly envisions a scribal group from Babylonia returning to impose its will on the people of Yehud, implicitly creating some competition for whatever scribal group already existed there—that is, the scribal group descended from those who returned under Zerubbabel. Therefore, competing scribal groups in the same location using different writing styles is not implausible. Second, addressing Zevit's first criticism concerning mixed language containing both archaisms and neologisms, Young, Rezetko, and Ehrensvärd provide evidence of competing writing styles found in documents from one location—that is, in the Elephantine letters, some of which can be characterized as "eastern" Aramaic and others as "western." Furthermore, the study of oral traditions has demonstrated that, even in oral traditions produced by illiterate bards, archaic linguistic forms and neologisms can exist within the same oral performance, because of the traditional character of the performance. Therefore, texts that have a mixed language of what Zevit calls a "living language" and archaisms can simply reflect the primarily oral culture in which they were written—at least this is the argument made for some of the great "literary" texts, including Homeric epic, *Beowulf*, the *Cid*, and the *Song of Roland*.[60]

---

60. For a brief discussion of epic language and some further references, see Foley, "Analogues," 202–3.

2

THE SCRIBES OF ANCIENT ISRAEL
IN THEIR ORAL WORLD

Beginning with Martin Noth, scholars have generally striven to identify the specific individuals behind the Deuteronomic History and Chronicles–Ezra–Nehemiah. Noth identified two separate individuals, the Deuteronomistic Historian and the Chronicler. The various revisions of Noth have identified additional redactional layers but often continue to identify specific individuals with these layers—for example, Dtr¹ and Dtr²; DtrG, DtrP, and DtrN; and two authors for Chronicles and Ezra–Nehemiah.

This individualistic notion of writing in the ancient world certainly continues to influence the typical understanding of how sources are used in the writing of biblical texts. For example, Steven McKenzie has returned to Noth's understanding of only one Deuteronomist, even though he acknowledged that there are ad hoc additions to the text.

My thesis is that 1 Samuel 8–12* is a unified composition by a single author/editor, the Deuteronomist (Dtr). The sources behind these chapters had not previously been redacted together, and while additions have been made to Dtr's version of these chapters, there is no evidence of later, systematic editing. In other words, I think that Noth was basically correct that 1 Samuel 8–12* was Dtr's composition.[1]

---

1. McKenzie, "Trouble with Kingship," 286. McKenzie has specifically criticized the idea of collective authorship in the work of Thomas Römer on the Deuteronomistic History ("A Response to Thomas Römer, *The So-Called Deuteronomistic History*," in "In Conversation with Thomas Römer, *The So-Called Deuteronomistic History: A Sociological, Historical, and Literary Introduction*," *Journal of Hebrew Scriptures* 9 [2009]: Article 17, 18–19). He wrote: "[Römer's] ascription of the Deuteronomistic History to a school of scribes traversing centuries begs for an analogous parallel. Where can one find a comparable school of writers? What social-scientific evidence exists for such a phenomenon?" I provided some such analogies in *Deuteronomic School*, especially in the mission of Udjahoresnet to reestablish the "House of Life" at Sais, Egypt, using exiled Egyptian scribes (chapter 3). I hope that some of what I provide in this chapter and the next helps further address McKenzie's questions. See also Römer's response to McKenzie ("Response," 44–45).

Although McKenzie is now in a minority with his view of only one Deuteronomist, his understanding of how the first Deuteronomist used his sources creatively is certainly consistent with the scholarly consensus. In the following words of Kai Peltonen, we see a similar understanding of the use of sources by the work of the Chronicler:

> A central result achieved by the source criticism of Chronicles at this point is the view—generally accepted today—that [the Chronicler] was a creative and sophisticated author with considerable literary talent, who skillfully treated older materials when he created a novel and original interpretation of the history of the people.[2]

Often the assumption behind the uses of sources by authors/redactors is that almost any change made to the source is intentional, probably determined by a theological or ideological difference that the author/redactor had with the author/redactor of the source. Although this is not always explicitly stated when the sources are no longer extant and, therefore, available for comparison, this assumption is often stated when commentators are discussing Chronicles in relationship to its sources. For example, Sara Japhet wrote:

> While the possibility of secondary elaboration during the course of transmission was not ruled out—in particular in the lists, which are most susceptible to change—it seemed that a better explanation of the book's variety and composition is the view that it is one work, composed essentially by a single author, with a very distinct and peculiar literary method. The author's penchant for citing existing texts, for expressing his own views through elaboration and change of such texts, and his being influenced by both the Pentateuch, the Deuteronomistic historiography and a plethora of earlier sources, yet going his own way, account best for the varieties of the book.[3]

Gary Knoppers presented a much more nuanced version of this assumption, seriously taking into account text-critical evidence:

> On the one hand, caution is dictated in attributing tendentious intention to a Chronicles text whenever it differs from Genesis or Samuel, as the alleged change may be due either to the textual tradition represented by the Chronicler's *Vorlage* or to textual corruption. On the other hand, when neither of these two options seems likely, especially in dealing with the text of Kings, one can with confidence

---

2. Peltonen, "Source Criticism," 65–66.
3. Sara Japhet, *I & II Chronicles: A Commentary* (OTL; Louisville: Westminster John Knox, 1993), 7.

more clearly recognize those instances in which the Chronicler consciously made a change in his text.[4]

Note, however, that once he eliminated the possibilities of the Chronicler using an earlier version of Samuel, for example, or the "textual corruption" of Chronicles itself, Knoppers stated confidently that one has an instance "in which the Chronicler *consciously* made a change in his text." Similar notions of intentionality on the part of the Chronicler's use of his sources are common—for example, John Van Seters wrote, "The nature of Chr's historiography is deliberately and consciously ideological."[5]

Our concern to identify specific individual authors/redactors and our tendency to assume that changes made to a source must be consciously and intentionally made for theological or ideological reasons are mostly likely based on our modern, individualistic notion of writing that comes from our highly literate society.[6] As we will see below, societies in which literacy is absent or limited to a small elite group have different understandings of writing and what constitutes an accurate reproduction of the tradition. That is, these societies are primarily oral, even though writing can be found in limited segments of the society. Below I will first briefly summarize the work of Milman Parry, Albert Lord, and John Miles Foley on oral traditions and their influence on recent work in biblical studies. I will then survey references to writing and scribes in the Deuteronomic History and Chronicles–Ezra–Nehemiah. My survey of these biblical texts will illustrate the interplay of the oral and the written in the context of the tradition shared by the Deuteronomic school and the Chronistic school, which minimizes the role of individual human authors even though it preserves memories of notable scribal figures such as Moses and Ezra.

SCRIBES IN THEIR ORAL WORLD

In contrast to modern Western society, societies based primarily on the oral transmission of culture rarely preserve information about who originated the

---

4. Knoppers, *I Chronicles 1–9*, 71. Ralph Klein reaches a similarly nuanced conclusion: "Of course there are also hundreds of changes in detail, sometimes for theological or ideological reasons, but others apparently because of literary or linguistic sensitivies" (*1 Chronicles: A Commentary* [Hermeneia; Minneapolis: Fortress, 2006], 37).

5. John Van Seters, "The Chronicler's Account of Solomon's Temple-Building: A Continuity Theme," in *The Chronicler as Historian* (ed. M. Patrick Graham, Kenneth G. Hoglund, and Steven L. McKenzie; JSOTSup 238. Sheffield: Sheffield Academic Press, 1997), 300.

6. For an excellent discussion of the different ancient and modern notions of authorship, see Karel van der Toorn, *Scribal Culture and the Making of the Hebrew Bible* (Cambridge, Mass.: Harvard University Press, 2007), chapter 2.

narratives that are repeatedly performed. This insight was first emphasized strongly in Western scholarship by Milman Parry.[7] At that time, in Homeric studies a debate was raging concerning who Homer was and even if he ever existed. The two sides of the debate were those who argued for a single author, Homer, and those who argued for a long redactional history of the Homeric epics in which numerous "Homers" systematically reworked the tradition. Parry saw that the discussion was at a complete impasse, since neither side seemed completely reasonable given the contradictory evidence. Parry's solution was to bypass the discussion of how many authors/redactors were responsible for the epics by emphasizing instead a continuing traditional process. In his master's thesis of 1923, Parry wrote:

> Just as the story of the Fall of Troy, the tale of the House of Labdakos, and the other Greek epic legends were not themselves the original fictions of certain authors, but creations of a whole people, passed through one generation to another and gladly given to anyone who wished to tell them, so the style in which they were to be told was not a matter of individual creation, but a popular tradition, evolved by centuries of poets and audiences, which the composer of heroic verse might follow without thought of plagiarism, indeed, without knowing that such a thing existed.[8]

This initial idea suggested that poets in oral traditional societies understand themselves not as authors who are creating something new but rather as performers of a long-standing tradition. However, they are more than mere performers in that they are also composers. Whereas many modern performers will generally repeat verbatim what they have memorized, the oral poets composed the traditional epics extemporaneously by drawing from the system of formulae, themes, and story patterns available in the tradition. As Albert Lord noted, "the picture that emerges is not really one of conflict between preserver of tradition and creative artist; it is rather one of the preservation of tradition by the constant re-creation of it."[9] On the one hand, one cannot speak of the original composer of a traditional oral epic because the tradition as a whole produced the epic. On the other hand, one can identify many composers of the

---

7. The discussion of Parry and Lord below is based on John Miles Foley, "Oral Theory in Context," in *Oral Traditional Literature: A Festschrift for Albert Bates Lord* (ed. John Miles Foley; Columbus: Slavica, 1981), 27–122, esp. 27–51.

8. Milman Parry, "A Comparative Study of Diction as One of the Elements of Style in Early Greek Epic Poetry," in *The Making of Homeric Verse: The Collected Papers of Milman Parry* (ed. A. Parry; Oxford: Oxford University Press, 1971), 421 (cited in Foley, "Oral Theory in Context," 30).

9. Lord, *Singer of Tales*, 29.

epic in every performance, including future performances that stand within the tradition.

Parry tested his own early notions of oral tradition concerning Homer by conducting fieldwork in the former Yugoslavia among the *guslars*, the oral poets of the Muslim Serbo-Croatian epic traditions. Parry was joined by his student Albert Lord, who continued Parry's work after his untimely death. The work begun by Parry and Lord has been expanded further by many others to include fieldwork in various contemporary cultures and the application of these observations to many other bodies of literature. Clearly the leader in this field today is John Miles Foley, who founded and edits the journal *Oral Tradition* and whose own research is primarily in Homeric epic, Old English literature, and Serbo-Croatian epic.[10]

Although biblical scholars have talked about oral traditions behind the biblical text for many years, especially since Hermann Gunkel, it was not until the 1970s and the 1980s that the Parry-Lord approach to the study of oral traditions was applied to biblical texts. The early work of applying the Parry-Lord theory to biblical texts was done by Robert Culley, Robert Coote, Burke Long, Werner Kelber, and Albert Lord among others.[11] Below I will summarize the recent work of Susan Niditch and David M. Carr, both of whose work is informed by that of Foley and these earlier applications to biblical studies, and also summarize some of my own earlier work on this topic.[12]

In *Oral World and Written Word*, Susan Niditch concludes that "Israelite writing is set in an oral context."[13] From our modern, literate perspective, this

---

10. See the following works by Foley: *Theory of Oral Composition*; *Traditional Oral Epic*; *Immanent Art*; *Singer of Tales in Performance*; and *Homer's Traditional Art*.

11. For an excellent review of these studies and others, see Robert C. Culley, "Oral Tradition and Biblical Studies," *Oral Tradition* 1 (1986): 30–65.

12. Two other recent studies that are related to this issue should be mentioned: William M. Schniedewind, *How the Bible Became a Book: The Textualization of Ancient Israel* (Cambridge: Cambridge University Press, 2003); and van der Toorn, *Scribal Culture*. However, I have not included a discussion of their work here because both Schniedewind and van der Toorn depend too much on earlier studies of the "great divide thesis" of orality versus literacy, and therefore their conclusions are often, in my opinion, skewed. For an excellent critique of Schniedewind on this problem, see David M. Carr, "Response to W. M. Schniedewind, *How the Bible Became a Book: The Textualization of Ancient Israel*," in "In Conversation with W. M. Schniedewind, *How the Bible Became a Books: The Textualization of Ancient Israel*," *Journal of Hebrew Scriptures* 5 (2004–5): Article 18, 1–19. Although I do not summarize their work here, I will discuss them below when appropriate.

13. Susan Niditch, *Oral World and Written Word: Ancient Israelite Literature* (Louisville: Westminster John Knox, 1996), 88. See also M. C. A. McDonald, "Literacy in an Oral Environment," in *Writing and Ancient Near Eastern Society: Papers in Honor of Alan R. Millard* (ed. Piotr Bienkowski, Christopher Mee, and Elizabeth Slater; Library of Hebrew

conclusion may sound contradictory—that is, how can writing be understood in an oral context? In fact, until recently scholars of orality and literacy emphasized what Werner Kelber has called "the great divide thesis"[14]—that is, a tremendous gulf was envisioned between oral cultures and literate cultures. It was as if, when an oral epic was written down, it was completely removed from its traditional culture, never again to be influenced by that culture, and even the earliest readers of this new text were ignorant of its traditional culture. Recent studies, however, discuss an oral–literate continuum, thereby narrowing the supposed gap between oral and literate cultures, especially as it relates to the interaction of orality and literacy in transitional cultures like ancient Greece and medieval Europe.[15] Even though Niditch's conclusion *seems* contradictory from our modern perspective, it is consistent with contemporary scholarly understandings of the interaction of literacy and orality in ancient and transitional cultures. Therefore, as Niditch states, "Israelite literacy in form and function is not to be confused with modern literacy and . . . ancient Israelite literacy has to be understood in the context of an oral-traditional culture."[16]

Niditch's conclusions have implications for how the composition and transmission of the Hebrew Bible are understood. She offers four models for the "genesis of the Hebrew Bible":

> (1) the oral performance, which is dictated to a writer who preserves the text in an archive, creating a fixed text out of an event; (2) the slow crystallization of a pan-Hebraic literary tradition through many performances over centuries of increasingly pan-Israelite tales to audiences with certain expectations and assumptions about shared group identity; late in the process authors write down the shared stories; (3) a written imitation of oral-style literature to create portions of the

---

Bible/Old Testament Studies 426; London: T&T Clark, 2005), 49–118. McDonald provides a wealth of comparative evidence for the relationship of writing in primarily oral societies.

14. Werner Kelber, "Scripture and Logos: The Hermeneutics of Communication" (paper presented at the annual meeting of the SBL, Kansas City, November 1991). See also John Miles Foley, "Comparative Oral Traditions," in *Voicing the Moment: Improvised Oral Poetry and Basque Tradition* (ed. Samuel G. Armistead and Joseba Zulaika; Center for Basque Studies Conference Papers 3; Reno: University of Nevada at Reno, 2005), 72–73.

15. For example, M. T. Clanchy, *From Memory to Written Record: England, 1066–1307* (Cambridge, Mass.: Harvard University Press, 1979); Brian Stock, *The Implications of Literacy: Written Language and Models of Interpretation in the Eleventh and Twelfth Centuries* (Princeton: Princeton University Press, 1983); idem, *Listening for the Text: On the Uses of the Past* (Parallax; Baltimore: Johns Hopkins University Press, 1990); Rosalind Thomas, *Oral Tradition and Written Record in Classical Athens* (Cambridge Studies in Oral and Literate Culture 18; Cambridge: Cambridge University Press, 1989).

16. Niditch, *Oral World*, 99. See similarly McDonald, "Literacy in an Oral Environment," 49–118; and Richard A. Horsley, *Scribes, Visionaries, and the Politics of Second Temple Judea* (Louisville: Westminster John Knox, 2007), 91.

tradition; (4) the production of a written text that is excerpted from another written text by a writer who deftly edits or recasts the text in accordance with his own view of Israelite identity.[17]

Although each of these models moves from one end of the oral–literate continuum to the other, Niditch capably demonstrates that even the most literate of these models—that is, a written composition based on written sources—is nevertheless influenced by an oral mind-set. For example, she argues that even though Chronicles is based on Samuel–Kings, it does not displace or replace it, as would be expected in a culture with a literate mind-set.[18] Therefore, even if the biblical text being studied was created by a literate redactor working with various written sources, the redactor and the redactor's work were still heavily influenced by the contemporary oral culture.

Niditch's emphasis is clearly on the composition of the Hebrew Bible. After referring to some recent text-critical work, however, she suggests that the "transmission of this tradition may well have involved complex interplays between written and oral processes."[19]

In "The Ancient Israelite Scribe as Performer," I made arguments very similar to Niditch's, but placed more emphasis on the transmission of texts.[20] Admittedly, the modern distinction between composition and transmission is somewhat artificial because many ancient scribes were not mere copyists. Michael Fishbane has written that "the boundary-line between scribes and authors is often quite difficult to draw in biblical literature, and, in some cases, involves precarious judgments."[21] By drawing from both the text-critical study of the Hebrew Bible and the study of oral traditions, I concluded the following:

> The ancient Israelite scribes were literate members of a primarily oral society. As members of a primarily oral society, they undertook even their literate activity— that is, the copying of texts—with an oral mindset. When they copied their texts, the ancient Israelite scribes did not slavishly write the texts word by word, but preserved the texts' meaning for the on-going life of their communities in much the same way that performers of oral epic re-present the stable, yet dynamic, tradition to their communities. In this sense, the ancient Israelite scribes were not mere copyists, but were also performers.[22]

17. Niditch, *Oral World*, 130.
18. Ibid., 130.
19. Ibid., 77.
20. Person, "Ancient Israelite Scribe as Performer," 601–9.
21. Michael Fishbane, *Biblical Interpretation in Ancient Israel* (Oxford: Oxford University Press, 1985), 85; see also 27, 37, 41, 78–79, 83–88.
22. Person, "Ancient Israelite Scribe as Performer," 602.

This conclusion is significantly influenced by the comparative evidence of what constitutes a "word" or a unit of meaning in primarily oral cultures.

As Niditch argues so well, ancient Israelite literature must be understood from the perspective of the aesthetics of an oral tradition. One aspect of oral traditions concerns the understanding of the basic unit of meaning. Studies in oral traditions demonstrate that the understanding of "word" differs from our own highly literate understanding—that is, a unit of meaning in a primarily oral culture may be equivalent to what we would call a line, a stanza, or even the entire epic.[23] This general observation is illustrated well in the interview of the Serbo-Croatian oral poet (*guslar*) Mujo Kukuruzovic by Milman Parry's Yugloslavian assistant Nikola Vujnovic:

> NIKOLA: Let's consider this: "Vino pije licki Mustajbeze" ("Mustajbeg of Lika was drinking wine"). Is this a single word?
> MUJO: Yes.
> N: But how? It can't be *one*: "Vino pije licki Mustajbeze"
> M: In writing it can't be one.
> N: There are four words here.
> M: It can't be one in writing. But here, let's say we're at my house and I pick up the *gusle* [a traditional single-stringed instrument]—"Pije vino licki Mustajbeze"—that's a single word on the *gusle* for me.
> N: And the second word?
> M: And the second word—"Na Ribniku u pjanoj mehani" ("At Ribnik in a drinking tavern")—there.[24]

In this interview, we can see a clash of cultures as the literate Yugoslav insists that "Vino pije licki Mustajbeze" is not one word but four, while the oral poet insists that it is only one word. In fact, the oral poet's conception of the entire phrase being one word even allows for some variation. Notice that Nikola is discussing the phrase "Vino pije licki Mustajbeze," but, when Mujo imagines playing his *gusle* (a one-string instrument) and singing this phrase, he says what from a highly literate viewpoint might be considered a different phrase because of the inversion of the first two "words," that is, "Pije vino licki Mustajbeze." For Mujo, the oral poet, both "Vino pije licki Mustajbeze" and "Pije vino licki Mustajbeze" are not only one "word" but the *same* "word."

We can see a similar phenomenon in the semantic range of the Hebrew word דבר. דבר is the closest Hebrew equivalent to the English term "word," but it can also mean "utterance," "speech," or "message." For example, in Deut 4:13

---

23. See especially John Miles Foley, "Editing Oral Epic Texts: Theory and Practice," *Text* 1 (1981) 77–78; idem, *Traditional Oral Epic*, chapters 4–6; idem, "Comparative Oral Traditions," 67–68.

24. Cited in Foley, "Editing Oral Epic Texts," 92 n. 11.

and 10:4, we can translate עשׂרת הדברים literally as "the ten words" and imagine an analogous argument concerning how many "words" there are in each of
"the ten commandments" (as it is usually translated). Is "observe the sabbath
day and keep it holy" (Deut 5:12) only one "word" among "the ten words"?
It certainly looks like more than one "word" to us modern, literate readers!
We must keep in mind, however, that the ancient Israelite unit of meaning
or "word" may not correspond to our own highly literate understanding of
"word" as we struggle to understand more about the primarily oral culture in
which the ancient Israelite scribes lived and worked.[25] To continue my critique
of Knoppers and others above, even if we have eliminated changes to the text
that can be explained by an earlier version of Samuel used by the Chronicler
or textual corruption of the text of Chronicles, what *we* may perceive as a "conscious" or "intentional" "change" may not even be considered a change at all by
the ancient author/redactor(s) and the ancient audience. Rather, the ancient
author/redactor(s) may still understand it to preserve accurately the meaning
of the source text.

In *Writing on the Tablet of the Heart*, David M. Carr provides an impressive survey of comparative evidence in the ancient Near East to demonstrate
that ancient texts were composed and transmitted primarily as mimetic aids.[26]
The emphasis of ancient education—whether as early as Sumer or as late as
Athens or Qumran—was not on the texts themselves but on mastering the
meaning of those texts. In fact, Carr notes that ancient texts were often written
in such a way that someone who did not already know the content well would
have difficulty reading the texts—for example, there were no spaces between
the words. Therefore, he concluded that

> this element of visual presentation of texts is but one indicator of the distinctive
> function of written copies of long-duration texts like the Bible, Gilgamesh, or
> Homer's works. The visual presentation of such texts presupposed that the reader
> already knew the given text and had probably memorized it to some extent.[27]

---

25. For further discussion of what constitutes a "word" especially as it relates to text-
critical variants (such as synonymous readings and additions of titles and proper names),
see Person, "Ancient Israelite Scribe as Performer."

26. David M. Carr, *Writing on the Tablet of the Heart: Origins of Scripture and Literature* (Oxford: Oxford University Press, 2005). For a good discussion of memory from the
perspective of oral traditional studies, see John Miles Foley, "Memory in Oral Tradition,"
in *Performing the Gospel: Orality, Memory, and Mark: Essays Dedicated to Werner Kelber*
(ed. Richard A. Horsley, Jonathan A. Draper, and John Miles Foley; Minneapolis: Fortress,
2006), 83–96.

27. Carr, *Writing on the Tablet of the Heart*, 5. On the basis of comparative evidence,
van der Toorn reached a similar conclusion concerning the composition of texts: "On the
whole, scribes were trained to produce stock phrases from memory and to compose their

After reviewing both the biblical and nonbiblical evidence, Carr concluded that in ancient Israel as early as the monarchic period literate elites existed and used texts in some form of education and enculturation as mimetic aids. In Carr's own words, "the focus was as much or more on the transmission of texts from mind to mind as on transmission of texts in written form."[28] Therefore, if what is in the new written copy of a text corresponds to what is in the mind of the copyist, then the copy is an accurate re-presentation of the original, even if the actual words and phrases in the text differ to some degree from its written source. In other words, what we might consider a "change" in the meaning of a text as a result of the addition, omission, or substitution of a couple of words here and there may nevertheless have been understood by the ancient scribes not as a change at all but rather as a faithful copy of the original.

Ancient authors/redactors/scribes in their oral worlds did not identify themselves as authorizing the text or the tradition. Pseudonymity and anonymity were generally the rule. In this way, texts were related to the ongoing traditional culture rather than to individual creative literary geniuses.[29] Furthermore, what the ancients would have understood as a faithful re-production/re-presentation of the tradition allowed for variation in ways that, from our modern perspective, suggest changes in the tradition but from the ancient perspective may not have been understood as changes at all. Although what we would understand as individual words may have been added, subtracted, or substituted in the copying of a text, we are thinking at too much of a micro-level to comprehend how the ancient scribes would have understood the basic unit of meaning. As long as the copy of the text re-presented what the scribes understood as the meaning of the text in their mind, then the copy was a faithful reproduction of the original text.[30]

The importance of this insight concerning variation in the interpretation of the Deuteronomic History, the book of Chronicles, and their interrelation-

---

text before they committed it to papyrus. The scroll served as the repository of a completed text. The composition of a text normally preceded its fixation in writing" (*Scribal Culture*, 21–22).

28. Carr, *Writing on the Tablet of the Heart*, 5.

29. Foley commented on our modern drive to identify individual authors of ancient epics: "Conventional literary history abhors a vacuum of authorship, of course, preferring to impute a supremely gifted individual as the ultimate source of each of the works that constitute a tradition, but that desperate search for an author-like figure may well obscure the process behind the product" ("Analogues," 200).

30. Although there is evidence that some scribes corrected their own copied texts and different scribes sometimes corrected others' copied texts in the Qumran materials, this does not necessarily lead to a rejection of the position stated here. For my discussion of the interplay of the oral and written in such scribal "corrections," see Person, *Deuteronomic School*, 94–95.

ship will be discussed further in the following chapters. Before that, however, we will look carefully at how scribes, the act of writing, and written texts are referred to in the Deuteronomic History, Chronicles, and Ezra–Nehemiah.

Scribes as Portrayed in the Deuteronomic History and Chronicles–Ezra–Nehemiah

Arguments for the existence of some form of formal training of scribes in ancient Israel as early as the monarchy are based on four kinds of evidence: (1) The Hebrew Bible itself contains three kinds of evidence: (a) narratives that describe the activity of professional scribes (for example, 2 Kgs 22:8–13),[31] (b) the mention of the existence of source materials, which presumably would have come from the royal court,[32] such as "the Book of the Annals of the Kings of Israel" (for example, 1 Kgs 14:19) and "the Book of the Annals of the Kings of Judah" (for example, 1 Kgs 14:29); and (c) vocabulary reflecting the technical language of scribalism.[33] (2) The administrative complexity of the institution of the monarchy required the service of professional scribes; therefore, in order to fulfill this need, scribal schools were established.[34] (3) Scribal schools existed throughout the ancient Near East; hence, by analogy, ancient Israel may have also had scribal schools.[35] (4) Archaeological evidence, especially epigraphic sources, increasingly suggests the existence of professional scribes who were trained with some amount of standardization.[36] Although such

---

31. For example, Joseph Blenkinsopp, "The Sage, the Scribe, and Scribalism in the Chronicler's Work," in *The Sage in Israel and the Ancient Near East* (ed. John G. Gammie and Leo G. Perdue; Winona Lake, Ind.: Eisenbrauns, 1990), 308–9; Carr, *Writing on the Tablet of the Heart*, 112, 116–22; Fishbane, *Biblical Interpretation*, 25; Eric Heaton, *The School Tradition of the Old Testament* (Oxford: Clarendon, 1994), 32–36; and van der Toorn, *Scribal Culture*, 76–77.

32. For example, Carr, *Writing on the Tablet of the Heart*, 112; Philip R. Davies, *Scribes and Schools: The Canonization of the Hebrew Scriptures* (Louisville: Westminster John Knox, 1998), 86.

33. Fishbane, *Biblical Interpretation*, 29–32.

34. For example, P. Davies, *Scribes and Schools*, 15–19; Niditch, *Oral World*, 4; Katherine Dell, "Scribes, Sages, and Seers in the First Temple," in *Scribes, Sages, and Seers: The Sage in the Eastern Mediterranean World* (ed. Leo G. Perdue; FRLANT 219; Göttingen: Vandenhoeck & Ruprecht, 2008), 132.

35. For example, Carr, *Writing on the Tablet of the Heart*, 111–12; P. Davies, *Scribes and Schools*, 15–30; Heaton, *School Tradition*, esp. 24–64; André Lemaire, "The Sage in School and Temple," in *The Sage in Israel and the Ancient Near East* (ed. John G. Gammie and Leo G. Perdue; Winona Lake, Ind.: Eisenbrauns, 1990), 168–70; and van der Toorn, *Scribal Culture*, 76.

36. For example, Carr, *Writing on the Tablet of the Heart*, 112, 122–24; Heaton, *School Tradition*, 30–32; P. Davies, *Scribes and Schools*, 77–78; David W. Jamieson-Drake, *Scribes*

reasoning has been used to make what James Crenshaw has justifiably called "extravagant claims,"[37] it nevertheless suggests that schools for the training of a small cadre of professional scribes existed in preexilic Judah. Certainly some scribes would have been low-level functionaries involved in reading and writing more mundane texts (for example, letters, tax records, inventories), but the comparative evidence combined with the biblical evidence strongly suggests that scribes were also part of the royal officials whose tasks were not only related to the act of reading and writing but also to providing advice and counsel. Thus, Leo Perdue can conclude:

> The scribes (ספר) and sages (חכם) of Israel and Judah comprised a professional social class of intellectuals, composers, officials, and clerks from their origins in the monarchic period until the emergence of Rabbinic Judaism during the early centuries of the Common Era (the Tannaitic and Amoraic periods).[38]

As one can see from this summary of arguments for scribes and scribal institutions in ancient Israel, the Deuteronomic History and Chronicles–Ezra–Nehemiah play important roles in these discussions owing to the relatively high prevalence of references to scribes and written texts. Below I will survey selected passages concerning scribes and texts in the Deuteronomic History, in the book of Chronicles, and then in Ezra–Nehemiah. In my survey I will continue to keep in mind the perspective given above for scribal culture in a primarily oral world. That is, I will heed Niditch's directive: "Exploring the

---

and *Schools in Monarchic Judah: A Socio-Archeological Approach* (JSOTSup 109; Sheffield: Almond, 1991); Graham Davies, "Were There Schools in Ancient Israel?" in *Wisdom in Ancient Israel: Essays in Honor of J. A. Emerton* (ed. John Day, Robert P. Gordon, and H. G. M. Williamson; Cambridge: Cambridge University Press, 1995); idem, "Some Uses of Writing in Ancient Israel in the Light of Recently Published Inscriptions," in *Writing and Ancient Near Eastern Society: Papers in Honor of Alan R. Millard* (ed. Piotr Bienkowski, Christopher Mee, and Elizabeth Slater; Library of Hebrew Bible/Old Testament Studies 426; London: T&T Clark, 2005), 155–74; Émile Puech, "Les écoles dans l'Israël préexilique: données épigraphiques," in *Congress Volume: Jerusalem 1986* (ed. J. A. Emerton; VTSup 40; Leiden: Brill, 1988), 189–203; Niditch, *Oral World*, 39–59; James L. Crenshaw, *Education in Ancient Israel: Across the Deadening Silence* (Anchor Bible Reference Library; New York: Doubleday, 1998), 34–35.

37. James L. Crenshaw, "Education in Ancient Israel," *JBL* 104 (1985): 601. Crenshaw used "extravagant claims" in reference to Lemaire's reconstruction of schools for the general population at all of the major cities of the preexilic Judah.

38. Leo G. Perdue, "Sages, Scribes, and Seers in Israel and the Ancient Near East: An Introduction," in *Scribes, Sages, and Seers: The Sage in the Eastern Mediterranean World* (ed. Leo G. Perdue; FRLANT 219; Göttingen: Vandenhoeck & Ruprecht, 2008), 3. See similarly Blenkinsopp, "The Sage, the Scribe, and Scribalism"; van der Toorn, *Scribal Culture*, chapters 3–4; and Carr, *Writing on the Tablet of the Heart*, 116–22.

interplay between orality and literacy is essential to understanding the social contexts of reading and writing in a traditional culture."[39] Furthermore, my approach here is synchronic as a means of trying to discern what the authors/redactors' cultural understanding was of the relationship of oral and written discourse. We will see that none of the major figures associated with the law is understood as an author of the law. Moses, Joshua, Josiah, and Ezra did not originate the law; they simply recited it aloud to the people, taught the people what the law required, and led the people of Israel in their obedience to the law. References to source material on royal histories (for example, "the Book of the Acts of Solomon" [1 Kgs 11:42], "the Commentary on the Book of Kings" [2 Chr 24:27], and "the directions of King David of Israel" [Ezra 3:10]) refer not to their authors but to the main character(s). Even though there is tremendous variety in the phrases used to refer to the royal, prophetic, and liturgical sources, the source citations (at least) in Chronicles probably refer to various sections of one primary source, either an earlier form of Samuel–Kings or another common source. The only written documents that are specifically associated with their individual originators are letters and royal edicts, but even in these cases the originators are often not understood to be the actual writers. Scribes wrote the letters and edicts; scribes or heralds read them aloud to the addressees.[40]

SCRIBES AS PORTRAYED IN THE DEUTERONOMIC HISTORY

All of the major characters in the book of Deuteronomy are portrayed as scribes of the law. God writes the law tablets twice (5:22; 10:4); Moses writes down "this law" (31:9, 24); the future king writes a copy of the law (17:18); and the people are commanded to write the law on their doorposts and gates (6:9; 11:20).[41] All of these forms of writing are closely related to the spoken word.[42] The book of Deuteronomy begins, "These are the words that Moses spoke to all Israel beyond the Jordan" (1:1). The law that God wrote down consists of that which he first spoke to Israel: "These words the LORD spoke to your whole assembly at the mountain. . . . He wrote them on two stone tablets" (5:22). The book ends with Moses completing both the writing and the speaking of these words: "When Moses had finished writing down the words of this law in a book to the end" (31:24) and "Moses finished speaking all these words to all Israel" (32:45). In the book of Deuteronomy, the oral and written characteris-

---

39. Niditch, *Oral World*, 98.

40. See similarly Niditch, *Oral World*, 90–91.

41. Jean-Pierre Sonnet, *The Book within the Book: Writing in Deuteronomy* (Biblical Interpretation Series 14; Leiden: Brill, 1997), 262.

42. On Deut 6:4–9 and 17:14–20, see Niditch, *Oral World*, 99–102.

tics of the Torah are not in opposition to each other but clearly work together to ensure the proper internalization of God's law: "Teach them [these words] to your children, talking about them when you are in your house and when you are on the road, when you lie down and when you get up. Write them on the doorposts of your house and on your gates" (11:19–20).[43] Thus, we can conclude in the words of David Carr, "[r]ecitation, writing, and other forms of reminder are all forms of cultural circulation, ensuring—in the Deuteronomic vision—that Israelites do not 'forget' YHWH and the commandments he has given them (Deut 6:12)."[44]

The close connection between the spoken law and the written law continues in the book of Joshua.[45] The book opens with these words of instruction from God to Joshua:

> Only be strong and very courageous, vigilantly acting according to all the law that
> my servant Moses commanded you; do not turn aside from it to the right hand

---

43. My reading of Deuteronomy here is influenced by the work of Sonnet (*Book within the Book*) and Joachim Schaper ("A Theology of Writing: The Oral and the Written, God as Scribe, and the Book of Deuteronomy," in *Anthropology and Biblical Studies: Avenues of Approach* [ed. Louise J. Lawrence and Mario I. Aguilar; Leiden: Deo, 2004], 97–119; and idem, "The Living Word Engraved in Stone: The Interrelationship of the Oral and the Written and the Culture of Memory in the Books of Deuteronomy and Joshua," in *Memory in the Bible and Antiquity: The Fifth Durham-Tübingen Research Symposium (Durham, September 2004)* [ed. Stephen C. Barton, Loren T. Stuckenbruck, and Benjamin G. Wold; WUNT 212; Tübingen: Mohr Siebeck, 2007], 9–23). However, both Sonnet and Schaper assume the "great divide thesis" of orality versus literacy, thereby skewing some of their conclusions. For example, Sonnet criticized others for emphasizing the oral dimension in the text and then concluded: "Moses, while speaking, is projecting written communication at the horizon of his ongoing speech act. His addressees, and their descendants in the land, will write: they will transcribe his words—Israel's essential words. In so doing, Moses transfers to 'the end' (the reception of his words in the land) what was equally present at the beginning of the Horeb-Moab communication process: commitment to writing. Before Moab (that is, at Horeb) and after Moab (that is, in the land), writing is thus *de rigueur*" (41). Schaper concluded that memory is irrelevant to the discussion of Deuteronomy because memory is a feature of oral societies and "ancient Israel . . . was a literate society . . . [and] never was a primary oral society" ("Living Word Engraved," 10). The dichotomy that both Sonnet and Schaper create is a false one based on their own literate notions of language and not the text of Deuteronomy.

44. Carr, *Writing on the Tablet of the Heart*, 135.

45. My reading of Joshua here is influenced by the work of Donald C. Polaski ("What Mean These Stones? Inscriptions, Textuality and Power in Persia and Yehud," in *Approaching Yehud: New Approaches to the Study of the Persian Period* (ed. Jon L. Berquist; SemeiaSt 50; Atlanta: Society of Biblical Literature, 2007], 37–48). See especially his interpretation of the Behistun Inscription as an iconic use of writing analogous to the use of writing and/or stones in Josh 8; 22; 24.

or to the left, so that you may be successful wherever you go. This book of the law shall not depart from your mouth; you shall meditate on it day and night, so that you may vigilantly act according to all that is written in it. (1:7–8)

Although it is written, the law is also something that came from Moses' mouth and should not depart out of the mouths of the Israelites. The Israelites must meditate on the law continuously. In order to facilitate this meditation, Joshua writes the law on stone.

> And he wrote there on the stones a copy of the law of Moses, which he had written in the presence of the Israelites. . . . And afterward he called out all the words of the law, blessings and curses, according to all that is written in the book of the law. There was not a word of all that Moses commanded that Joshua did not call out in front of all the assembly of Israel and the women, and the little ones, and the aliens who go among them. (8:32, 34–35)

The writing of the law is accompanied by its public recitation. In this act, Joshua and the people are fulfilling the commandments made first in Deuteronomy and then in Josh 1:7–8.

As is well known, the book of Kings refers to various books as sources: "the Book of the Acts of Solomon" (1 Kgs 11:42), "the Book of the Annals of the Kings of Israel" (1 Kgs 14:19; 15:31; 16:5, 14, 20, 27; 22:39; 2 Kgs 1:18; 10:34; 13:8, 12; 14:15, 28; 15:11, 15, 21, 26, 31), and "the Book of the Annals of the Kings of Judah" (1 Kgs 14:29; 15:7, 23; 22:45; 2 Kgs 8:23; 12:19; 14:18; 15:6, 36; 16:19; 20:20; 21:17, 25; 23:28; 24:5). These references appear at the end of narratives concerning the kings and state that additional information can be found in these sources—for example, "Now the rest of the acts of Jeroboam, how he warred and how he reigned, are written in the Book of the Annals of the Kings of Israel" (1 Kgs 14:19).

In *Why Did They Write This Way?* Katherine Stott undertook an extensive comparison of references to written documents in biblical texts and in classical literature. Her review of classical literature, including especially Herodotus and Thucydides, led her to the following conclusions: a reference to a source does not necessarily demonstrate that the author used the source; the lack of a reference to a source does not necessarily demonstrate that no source was used; and references are not necessarily due to firsthand knowledge of the source.[46] On the basis of this comparative evidence, she concluded concerning the source citations in Kings:

---

46. Katherine M. Stott, *Why Did They Write This Way? Reflections on References to Written Documents in the Hebrew Bible and Ancient Literature* (Library of Hebrew Bible/ Old Testament Studies 492; New York: T&T Clark, 2008), chapter 2, esp. 50–51.

While the numerous citations in Kings might suggest that this author was more interested in documentary sources than the vast majority of classical historians, he was not necessarily exceptional in his treatment of this material. He may have used this material for information about the past, but his lack of critical engagement with these texts (though typical of biblical methods in general) is reminiscent of classical approaches. In fact, the way in which he cites these documents, often in the form of a rhetorical question, and without explicit link between the account and the source cited for it, bears resemblance to the use of inscriptions in classical historiography as a confirmatory device.[47]

When combined with the understanding of writing in a primarily oral culture discussed above, Stott's conclusions are especially interesting. Stott seems to have an implicit criticism of "this author" for "his lack of critical engagement" and his lack of explicit link (= quotations?) with these sources. However, what Stott appears to expect implies a more literate understanding of written texts. She seems to acknowledge this contrast when she writes elsewhere that "Herodotus' attitudes and approach to written material seem to reflect the predominantly oral society in which he operated,"[48] but does not carry this insight over to her discussion of the biblical texts. Certainly if the authors/redactors of Kings parallel Herodotus's use of source citations, then this also may be due to the "predominantly oral society in which [they] operated." That is, the authors/redactors know of a connection between their own text and a source text based on their memory of the meanings represented by the source text; therefore, a reference to the source text can simply be a reference to the memory of the meaning taken from that source text rather than an indication that the author double-checked the written source text for the sake of accuracy according to our own highly literate standards.[49] To paraphrase the words of Carr, source citations are more about the transmission of sources from mind to mind than the transmission of source material in its written form.[50]

As discussed above, Deut 17:18 requires the king to write a copy of the law, so that he can meditate on it continuously; 2 Kgs 22–23 portrays King Josiah as obeying the Deuteronomic commandment.[51] A law book is found

---

47. Ibid., 60.

48. Ibid., 27.

49. For an excellent discussion of how the material conditions of writing in the ancient world—for example, the use of heavy leather scrolls—influenced the type of literature produced (including the quotation of sources from memory), see van der Toorn, *Scribal Culture*, 20–23.

50. Carr, *Writing on the Tablet of the Heart*, 5.

51. My reading of 2 Kgs 22–23 here is influenced by the work of Stott (*Why Do They Write This Way?* chapter 5), Niditch (*Oral World*, 102–4), and Carr (*Writing on the Tablet of the Heart*, 140). See below pp. 121–25 for my further discussion of 2 Kgs 22–23//2 Chr 33–34.

and read aloud to Josiah by his secretary Shaphan. Josiah consults the prophet Huldah, who confirms the law book's validity. Then Josiah, like Moses and Joshua before him, read the law book aloud to the people, reconstituting the covenant based on this law. Once again the interplay between the oral and the written is evident. The law book is determined to be authoritative, not simply because it was written but because of its relationship with the past in time and the temple in space, and, more importantly, because its authority is confirmed by the spoken word of God through the prophet Huldah. The written text is then read aloud to all of the people.

Scribes as Portrayed in the Book of Chronicles

The book of Chronicles certainly refers to the written law of Moses—for example, "according to all that is written in the law of the Lord that he commanded Israel" (1 Chr 16:40). However, some have made too much of this observation. For example, William Schniedewind concluded: "Although the term 'Torah' (תרה) originally had the meaning of 'instruction' and hence originally had an oral context, this oral Torah or 'instruction' is transformed into the textual and written Torah in Chronicles (and other Second Temple literature)."[52]

This leads to his contention that "Chronicles reflects the transition to a religion of the book."[53] Although the law of Moses is sometimes referred to in ways that highlight its textual character, Schniedewind could reach his conclusion only by overlooking the other references to the law in Chronicles that refer to its oral dimension but not necessarily its textual character or by assuming a textual interpretation even where the reference may be ambiguous. Here I provide just a selection:

> according to all that Moses the servant of God had commanded (1 Chr 6:49)
> as Moses has commanded according to the word of the Lord (1 Chr 15:15)

---

52. William M. Schniedewind, "The Chronicler as an Interpreter of Scripture," in *The Chronicler as Author: Studies in Text and Texture* (ed. M. Patrick Graham and Steven L. McKenzie; JSOTSup 263; Sheffield: Sheffield Academic Press, 1999), 161.

53. Ibid. Ehud Ben Zvi makes similar statements about Persian-period Yehud as a "text-centered community" in his discussion of both Kings ("Imagining Josiah's Book and the Implications of Imagining It in Early Persian Yehud," in *Berührungspunkte: Studien zur Sozial- und Religionsgeschichte Israels und seiner Umwelt: Festschrift für Rainer Albertz zu seinem 65. Geburtstag* [ed. Ingo Kottsieper, Rüdiger Schmitt, and Jakob Wöhrle; AOAT 350; Münster: Ugarit-Verlag, 2008], 197) and Chronicles ("Observations on Josiah's Account in Chronicles and Implications for Reconstructing the Worldview of the Chronicler," in *Essays on Ancient Israel in Its Near Eastern Context: A Tribute to Nadav Na'aman* [ed. Yairah Amit, Ehud Ben Zvi, Israel Finkelstein, and Oded Lipschits; Winona Lake, Ind.: Eisenbrauns, 2006], 101).

in all that we have heard with our ears (1 Chr 17:20)
when the king heard the words of the law he tore his clothes (2 Chr 34:19)
according to the word of the LORD by Moses (2 Chr 35:6)

These references seem to refer to the oral context of instruction. But again we should not make too much of this by, for example, concluding that the law was only oral and not written. When taken together, the many references to the law betray a close interaction between its oral and written aspects. For example, I would interpret 2 Chr 33:8 ("all that I commanded them—all the law, the statutes, and the ordinances—by Moses") as containing a reference to God's oral presentation of the law to Moses on Horeb (see 2 Chr 5:10), the writing down of the law (whether by God and/or Moses), *and* Moses' oral instruction of the law to the people. That is, from the perspective of the book of Chronicles, it seems that these references necessarily share an understanding of the law that requires the interplay between the oral and the written.

Other references to God's will and/or God's commands show the same type of interplay between the oral and the written.

according to the word of the LORD by Samuel (1 Chr 11:3)
according to the ordinance of David his father (2 Chr 8:14)
according to all that Jehoiada the priest commanded (2 Chr 23:8)
according to the commandment of David and of Gad the king's seer and of
        Nathan the prophet (2 Chr 29:25)
according to the command of the king Josiah (2 Chr 35:16)

These references must be understood as potentially involving both the oral and the written. "The command of the king Josiah" in 2 Chr 35:16 is clearly an oral command given on the basis of a written law book.

In 1 Chr 28 David plans to build a temple in Jerusalem, but God tells him that his son Solomon will build the temple, not David. However, the plan for the temple is given to Solomon through David.

Then David gave to Solomon his son the plan of the vestibule, its houses, its treasuries, its upper rooms, its rooms, its inner chambers, and the room for the mercy seat; and the plan of all that he had in mind: for the courts of the house of the LORD, all the surrounding chambers, the treasuries of the house of God, and the treasuries for dedicated gifts; . . . [David said,] "All this, in writing at the LORD's direction, he made clear to me—the plan of all the works." (1 Chr 28:11–12, 19)

The plans are referred to as being in David's "mind" (literally "in spirit with him") and being imparted to Solomon both in David's words of instruction and in written plans. In the narrative of Solomon's building of the temple (2 Chr 2–6), Solomon carefully follows David's plans. He builds the temple where David instructed him (2 Chr 3:1) and furnishes the temple with items provided by and dedicated by David (2 Chr 5:1). Solomon's prayer includes various references to David to connect his work explicitly to that of his father (2 Chr 6:15, 16, 17, 42). However, it is interesting that nowhere in 2 Chr 2–6 is there another reference to the written plans that David gave to Solomon. The narrative asserts that Solomon's temple followed David's plans carefully, but it does so without once referring to the written document given to Solomon by David for the building of the temple. From the perspective of the narrative itself, Solomon requested wisdom to complete David's plans and God granted his request (2 Chr 1:7–13), so the plans were once again transmitted from mind to mind with the aid of a written text that in this case plays virtually no role in the narrative.

As is well known, the book of Chronicles also refers to a variety of written documents, in addition to the law: "the Book of the Kings of Israel" (1 Chr 9:1; 2 Chr 20:34), "the Annals of King David" (1 Chr 27:24), "the records of the words of Samuel the seer, the words of Nathan the prophet, and the words of Gad the seer" (1 Chr 29:29), "the records of the words of Nathan the prophet, the prophecy of Ahijah the Shilonite, and the visions of Iddo the seer" (2 Chr 9:29), "the records of the words of Shemaiah the prophet and Iddo the seer" (2 Chr 12:15), "the story of the prophet Iddo" (2 Chr 13:22), "the Annals of Jehu" (2 Chr 20:34), "the Commentary on the Book of Kings" (2 Chr 24:27), "the Book of the Kings of Judah and Israel" (2 Chr 16:11; 25:26; 28:26; 32:32), "the Book of the Kings of Israel and Judah (2 Chr 27:7; 35:27; 36:8), "the words of David and Asaph the seer" (2 Chr 29:30), "the vision of Isaiah son of Amoz the prophet" (2 Chr 32:32), "the Annals of the Kings of Israel" (2 Chr 33:18), "the writing of David king of Israel and the writing of Solomon his son" (2 Chr 35:4), and "the Laments" (2 Chr 35:25). Most of these references, as in the book of Kings, occur in the concluding formulas for the king—for example, "Now the rest of the acts of Jehoshaphat, from first to last, are written in the Annals of Jehu son of Hanani, which are recorded in the Book of the Kings of Israel" (2 Chr 20:34).[54] The references are to what appear to be royal histories (or one royal history), but they also contain other material—prophetic material (see 2 Chr 20:34; 32:32; 33:18), genealogical information (see 1 Chr 9:1), and possibly laments and psalms (see 2 Chr 29:30; 35:25). In fact, because of the connections between some of the purported sources (for example, 2 Chr 20:34 and 32:32, where the prophetic material is recorded in a royal history), most of these references are often understood to refer to one extended written document, either an early form of Samuel–Kings or another common source.[55]

---

54. Those not occurring in the concluding formulas are 1 Chr 27:24; 2 Chr 29:30; 34:14; 35:4.

55. For an excellent discussion of the various interpretations of these references, see Stott, *Why Did They Write This Way*, 60–67.

Drawing from her comparative research on references to written documents, Stott also reached a conclusion concerning the Chronicler's use of sources that is similar to that which she reached concerning sources in Kings:

> the Chronicler, in relying extensively on the work of his predecessor, did what any classical historian might do in writing about the non-contemporary past. Furthermore, in using this material he exploited the full range of techniques that his classical counterparts also exhibit. Just as classical historians could quote from, rephrase, elaborate up, abridge, and imitate older texts, so too it seems did the Chronicler.[56]

Concerning the possible use of nonbiblical sources, Stott concluded:

> Basing our judgment on the practices of classical historians who wrote about the non-contemporary past, it is likely that the Chronicler was chiefly dependent on the received literary tradition. However, it is not beyond the realm of possibility that he engaged (at least to some extent) in "primary" research, utilizing information from both written and oral sources and perhaps even travelling to research his account.[57]

Although here Stott explicitly allowed for the Chronicler's use of "oral sources," she did so in a way that may still imply the type of intentional research of written documents that betrays a highly literate model. It seems that, if he used nonbiblical sources, it was because the Chronicler decided that some "primary" research was necessary to "correct" the record and, therefore, set out to do so. Stott does not seem to imagine the possibility of her Chronicler simply drawing from the literary tradition that existed primarily in his memory, a tradition that was certainly steeped in biblical texts but may have included some nonbiblical texts (a distinction that is itself anachronistic). In other words, the literary record that existed in his mind was mostly influenced by what we would call biblical texts but was most likely also influenced by other texts that he had read and to some extent memorized. As Stott herself implies, if the Chronicler was not directly copying from written sources but was referring to them by memory (or invention), then the influence of other sources, including his own creative imagination, may be the cause of what we might consider "changes," whereas he could understand himself simply to be reproducing the tradition faithfully. For example, "the Book of the Kings of Israel," "the Book of the Kings of Judah and Israel," "the Book of the Kings of Israel and Judah," and "the Annals of the King of Israel" very well may refer to only one literary tradition in the mind of the Chronicler(s) and the ancient audience, even though

---

56. Ibid., 66–67.
57. Ibid., 67.

from our highly literate perspective we would insist on picking only one of these and consistently using it so as to avoid confusion.

The account of Josiah's reforms and the discovery of the law book (2 Chr 34–35) also includes the interplay of the oral and the written, although the order of events differs from the account in 2 Kgs 22–23.[58] In his eighth year, Josiah began his religious reforms (2 Chr 34:3–7), destroying the high places of worship to foreign gods. In his eighteenth year, after cleansing the land of pagan worship, Josiah renovated the Jerusalem temple (2 Chr 34:8–17). In the process, "Hilkiah the priest found the book of the law of the LORD by Moses" (2 Chr 34:14). Hilkiah then reported to the scribe Shaphan about the discovery of the law book. Shaphan then reported the finding of the book to Josiah and "called it out to the king" (2 Chr 34:18). "When the king heard the words of the law he tore his clothes" (2 Chr 34:19); he commanded Hilkiah, Shaphan, and others to consult a prophet for God's will in relation to the law book. Huldah the prophet confirmed that the curses written in the law book will occur, but Josiah himself would be spared (2 Chr 34:22–28). Josiah then sent word for all the people to gather, so that he could read the law book to the gathered people (2 Chr 34:29–30). After reading the law book, Josiah "made a covenant before the LORD, to follow the LORD, keeping his commandments, his decrees, and his statutes, with all his heart and all his soul, to do the words of the covenant written in this book" (2 Chr 34:31) and required the people to take the same pledge. Josiah thereafter led the people in the observance of the Passover, following "the writing of David king of Israel and in the writing of Solomon his son" (2 Chr 35:4), "according to the word of the LORD by Moses" (2 Chr 35:6), "as it is written in the book of Moses" (2 Chr 35:12), and "according to the command of David and Asaph" (2 Chr 35:15). Everything occurred "according to the command of King Josiah" (2 Chr 35:16). Once again the written law book was portrayed in a complex interrelationship between the oral and the written.[59] Josiah's early reforms (not based on the law book) were confirmed by the contents of the law book, once it is found. The law book itself found confirmation in the oral prophecy of Huldah. The power of the law book was presented in recitation, first by Shaphan to Josiah and then by Josiah to the people. Both Josiah and the people pledged themselves to following God's will

---

58. For my discussion of the synoptic relationship between 2 Kgs 22–23 and 2 Chr 34–35, see chapter 4 below, pp. 121–25.

59. Contra Schniedewind, "Chronicler as an Interpreter of Scripture," 162. Schniedewind minimized the role of the oral in Chronicles by emphasizing the subtle differences between the references to the scroll in Kings and Chronicles as evidence of increasing dominance of the written. For example, he wrote, "the substitution of 'the words of this scroll' (2 Kgs 22.13) with 'the word of YHWH' (2 Chr 34.21) is critical because it belies a general textualization" (162).

as given in the law book. Then the Passover occurred according to the king's commands, which were also based on the law book.

The book of Chronicles ends with the edict of Cyrus:

> In the first year of Cyrus king of Persia, to fulfill the word of the LORD spoken by Jeremiah, the LORD stirred up the spirit of Cyrus king of Persia so that he sent a herald throughout all his kingdom and also in writing declared: "Thus says Cyrus king of Persia: The LORD, the God of heaven, has given me all the kingdoms of the earth, and he has appointed me to build him a house in Jerusalem, which is in Judah. Whoever is among you of all his people, may the LORD his God be with him! Let him go up." (2 Chr 36:22–23)

Cyrus's written edict was proclaimed throughout the kingdom by a herald. The edict itself was the textualization of what Cyrus himself said and continued to say through the herald's words. Moreover, all of this was to fulfill "the word of the LORD spoken by Jeremiah," which, although it seemed to emphasize the spoken word, likely also referred to an early form of the written book of Jeremiah.

SCRIBES AS PORTRAYED IN EZRA–NEHEMIAH

Written texts play an important role in Ezra–Nehemiah—for example, both Ezra and Nehemiah have authorizing letters for their missions. However, some have overemphasized the role of written texts in Ezra–Nehemiah. Tamara Cohn Eskenazi, for example, contrasts Ezra–Nehemiah with Chronicles: "The importance of the book of Torah and of texts in Ezra–Nehemiah provides a striking contrast to Chronicles, wherein concerns with the text are peripheral."[60] Her conclusion concerning Chronicles directly contradicts that of Schniedewind, but ironically she made a similar mistake: like Schniedewind, Eskenazi overemphasized the role of texts in Ezra–Nehemiah by not recognizing the oral dimension of the texts in the narrative. We will see below that both the oral and the written dimension must be considered, in order to understand fully the role of texts in Ezra–Nehemiah.

Ezra–Nehemiah begins where the book of Chronicles ends, with reference to the edict of Cyrus (Ezra 1:1–4). The written edict represents the textualization of Cyrus's words that are declared throughout the kingdom by a herald, in order to fulfill "the word of the LORD by Jeremiah" (Ezra 1:1), which is preserved also in the book of Jeremiah.

---

60. Tamara Cohn Eskenazi, *In an Age of Prose: A Literary Approach to Ezra–Nehemiah* (SBLMS 36; Atlanta: Scholars Press, 1988), 179.

As we have seen already in Ezra 1:1, Ezra–Nehemiah continues with references to written documents that are presented as sources. The following are selected examples of references to the law and, in one case, a royal history:

as written in the law of Moses the man of God (Ezra 3:2)
according to the hand of David king of Israel (Ezra 3:10)
according to the law of your God, which is in your hand (Ezra 7:14)
the word that you commanded Moses your servant (Neh 1:8)
the book of the law of Moses, which the LORD had commanded Israel (Neh 8:1)
commandments and statues and a law you commanded them by Moses your
    servant (Neh 9:14)

As we have seen with both the Deuteronomic History and the book of Chronicles, these references betray an interplay of the oral and the written. Some have explicit references to written documents (for example, Neh 8:1); others seem to emphasize the oral aspect (for example, Neh 1:8). Furthermore, Ezra–Nehemiah includes references to sources in the form of edicts and letters that are "quoted" in the narrative.[61] Shimshai the scribe writes a letter to Artaxerxes opposing the rebuilding of Jerusalem (Ezra 4:7–16), and Artaxerxes responds in a letter (Ezra 4:17–24). Tattenai inquires of Darius about the rebuilding of the temple (Ezra 5:6–17), and, after finding a "record" of Cyrus's written edict, Darius issues a decree (presumably accompanied with a letter), allowing the rebuilding of the temple to continue (Ezra 6:1–12). Artaxerxes gives Ezra a letter commissioning him for his mission (Ezra 7:11–26). Likewise, Nehemiah requests letters of commission from Artaxerxes, who grants his request (Neh 2:1–20). Nehemiah's mission generates opposition, leading to an exchange of letters (Neh 6:1–19). Although such letter writing seems to emphasize the written dimension, we must remember that letters are simply vehicles for transporting words over long distances. Furthermore, the oral dimension of the written letters was explicitly referred to when Artaxerxes' letter was read aloud to Rehum and Shimshai the scribe (Ezra 4:23).

The narrative concerning the rebuilding of the temple demonstrates the interplay of the oral and the written, not only because of the letters, the

---

61. Stott drew a sharp contrast between Ezra–Nehemiah, on the one hand, and Kings and Chronicles, on the other. She noted that, in contrast to Kings and Chronicles, "the documents in Ezra are 'quoted' and thus more explicitly incorporated into the narrative" (*Why Did They Write This Way*, 67). However, she overstated the case. The references to the law and royal histories in the Deuteronomic History, Chronicles, and Ezra–Nehemiah are treated in very much the same way—that is, without such obvious quotations. Furthermore, although the "quotation" of edicts and letters is more important in Ezra–Nehemiah, such "quotations" exist also in the Deuteronomic History (2 Sam 11:14–15; 1 Kgs 21:8–14; 2 Kgs 5:5–7; 10:1–7) and Chronicles (2 Chr 2:11–12; 21:12–15; 30:6–9; 32:17–19; 36:22–23).

"record" of Cyrus's edict, and Darius's edict. Jeshua the high priest and Zerub-babel the governor build an altar, in order to offer burnt offerings "as written in the law of Moses the man of God" (Ezra 3:2); however, they also depended on the oral prophecies of Haggai and Zechariah (Ezra 5:1; 6:14). Again, the written law is confirmed by the oral word of God through a prophet.

The most prominent scribe in the Hebrew Bible is the character of Ezra. Although Ezra was "the scribe par excellence in Second Temple history,"[62] he did not work alone. He was accompanied from Babylonia by "some of the Israelites, and some of the priests and Levites, the singers and gatekeepers, and the temple servants" (Ezra 7:7), many of whom directly assisted in his mission. For example, the Levites helped Ezra by reading the law and interpreting it to the people, so that they could understand it (Neh 8:7–8)—that is, the Levites function as lower-level scribes under Ezra's leadership.

As the leader of this group, Ezra is variously described as scribe and priest, so much so that, at least as these terms apply to Ezra, they seem interchangeable:

> a scribe skilled in the law of Moses that the LORD the God of Israel had given
>   (Ezra 7:6)
> Ezra the priest, the scribe, a scholar of the words of the commandments of the
>   LORD and his statutes for Israel (Ezra 7:11; see also Neh 8:9; 12:26)
> Ezra the priest, the scribe of the law of the God of heaven (Ezra 7:12, 21)
> Ezra the scribe (Neh 8:1, 4, 13; 12:36)
> Ezra the priest (Ezra 10:10, 16; Neh 8:2)

Certainly Ezra performs priestly duties: he proclaims a fast (Ezra 8:21–23); he entrusts the sacred temple vessels to chosen priests who deliver them safely to the Jerusalem temple (Ezra 8:24–30); the returnees offer burnt offerings (Ezra 8:35–36); and he oversees the divorce of foreign wives (Ezra 9–10). However, even in these priestly roles, his role as a scribe of the law is at least implicitly involved and, in the case of the divorce decree, explicitly involved ("let it be done according to the law" [Ezra 10:3]). Ezra also performs scribal duties: he

---

62. Jacob L. Wright, "Writing the Restoration: Compositional Agenda and the Role of Ezra in Nehemiah 8," in "Scribes Before and After 587 BCE: A Conversation," *Journal of Hebrew Scriptures* 7 (2007): Article 10, 19. Other works consulted on the role of Ezra as scribe are the following: Blenkinsopp, "Sage, the Scribe, and Scribalism," 312–15; Niditch, *Oral World,* 105–6; Reinhard G. Kratz, "Ezra—Priest and Scribe," in *Scribes, Sages, and Seers: The Sage in the Eastern Mediterranean World* (ed. Leo G. Perdue; FRLANT 219; Göttingen: Vandenhoeck & Ruprecht, 2008), 163–88; Christine Schams, *Jewish Scribes in the Second-Temple Period* (JSOTSup 291; Sheffield: Sheffield Academic Press, 1998), 46–60; Jacob L. Wright, "Seeking, Finding and Writing in Ezra–Nehemiah," in *Unity and Disunity in Ezra–Nehemiah: Redaction, Rhetoric, and Reader* (ed. Mark J. Boda and Paul L. Redditt; Sheffield: Sheffield Phoenix, 2008), 277–304.

studies the law, brings the law to the people, reads it aloud, and oversees its proper interpretation (Neh 8:1–12; see also Ezra 7:25), and then he leads the people in a written covenant (Neh 9:38). However, even in these scribal roles, his role as priest is at least implicitly involved, because a better understanding of the law by the people leads to proper obedience to the law—divorce in Ezra 9–10, the festival of booths in Neh 8:13–18—as well as a written agreement to continue to obey the law (Neh 9:38). In short, Ezra as both scribe and priest symbolizes the close connection between law and temple.[63]

The interplay of the oral and the written are evident in Ezra's scribal roles. He studies the written law and reads it aloud to the people. Ezra and the Levites not only read the law but interpret it in their teaching. As Susan Niditch concluded:

> Torah is mysterious writing in need of interpretation and clarification, hidden either because of a language barrier—these Jews may use Aramaic and not Hebrew as their vernacular—or because of the complexity of the material or because such texts, especially legal rather than homiletical ones, are unfamiliar and not easily digestible. [64]

The oral agreement to obey the law is made into "a firm agreement in writing" contained in a "sealed document" on which the names of the officials, Levites, and priest were inscribed (Neh 9:38). Note that the sealed document itself would act as an iconic, mimetic aid, in that it could not be read without destroying the seal. Of course, its content is divulged in Ezra–Nehemiah, so that whenever Ezra–Nehemiah is read aloud, the contents of the "sealed document" will be made known.

CONCLUSION: SCRIBES IN THEIR ORAL WORLD

Like all ancient and medieval societies, ancient Israel was primarily an oral culture. Despite the presence of writing, most of the members of society functioned without writing, and even the most literate individuals approached writing from more of an oral mind-set than a literate one. The combination of biblical, comparative, and epigraphic evidence strongly suggests that there was some form of education for the training of a small cadre of professional

---

63. Contra Jacob Wright, "Writing the Restoration," 19–29. Wright understands Ezra–Nehemiah as setting up "competing agendas" between the scribal institutions that preserve the law and the sacrificial cult of the temple. Even Wright seems to be uncomfortable with this opposition when in a brief remark in his conclusion he wants to "avoid any misunderstandings" implied by this opposition ("Writing the Restoration," 28). See also idem, "Seeking, Finding and Writing in Ezra–Nehemiah," 277–304.

64. Niditch, *Oral World*, 106.

scribes as early as the late monarchy. The comparative evidence combined with the biblical portrayal of scribes strongly suggests a hierarchy of scribes with some acting as low-level functionaries responsible for more mundane tasks (for example, inventories, letter-writing) and other higher-ranked scribes acting as royal officials, providing advice and counsel as well as tasks related to reading and writing.

The ancient Israelite scribes did not function as independent creative artists; they were members of scribal guilds, in which they probably received their education. This does not mean that scribes never left the confines of the guild to meet needs elsewhere in society; however, their self-identification would have been as part of a scribal group or school and their tasks would have been defined primarily by that guild.[65] They did not identify themselves as authorizing the text or the tradition; in fact, the tradition authorized them. Pseudonymity and anonymity were generally the rule for oral traditions and literary works. In this way, texts were related to the ongoing traditional culture rather than to individual creative literary geniuses.

In the survey of the Deuteronomic History, Chronicles, and Ezra–Nehemiah above, we saw that none of the major figures associated with the law—Moses, Joshua, Josiah, and Ezra—were portrayed as the authors of the law. Rather they received the law, read it aloud to the people, instructed the people concerning the legal requirements, and led the people in their obedience to the law. The royal histories (for example, "the Book of the Annals of the Kings of Israel" [1 Kgs 14:19] and "the Annals of King David" [1 Chr 27:24]) refer to the main character(s), not to the authors. Even though Chronicles contains significant variety in the phrases used to refer to the royal, prophetic, and liturgical sources, the source citations (at least) in Chronicles could refer to various sections of one primary source. The only written documents specifically associated with their individual originators are letters and royal edicts; however, even in these cases scribes wrote the documents on behalf of the originators, often kings, and scribes or heralds read them aloud to the addressees. In this way, the major characters who act as scribes (especially Moses and Ezra) represent the collective scribal tradition as understood by the tradents, and the written documents represent the products of this same tradition, which are read aloud and used as the basis of the oral instruction of the people.

Furthermore, the ancient understanding of a faithful re-production/re-presentation of the tradition allowed for variation in ways that are quite foreign to our modern perspective. When we perceive changes in the addition or subtraction of individual words, we are thinking at too much of a micro-level to comprehend how the ancient scribes would have understood the basic unit

---

65. See Christian, "Priestly Power that Empowers," 17–18 n. 49.

of meaning. For the ancients, as long as the copy of the text re-presented the meaning of the tradition in their mind, the copy was a faithful reproduction of the original text, which also represented the fuller tradition beyond itself. For example, the way in which the law of Moses is referred to differs significantly, when we look at the various phrases used at a micro-level. Also, the phrases used in Chronicles to refer to what was probably one source document on the history of Israel demonstrates tremendous diversity.

Thus, I am advocating for a third possibility for how to imagine what individual ancient authors were doing when they "copied" texts, whether the result is what we might understand as a faithful reproduction, a midrash, an exegetical work, or a new historiography based on earlier source material. Currently, we tend to consider only two options, as seen in the words of Isaac Kalimi:

> The books of Samuel–Kings were not simply canonical for the Chronicler, who did not treat them as immutable, sealed books that one could only strive to explain and to comprehend in their given form. On the contrary, these books served him as raw material to be manipulated as he saw fit: he adapted them, adding to them and deleting from them in accordance with his ideological-theological outlook, his literary and historiographical methods, and his linguistic and stylistic taste.[66]

These two options are a verbatim copy (allowing for some unintentional errors) or an ideologically motivated manipulation of earlier material that produces a new literary work. The third option, the option rarely considered in biblical studies, is a work that allows for some multiformity and fluidity that would nevertheless be considered by the ancients as a faithful presentation of the tradition, although never re-presenting the tradition in its entirety. If this third option is an accurate model for understanding the copying of ancient texts, then any text that has undergone multiple occasions of such copying could certainly diverge significantly, according to our modern perspective, from its earliest version, as what the ongoing tradition required as the meaningful context of the literature continued to change. This third option, therefore, allows for ways of explaining what from our perspective appears to be significant change without requiring the type of ideological manipulation that is often attached to Chronicles. In this way, I agree with Kalimi that the Chronistic school "did not treat [Samuel–Kings] as immutable, sealed books that one could only strive to explain and to comprehend in their given form," because this is clearly an anachronistic understanding of ancient texts. However, the only other option that Kalimi imagines is likewise anachronistic:

---

66. Kalimi, *Reshaping of Ancient Israelite History*, 7.

a creative writer, a historian, in the sense of being a writer who *selected* his mate-rial from earlier books, *reorganized* it and *edited* it in the order, context and form he found appropriate. He also made *connections* between the texts. He stylized, reshaped and *explained* some of them. Others he brought into harmony in accor-dance with his unique beliefs, thoughts and "philosophy" of history.[67]

The intentionality that Kalimi attaches to his Chronicler seems to run counter to, for example, the multiplicity of ways the law of Moses is referred to in the Deuteronomic History, Chronicles, and Ezra–Nehemiah or to the references to written documents as source material. If the ancient authors/redactors of the Deuteronomic History, Chronicles, and Ezra–Nehemiah allow such inter-nal multiformity, then we certainly should explore the possibility that such multiformity existed between written documents within the same theological/literary/historiographical traditions.

---

67. Isaac Kalimi, *An Ancient Israelite Historian: Studies in the Chronicler, His Time, Place, and Writing* (SSN 46; Assen: Van Gorcum, 2005) 10 (emphasis his). See similarly idem, *Reshaping of Ancient Israelite History*, 7.

3

MULTIFORMITY IN THE DEUTERONOMIC HISTORY
AND THE BOOK OF CHRONICLES

In the previous chapter I discussed how oral traditions and literature in primarily oral societies allow for what appears, from our modern, highly literate perspective, to be significant variations in meaning, but from the perspective of the oral culture, the re-presentation may be considered a faithful copy. Thus, one of the distinguishing features of oral traditions is multiformity. In the following quotation from *The Singer of Tales* Albert Lord contrasts well the idea of fluidity and multiformity in oral traditions with our modern understanding of literary texts.

> Whereas the singer thinks of his song in terms of a flexible plan of themes, some of which are essential and some of which are not, we think of it as a given text which undergoes change from one singing to another. . . . Our real difficulty arises from the fact that, unlike the oral poet, we are not accustomed to thinking in terms of fluidity. We find it difficult to grasp something that is multiform. It seems to us necessary to construct an ideal text or to seek an original, and we remain dissatisfied with an ever-changing phenomenon.[1]

As is clear from Lord's observation, an individual singer does not reproduce an exact replica each time he performs the same song. Furthermore, different communities may have slightly different understandings of what is "essential," thereby producing more multiformity. Building on Lord's observations, John Miles Foley has proposed that the way that we use the Internet is analogous to the role of memory navigating an oral tradition in that "they both operate via negotiation of multifaceted networks."[2] Foley also provided an excellent description of how memory produces multiplicity within oral traditions:

> the *aoidoi* [the bards as portrayed in Homeric epic] exercise not a rote, text-like memory but a plastic, generative process of recall, not a static knowledge of a

---

1. Lord, *Singer of Tales*, 99–100.
2. Foley, "Memory in Oral Tradition," 95.

preexisting inventory but rather an ability to negotiate networks with multiple possibilities. This negotiation, undertaken . . . in the company of the co-creating audience(s), is a process that leads to the products we call 'performances.' Each performance will take shape as both a singular, time- and space-bound experience and concurrently a version of a larger, inexpressibly plural set of potentials. Successful performance means remembering how to travel the pathways.[3]

Thus, no performance—no matter how successful—can re-present the broader oral tradition in its entirety. Multiplicity is therefore the norm.

Below I first spend more time discussing this concept of multiformity in living oral cultures for which we have ethnographic fieldwork from the twentieth century to provide some good comparative evidence. I will discuss two examples, one from Serbo-Croatian epic and one from the Luo people of Kenya. Then I discuss multiformity in the Deuteronomic History and in Chronicles before giving some brief remarks about the multiformity evident when we consider the Deuteronomic History and the book of Chronicles together.

MULTIFORMITY IN MODERN ORAL TRADITIONS

MULTIFORMITY IN SERBO-CROATIAN EPIC

Milman Parry and Albert Lord first studied the Muslim Serbo-Croatian epic tradition, because in their judgment it was a close analogue to Homeric epic. Later, others, including John Miles Foley, expanded the fieldwork in the former Yugoslavia to include the Christian Serbo-Croatian epic traditions as well as other genres. Below I will discuss multiformity in Serbo-Croatian epic in the Christian tradition with a brief analysis of three performances of "Marko Recognizes His Father's Sword."[4] The commonalities between these three performances can be outlined as follows:

The Turk and Marko interact.
> Marko recognizes Vukasin's sword in the Turk's possession because of three Christian letters.
> They go to a private place.
> Marko asks of the sword's origin.
> The Turk answers truthfully.

---

3. Ibid., 94.

4. I was introduced to the English translations of these three performances at a National Endowment for the Humanities Summer Seminar directed by John Miles Foley at the University of Missouri in 1992. One is published in his book *Immanent Art*, 253–56 (II.56); the other two are his unpublished translations (II.38; II.57). All quotations of these works are from these translations by Foley.

> The Turk and Vukasin interact.
> Vukasin is injured from an earlier battle.
> The Turk finds Vukasin with the sword.
> Vukasin begs for help.
> The Turk kills Vukasin and takes the sword.
> Marko kills the Turk and takes the sword.

In addition to this outline, some details also are common but nevertheless demonstrate some fluidity. In all three versions, the reason Marko recognizes the sword is that it has three "Christian" letters on it; however, what the three letters represent differs in each of the versions:

> On the saber were three Christian letters:
> One letter for Novak the blacksmith,
> The second letter for King Vukasin,
> The third letter for Kraljevic Marko. (II.56 lines 87–90 in *Immanent Art*, p. 255)

> And on the sword were three Christian letters:
> One letter for St. Demetrius,
> The second letter for St. Arandjele,
> The third letter for King Vukasin. (II.57 lines 39–41)

> He saw three Christian letters:
> One letter for King Vukasin,
> Even Marko's elderly parent himself;
> The second letter for St. George of the summer,
> Even Marko's beautiful baptismal name itself;
> The third letter for St. Demetrius. (II.38 lines 43–48)

Furthermore, all three performances include a reference to a large sum of money (300 + 300 + 300 ducats) or items worth the same amount. In one, the wounded Vukasin has three money belts and he uses them to beg for help from a Turkish maiden who has found him.

> With me I have three belts of riches,
> And in each is some three hundred ducats:
> I will give one of them to you,
> The second to Mustafaga [her brother, the Turk],
> But the third will remain with me (II.56 lines 37–41 in *Immanent Art*, p. 254)

In the other two, the reference to 300 + 300 + 300 ducats occurs in the Turk's asking price for the sword.

> The naked sword worth three hundred ducats,
> Its scabbards three hundred ducats,
> And its braids three hundred ducats. (II.57 lines 6–8)

The price of the sword is three hundred ducats,
And its hilt and scabbard
Will cost another three hundred ducats each,
Altogether some nine thousand! (II.38 lines 8–11)

In both of these performances, Marko appears to have 300 + 300 + 300 ducats to buy the sword and in one Marko carries the ducats in three money-belts (II.57 line 26).

Other differences occur among these three performances. In one of them Vukasin is identified as Marko's father (II.38 lines 45, 88–89); in another as his grandfather (II.57 lines 93–94). In two, the river is identified as Marica (II.56; II.38); in one as Sitnica (II.57). In one there are elaborations—that is, additional themes—not found in the others: Vukasin is first saved by a Turkish maiden before being killed by her brother (II.56 lines 1–59) and the tsar threatens Marko for the murder but backs down when confronted by Marko (II.56 lines 115–141).

Taking Lord's understanding of multiformity seriously requires us to allow that all three versions are authoritative within the tradition itself and requires us not to try to determine, for example, which river was "original" or whether Vukasin was Marko's father or grandfather or what the 300 + 300 + 300 ducats "really" referred to. These details are simply not essential elements of the tradition, which allows for such fluidity and multiformity. In fact, we must be careful not to conclude that this brief analysis of only three performances has identified what is "essential" to "Marko Recognizes His Father's Sword," because the fluidity and multiformity of the tradition itself allow for some reinterpretation of the "essential," especially over time.

Multiformity in a Luo Genealogical Tradition

As he began his fieldwork among the Luo people of Kenya, Ben Blount understood that Luo society was based on patrilineal descent; therefore, he interviewed various individuals in order to create a genealogical chart for his use.[5] He was surprised that few individuals could trace their ancestors back very far and that some individuals were reluctant to reconstruct their ancestral lineage by themselves, preferring that such work be done within the context of a group of elders. Despite these challenges, Blount was able to gather enough information to discern that there were inconsistencies and gaps in the genealogical memories of the Luo people. In other words, once someone outside the Luo

---

5. This entire section is based on Ben G. Blount, "Agreeing to Agree on Genealogy: A Luo Sociology of Knowledge," in *Sociocultural Dimensions of Language Use* (ed. Mary Sanches and Ben G. Blount; New York: Academic Press, 1975), 117–35.

started to write down the genealogy for what may have been the first time, the fluidity of their oral genealogical "record" was clearly revealed. This revelation led to a gathering of the elders in order "to count their grandfathers" (*kwano kware*).

Beyond the obvious fact that he had no written record of the Luo genealogy available to him when he began his work, Blount's observations reveal the oral traditional setting of Luo genealogy. That few individuals, including elders, wanted to speak authoritatively as individuals demonstrates the oral traditional setting in which the tradition must be defined by the community through its appropriate representatives. Thus Blount observed: "Inquiries among informants showed unanimous agreement that genealogies should be discussed only by a group of elders . . . [meeting] at the home of one elder who would serve as host and provide food and drink for the visitors."[6]

Not only were the elders identified by the community as authorities on such matters, but the elders themselves had a hierarchy based on their own patrilineal descent. That is, the expertise of the elders was understood to be a combination of genealogical knowledge and social status based on an agreed kinship relationship.

Within this social hierarchy of elders the genealogies were told, challenged, and reconstructed by agreement. Blount concluded:

> Combinations of these factors yielded a genealogy that was a product of negotiation, based on Luo history but history as a partially dictated and a partially arbitrated synthesis. In effect, the genealogies as history were created by the elders in competition, cooperation, and occasionally by fiat within a framework of Luo social interaction.[7]

During the discussion an elder would sometimes ask another elder for confirmation of what he had stated. Confirmation sometimes came in the form of references to physical objects or geographical features associated with the ancestor under discussion. Many times these references would be connected to a folktale, which would then be performed. In this way the discussion was not "simply" about a genealogical chart of ancestors but was in many ways a summary of the Luo culture and social structure.

As oral traditional lore, the genealogical "record" definitely included multiformity. Not only was the multiformity that Blount identified the precipitating factor leading to the meeting in the first place, but disagreements among the elders occurred during the meeting itself. Blount discussed at some length a disagreement that occurred between two elders that had clear implications

---

6. Ibid., 123.
7. Ibid., 118.

for the social status of one of the disputing elders, based on whether his ancestor was adopted as a war captive or had assimilated voluntarily.

Although the social institution of *kwano kware* existed before he began his study, Blount's work as an outsider asking questions and trying to write a definitive account of the Luo genealogy precipitated the conflict that led to the meeting of the elders. Blount's own reflections betray his presuppositions based on his literate culture. He expected a fixed, authoritative genealogy and that the elders would concentrate their discussion on the gaps and inconsistencies he had identified rather than reconstruct the entire genealogy. He was also surprised by the reticence of the elders to speak authoritatively as individuals. In this way, we can see how his interaction with the Luo was a clash of cultures. However, the Luo used a traditional social institution to resolve the conflict within their own cultural environment.

The result of the elders' meeting was not the type of definitive genealogy that Blount seemed to be looking for at first. The genealogy was stated authoritatively in that particular meeting for that particular time and place based on the agreement of the specific individuals involved.

> The final version of genealogy for any speech event is the product of what the elders agree to agree upon. . . . Whatever the final product of the reconstruction, its acceptability as the accurate genealogy is the end result of a creative process whereby a structure of individual relationships is defined by reference to sets of rules and by individual initiative.[8]

Obviously, the genealogy may be reconstructed differently at a later time according to a similar process but with different individuals involved because of the death of some of the elders and the elevation of others as elders. In this way, the "final" version of the genealogy was final only for that particular speech event, and, therefore, multiformity and fluidity remained the norm for the Luo tradition.

MULTIFORMITY IN THE DEUTERONOMIC HISTORY

Most scholars of Samuel understand the relationship of MT 1 Sam 16–18 and LXX 1 Samuel 16–18 as follows: the LXX is the earlier text, preserving one version of the story of David and Goliath, and the MT is an expansion of the tradition, conflating the earlier version found in the LXX with another version of the story of David and Goliath. The conflation of these two versions in the MT produced some repetitions and inconsistencies owing to the differences found in the once-independent versions.

---

8. Ibid., 134.

Since the textual and literary relationship between the MT and the LXX has been discussed widely elsewhere,[9] here I will assume the validity of this broadly held conclusion in order to examine what the preservation and then conflation of variant versions of the story of David and Goliath may show about the understanding of oral traditions in ancient Israel and their relationship to the early forms of these same traditions preserved in writing. We will see that the evidence from the story of David and Goliath suggests that ancient Israelite writing was produced and interpreted within a primarily oral society in which multiformity was the norm. That is, the ancient Israelites did not have one definitive version of the story of David and Goliath, but rather valued the tradition of David and Goliath in its diversity. Furthermore, this diversity is reflected even within one text, MT 1 Sam 16–18.[10]

Once the story of David and Goliath was written down, the process of oral transmission apparently did not cease. Regardless of whether the Hebrew *Vorlage* of LXX 1 Sam 16–18 preserves the very first instance of the story in its written form, the tradition continued to preserve at least one other version of the story, later incorporated into MT 1 Sam 16–18 either from an oral source or a written source. In fact, it is likely that many other versions of the story continued to exist in the oral tradition beyond the first written copy of the story, even though we have empirical evidence for only one other. In short, the act of writing down the story did not put an end to the multiformity and fluidity of the tradition; the oral performance of the story of David and Goliath continued.[11]

Furthermore, the first written version of the story (whether the Hebrew *Vorlage* of LXX 1 Sam 16–18 or an earlier, no longer extant text) did not become so authoritative as to disallow the authority of other versions. According to the "great divide thesis," one might imagine a scenario in which the oral tradition continued after the writing down of the story but then was so denigrated

---

9. For my own brief discussion of this issue and additional references, see Person, *Deuteronomic School*, 37–39.

10. An additional variation is the tradition that states that Elhanan killed Goliath (2 Sam 21:19).

11. Stanley Isser argues that "a popular fixed secular legend of David" or more simply "the fixed legend" was a source for the work of his Deuteronomist (*The Sword of Goliath: David in Heroic Literature* [Studies in Biblical Literature 6; Atlanta: Society of Biblical Literature, 2003], 53). Although Isser claimed to draw from the study of oral traditions, he did not adequately take account of the characteristics of multiformity and fluidity in oral traditions. He argued that the tradition reached a "fixed" form prior to its being written down and that the Deuteronomist then made changes to this "fixed legend," thereby displacing the authoritative version (the "fixed legend") with his own work (1 Sam 16–18). Isser's literate notion of authoritative version itself denies the critical importance of multiformity and fluidity as characteristics of oral tradition and literature in primarily oral cultures.

because of the authority of the written version that it eventually perished. This does not seem to have been the case, because a later version (preserved only in MT 1 Sam 16–18) was considered authoritative enough to be conflated with an earlier version (preserved in LXX 1 Sam 16–18). It is notable that the later version did not displace the earlier version but that the two versions were conflated into what became one text.

As we saw above, the Serbo-Croatian oral tradition preserved "Marko Recognizes His Father's Sword" in various versions, so that no one version can be understood to re-present the entire tradition. In other words, no one performance of an oral traditional work is understood to be so authoritative that it can adequately re-present the tradition in its multiformity. This can apply also to written texts in primarily oral cultures. The conflation of two versions into one text, thus, can be understood as an attempt to preserve the multiformity/fluidity of the tradition.

In the case of the Luo, when writing is introduced into the oral tradition, inconsistencies are sometimes more noticeable, and therefore they can be understood as problematic. This appears to be the case as well with the story of David and Goliath. The two versions share the following outline:

> David is at the scene of the battle (16:21, 32//17:12–31)
> David fights and kills Goliath (17:40, 42–48a, 49, 51//17:41, 48b, 50)
> Saul makes David an officer (18:13//18:5)
> Saul offers David his daughter as his wife (18:20–27//18:17–19)

As one would expect of oral traditions or texts influenced significantly by oral tradition, however, the two versions also have some inconsistencies because of the characteristic of multiformity. When they were conflated in MT 1 Sam 16–18, some of these repetitions and inconsistencies were preserved as well as evidence that the redactor of this conflation attempted to address some of these inconsistencies.[12] The following chart summarizes the repetitions and inconsistencies between the two versions.

---

12. The following analysis follows the generally accepted source-redactional understanding. See esp. Emanuel Tov, "The Composition of I Samuel 16–18 in the Light of the Septuagint Version," in *Empirical Models for Biblical Criticism* (ed. Jeffrey H. Tigay; Philadelphia: University of Pennsylvania Press, 1985), 97–130; and P. Kyle McCarter Jr., *I Samuel: A New Translation with Introduction, Notes, and Commentary* (AB 8; Garden City, N.Y.: Doubeday, 1980), 299–309.

Earlier Version (LXX and MT)	Later Version (MT Only)
Jesse and David are introduced (15:34–16:20)	Jesse and David are introduced again (17:12–15)
"Saul loved [David] greatly" (16:21)	Saul does not know David (17:55–58)
David is Saul's armor bearer (16:21)	David is a shepherd (17:12–31, 55–58)
Saul makes David an officer (18:13)	Saul makes David an officer (18:5)
Saul offers David his daughter, Michal (18:20–27)	Saul offers David his daughter, Merab (18:17–19)

When conflating the two versions, the redactor of the MT may have eliminated some repetitions and inconsistencies but preserved others. Furthermore, the redactor attempted to harmonize some of the inconsistencies. In 17:12, the redactor most likely added the demonstrative particle "this" to the phrase in his source so that it read "David was the son of an Ephrathite man, *this one*, from Bethlehem."[13] This addition created an ungrammatical construction that probably should be understood as referring back to the introduction of Jesse in the earlier version—that is, "this one" means "the aforementioned." The addition of 17:15 ("David went back and forth from Saul to feed his father's sheep at Bethlehem") is probably the redactor's attempt to explain how David is both Saul's armor bearer and the shepherd of his father's flocks. In 18:21b ("Saul said to David *a second time*, 'You shall today be my son-in-law.'"), the redactor calls attention to the newly created repetition of Saul's offering of his daughter to David as if trying again, this time with a different daughter.

In these redactional attempts at harmonization, we can see the influence of writing leading to the "correction" of the multiformity and fluidity of the tradition. However, this "correction" is still done in a way that preserves the multiformity of the tradition, at least to some extent. The redactor could have simply chosen one version and incorporated only those elements from the other version that would not create such repetitions and inconsistencies. In fact, at times when reading some redactional studies I get the impression that the modern commentator faults the redactor for not doing this very thing— that is, for not doing a better job as a redactor of producing what, from the perspective of our highly literate culture, would be a better (that is, consistent) literary text. The redactor attempted some "correction" but nevertheless preserved a certain number of repetitions and inconsistencies in the conflated text, thereby preserving to some degree the multiformity of the tradition.

In sum, the tradition behind the biblical text produced at least two versions of the David and Goliath story, probably many more. The influence of

---

13. Tov's translation; my emphasis (Tov, "Composition of I Samuel 16–18," 123).

writing on this tradition did not preclude some continuation of the multiformity within the tradition, so much so that two versions were conflated rather than one version displacing the other. However, the influence of writing may have contributed to the redactor's awareness of certain repetitions and inconsistencies, leading to some attempts at harmonizing the two versions. Nevertheless, these attempts at harmonization do not erase the multiformity preserved in the conflated text but can be seen as an attempt to preserve the multiformity of the tradition by allowing the two versions a certain degree of autonomy by explaining what could be understood as repetitions and inconsistencies between the two versions.

MULTIFORMITY IN THE BOOK OF CHRONICLES

In the previous chapter I discussed the source citations in Chronicles. I noted that the various phrases used for these sources very well may refer to either an earlier form of Samuel–Kings or another common source. For example, Sara Japhet concluded that the following general references refer to the same literary work on the broad history of Israel: "the Book of the Kings of Israel" (1 Chr 9:1; 2 Chr 20:34), "the Commentary on the Book of Kings" (2 Chr 24:27), "the Book of the Kings of Judah and Israel" (2 Chr 16:11; 25:26; 28:26; 32:32), "the Book of the Kings of Israel and Judah" (2 Chr 27:7; 35:27; 36:8), "the Annals of the Kings of Israel" (2 Chr 33:18). She wrote:

> The titles . . . would imply, at least on the face of it, that the Chronicler refers to six different works—a rather doubtful possibility in view of further considerations. Several of these works are mentioned only once, and none of them is very common. . . . Moreover, the fact that the Chronicler never mentions any two of these works together may indicate that these titles are not exclusive but interchangeable—a possibility supported by the great similarity of the titles, sometimes differing only in the order of their components or in the definition of genre. In fact, these titles show clear signs of stylistic variety and inconsistent terminology; they differ in the definition of genre ("book," "chronicles," and "commentary"), of topic ("the kings," "the kings of Israel," "the kings of Judah and Israel," "the kings of Israel and Judah"), and even of the order of the common elements ("Judah and Israel," "Israel and Judah"). It is obvious that the term "Israel" has various connotations; when juxtaposed with "Judah" (as "in the Book of the Kings of Israel and Judah"), it refers to the northern kingdom alone; when appearing alone (e.g., "the Chronicles of the Kings of Israel"), it may apply to either the northern kingdom or the people of Israel in general.[14]

---

14. Japhet, *I & II Chronicles*, 21.

Furthermore, Japhet observed that two other source references make it clear that the more limited source references could also be understood as part of these more general references—that is, "the Annals of Jehu son of Hanani, which are recorded in the Book of the Kings of Israel" (2 Chr 20:34) and "the vision of Isaiah son of Amoz the prophet in the Book of the Kings of Judah and Israel" (2 Chr 32:32). These "royal histories" also include prophetic material. Thus, Japhet can conclude:

> The final implication of these considerations would be that in his explicit references to sources in the context of the concluding formulas, the Chronicler had in mind only one work, to which he referred in every possible way, a variety indicated by both his literary inclination and theological presuppositions.[15]

Japhet then indicated that three options have been proposed for what this single document would have been: (1) a noncanonical and no longer extant book of the history of Israel, (2) an earlier form of Joshua–Kings, and (3) a literary fiction created by the Chronicler for the appearance of authority. Japhet noted that each of these possibilities has some support.[16]

Japhet made a strong argument for understanding the Chronicler's use of a multiplicity of phrases to refer to written document(s) in ways that do not make much sense "on the face of it" from our modern, highly literate perspective. Rather, she insisted that the Chronicler's use of various phrases to refer to this single source is simply part of "his literary inclination and theological presuppositions."[17]

From our modern literate perspective, we rightly ask the question about how such variations came about and what the motivating factors might have been in these changes. As Japhet argues concerning the source citations, however, these variations have less meaning than we may initially ascertain. That is, Japhet made an argument for the presence of multiformity and fluidity in Chronicles similar to that found in oral traditions. James Sparks made a similar argument in his recent monograph *The Chronicler's Genealogies: Towards an Understanding of 1 Chronicles 1–9.*[18] Sparks drew significantly from Robert Wilson's comparative work on genealogies.[19] Sparks produced helpful charts

---

15. Ibid., 22. See similarly Stott, *Why Did They Write This Way?* 60–67.

16. Japhet, *I & II Chronicles*, 22–23. See also Stott's review of scholarship on this issue (*Why Did They Write This Way*, 60–67).

17. Japhet, *I & II Chronicles*, 22. Stott reaches a similar conclusion (*Why Did They Write This Way*, 67).

18. James T. Sparks, *The Chronicler's Genealogies: Towards an Understanding of 1 Chronicles 1–9* (Academia Biblica 28; Atlanta: Society of Biblical Literature, 2008).

19. See especially Robert R. Wilson, *Genealogy and History in the Biblical World* (Yale Near Eastern Researches 7; New Haven: Yale University Press, 1977).

summarizing the descendants of Benjamin as preserved in the following texts: MT Gen 46:21; LXX Gen 46:21; Num 26:38–41; 1 Chr 8:1–7; and 1 Chr 7:6–11.[20] Even a quick review of his charts reveals various inconsistencies among these passages. After discussing the inconsistencies between these genealogies, Sparks concluded:

> As Wilson points out, . . . the differences that the different genealogies contain are not to be thought of as in conflict, for they each rightly reflect the historical social reality at the given point in time at which they were formulated. Wilson further indicates that it is probable that even if conflicting genealogies arose within the same historical context, that the society in which they were formulated would not view them as in conflict, but would recognize that the differences which they project are reflections of the different social, political or religious contexts which brought the differing genealogies into existence.[21]

Like the arguments I have given above from Blount's work with the Luo, Wilson's conclusions drew from comparative anthropological fieldwork. This comparative work influenced Sparks to conclude that what appear to be contradictory genealogies may not have been understood as contradictory by the ancient audience.

Although I find Sparks's arguments on the multiformity of the genealogies convincing, I believe that he too often operated under the highly literate notion of individual authorship. For example, he wrote:

> This diversity makes it apparent that the Chronicler's genealogies would never have operated as a united genealogy within the societies of Israel, Judah, or Yehud, for they do not express the relationships within the society at any one point. If, however, the Chronicler's genealogies are not the reflection of a society's relationships at a particular point in time, and are not the result of a haphazard growth as suggested by Noth, this only leaves the conclusion that the Chronicler's genealogies are a literary construction of the Chronicler himself. If this conclusion is accepted, then this indicates that the current content, arrangement, and structure are the result of the deliberate plan and purpose of the Chronicler, as he shaped the overall work.[22]

Sparks seemed to assume that the diversity could not have existed at one point in time in Israelite society, because "a united [consistent?] genealogy" was necessary. Therefore, the genealogies are "a literary construction of the Chronicler himself" that are "the result of the deliberate plan and purpose of the Chronicler." Certainly individuals were involved in the writing of the

---

20. Sparks, *Chronicler's Genealogies*, 265–68.
21. Ibid., 263.
22. Ibid., 22.

book of Chronicles; however, Sparks's understanding seems to assume an anachronistic quality of autonomy for his Chronicler. Although oral traditions are characterized by multiformity, this multiformity is not produced by autonomous individuals who have complete creative license. Again, recall the reluctance of Luo individuals to reconstruct their own genealogy, because this was a task to be accomplished by a group of elders. Such would also be the case with literature of primarily oral societies.

In "Who Was the Chronicler's Audience?" Yigal Levin reaches conclusions similar to those of Sparks.[23] Although he continues to use the terminology of the Chronicler as the author, Levin nevertheless took the oral world of ancient Israel more seriously. From his study of the genealogies, he concluded:

> Many of the genealogies exhibit a large degree of *segmentation*, varying degrees of *depth*, and—in the comparison of the different lineages sometimes given to the same clans or tribes—a large degree of *fluidity*. The resemblance to oral genealogies is unmistakable.[24]

> And the discrepancies among different "versions" of the same list (such as the *four* different Benjaminite lists in Gen 46:21; Num 26:38–40; 1 Chr 7:6–12; 1 Chr 8:1–40) represented the fluidity that was essential to that form of list.[25]

Levin, therefore, concluded that the genealogies were not simply the literary creation of the Chronicler, but that "these genealogies were adapted from the 'living' oral traditions of the people of Judah, Benjamin, Levi, Ephraim, Manasseh, and (southern) Asher in the late Persian period and were intended to reflect the situation of those tribes' clans at the time."[26] Thus, the Chronicler's audience was "the tribal, village society . . . in the hill country of Judah and Benjamin, but also those of Ephraim and Manasseh."[27]

Although I still think that Levin's notion of one individual author, the Chronicler, is problematic, I nevertheless appreciate his emphasis on how his Chronicler was significantly influenced by the living, oral traditions as well as by written documents. This interplay of the oral and the written is consistent with what we know about writing in primarily oral societies. So, even though I would reconstruct the writing of the book of Chronicles as involving various individuals in a school or guild, I agree with Levin's notion that individuals (his Chronicler, my Chronistic school) would have drawn from both oral and

---

23. Yigal Levin, "Who Was the Chronicler's Audience? A Hint from His Genealogies," *JBL* 122 (2003): 229–45.

24. Ibid., 235.

25. Ibid., 243.

26. Ibid., 242–43.

27. Ibid., 245.

written sources without making a necessary distinction between the two types of sources.[28]

MULTIFORMITY BETWEEN THE DEUTERONOMIC HISTORY AND THE BOOK OF CHRONICLES

As we have seen, multiformity exists in both the Deuteronomic History and the book of Chronicles that on face value could be understood as denoting ideological or theological differences representing conflicts between individuals and the groups they represent. This multiformity, however, is best understood as reflecting a different cultural understanding—one based on an oral culture—that allows such variation without having such loaded intentions. The observation that two versions of the story of David and Goliath were both considered authoritative enough to be preserved in a conflation that did not eliminate their inconsistencies and the observation that Chronicles has various phrases to refer to what was most probably one written document suggest that the ancient Israelites understood such variation quite differently. If this is the case in each of these literary works, we should explore the possibility that some of the "differences" between these literary works may also be inconsequential from the ancients' perspective.

For example, Sparks's and Levin's perspective on multiformity in genealogical material could also apply well to the differences in the genealogies between the Deuteronomic History and the book of Chronicles, some of which are given here:

(1)   1 Chr 2:6:   "The sons of *Zerah*: Zimri, Ethan, Heman, Calcol, and Dara"
       1 Kgs 4:31:   "Ethan the Ezrahite, and Heman, Calcol, and Dara, sons of *Mahol*"

(2)   1 Chr 2:13, 15:   "Jesse became the father of Eliab his firstborn . . . David the *seventh*.
       1 Sam 16:10:   "Jesse made seven of his sons pass before Samuel, but Samuel said to Jesse, 'The LORD has not chosen these.'" [This implies that David is the *eighth* son.]

(3)   1 Chr 2:13, 16:   "*Jesse* became the father of Eliab his firstborn . . . and their sisters were Zeruiah and Abigail."

---

28. Ehud Ben Zvi argued a similar position concerning multiformity in Chronicles (as well as Samuel–Kings), but he did so from a perspective that assumed that Samuel–Kings were authoritative texts that would have influenced the reading of Chronicles in a text-centered community. See Ehud Ben Zvi, *History, Literature and Theology in the Book of Chronicles* (London: Equinox, 2006), esp. chapter 3.

	2 Sam 17:25:	"Abigail daughter of *Nahash*, sister of Zeruiah"
(4)	1 Chr 3:1:	"These are the sons of David who were born to him at Hebron . . . the second *Daniel*, by Abigail the Carmelite"
	2 Sam 3:2–3:	"Sons were born to David at Hebron . . . his second, *Chileab*, of Abigail the widow of Nabal the Carmelite"
(5)	1 Chr 3:6–8:	[sons of David] "Ibhar, *Elishama*, *Eliphelet*, Nogah, Nepheg, Japhia, Elishama, Eliada, and Eliphelet, nine." [Elishama and Eliphelet are repeated]
	2 Sam 5:15–16:	[sons of David] "Ibhar, Elishua, Nepheg, Japhia, Elishama, Eliada, and Eliphelet"
(6)	1 Chr 3:6–8:	[sons of David] "Ibhar, Elishama, Eliphelet, *Nogah*, Nepheg, Japhia, Elishama, Eliada, and Eliphelet, nine."
	2 Sam 5:15–16:	[sons of David] "Ibhar, *Elishua*, Nepheg, Japhia, Elishama, Eliada, and Eliphelet"
(7)	1 Chr 9:39:	"*Ner* begot Kish"
	1 Sam 9:1:	"Kish son of *Abiel*"

The standard approach to such inconsistencies is illustrated well in Japhet's comments on example 1 concerning the difference between Zerah (1 Chr 2:6) and Mahol (1 Kgs 4:31) as the father of Ethan, Heman, Calcol, and Dara. She wrote:

> It is precisely these historical difficulties which emphasize the Chronicler's intentions: to establish some kind of genealogy for the Zerahites, and to weave into his genealogical fabric as many as possible of the historical figures appearing in his narrative sources but which he does not mention in his own narrative sections.[29]

Japhet assumes that the differences between 1 Chr 2:6 and 1 Kgs 4:31 were intentional on the part of the Chronicler, and as an intentional change this difference must be related to a broader ideological and/or historiographical purpose. From what I have argued above, however, we should not assume that such differences are "intentional" or that such "differences" were even noticed by all of the ancient readers and writers. That is, we must allow for the possibility that many of these apparent inconsistencies were so inconsequential from the perspective of the early tradents that they were not understood as inconsistencies at all.

We also should explore further the implication of the above discussions concerning the references to written documents in the Deuteronomic History

---

29. Japhet, *I & II Chronicles*, 75.

and the book of Chronicles. Many scholars assume that the source citations in Kings refer to no longer extant written sources that influenced the writing of Kings, for example, king lists, temple records, and royal chronicles.[30] However, with regard to the source citations in Chronicles, many scholars assume that they simply refer to an earlier form of Samuel–Kings.[31] Why the difference? If Japhet is justified in concluding that the many references in Chronicles are probably to one written document, then we should reconsider the possibility that the references in Kings and those in Chronicles also are referring to one written document, a common source for these two works. The multiplicity in Kings is actually far less than that in Chronicles, so why would we not conclude the same? In fact, if we take Carr's observations seriously that the transmission of texts was more about what was in the mind, we must consider that the evidence for one common source is really evidence for a written source that is simply understood as one re-presentation of the fuller tradition in all its multiformity. That is, no one text can possibly re-present the tradition as a whole and, therefore, must necessarily refer to the broader tradition in its written and oral forms.

This understanding would certainly be consistent with my reconstruction of the history behind the Deuteronomic History and the book of Chronicles. In the Babylonian exile, scribes wrote a common source for these two works on the basis of documents they carried with them from Jerusalem. Source citations in this early common source, therefore, may have referred to pre-exilic royal annals, king lists, prophetic stories, and the like, that survived the destruction of Jerusalem and were taken to Babylonia either by the Babylonians or by the exiled Israelite bureaucracy, thereby indicating that the one written document did not re-present the entire tradition. However, as this common source underwent further changes during the Babylonian exile and later in both Persian Babylonia and Yehud, these references may have lost their connection to such monarchical source material, especially if it was no longer extant. If this is the case, then the references may have taken on new meaning as relating to the common source behind both the Deuteronomic History and the book of Chronicles, again even though this one source may not have been understood to re-present the entire tradition. Of course, my reconstruction mirrors closely the consensus model that has the Deuteronomic History (especially Samuel–Kings) playing the role of the exilic common source and Chronicles as the late text with new meanings.

---

30. See the excellent survey of scholarship in Stott, *Why Did They Write This Way*, 52–60.

31. See the excellent survey of scholarship in Stott, *Why Did They Write This Way*, 60–67.

Above I have been critical of others for too often assuming that apparent differences are significant evidence of ideological conflict. Now let me be clear that I am not assuming the opposite, that every difference is necessarily unintentional and therefore inconsequential. In fact, Japhet's comments that the difference between 1 Kgs 4:31 and 1 Chr 2:6 (example 1 above) are ideologically motivated may be accurate. Blount describes a case of disagreement about the genealogy of the Luo people that had significant consequences for the social standing of one of the elders, so there are certainly differences in genealogies within primarily oral cultures that are ideologically motivated. However, I think that we must carefully assess our own assumptions and try to determine on the basis of the literature itself what inconsistencies may be consequential and what inconsistencies may be inconsequential rather than assuming that all (or even most) differences are intentional and consequential.[32]

In the following chapters I explore more fully how this insight of multiformity relates to the interpretation of the Deuteronomic History and the book of Chronicles. In chapter 4, I explore some selected synoptic passages, and in chapter 5 some of the nonsynoptic passages. For heuristic reasons, I will intentionally err on the side of assuming that apparent differences are inconsequential and that we have exaggerated these differences in ways that are anachronistic because of our own notions of writing and texts. I must admit, however, that I have struggled with developing some way in which to discern when an apparent difference is consequential (that is, due to an ideological or theological difference between the two schools of authors/redactors) or inconsequential (that is, having no value for reconstructing such ideological or theological differences), especially when the evidence for such possible ideological conflict is confined to only one or two passages.

---

32. Although this point was made years ago by Werner Lemke, it needs to be continually reasserted. See Werner E. Lemke, "The Synoptic Problem in the Chronicler's History," *HTR* 58 (1965): 349–63.

4

Multiformity and the Synoptic Passages

The multiformity of textual traditions is widely accepted as the norm for the transmission of biblical texts. The extant textual traditions—MT, LXX, Vulgate, Qumran, and so on—provide ample evidence that various Hebrew text-types circulated in Israel at least as late as the first century C.E. This multiformity operates also on a more micro-level within these text-types. For example, Shemaryahu Talmon concluded that the existence of doublets or conflate readings "illustrate the scribes' reverence for transmitted alternative readings."[1] Also commenting on conflate readings, Julio Trebolle noted that "copyists had great respect for every existing variant reading transmitted."[2]

Despite this consensus in text criticism, few redaction critics take seriously the implications of textual plurality upon their redaction-critical work. For example, Isaac Kalimi based his work on Chronicles primarily on a comparison of MT Chronicles with MT Samuel–Kings.[3] However, a growing number of scholars are making use of text-critical evidence in their redactional work on the Deuteronomic History and on the relationship between the Deuteronomic History and the book of Chronicles.[4] These scholars use principles developed from text criticism as more objective controls on their redaction-critical work. For example, in text criticism Emanuel Tov concluded:

> Differences in sequence often concern sections (short as well as long ones), whose position had not yet been fixed in the various traditions because of their secondary nature. These sections were added to the text at a relatively late period, and because of uncertainty over their position, were inserted in different places in [MT, the Targumim, Samaritan Pentateuch, Vulgate, and the Hebrew *Vorlage* of LXX].[5]

---

1. Shemaryahu Talmon, "Conflate Readings (OT)," *IDBSup*, 170.
2. Julio C. Trebolle, "Conflate Readings in the Old Testament," *ABD* 1:1125.
3. Kalimi, *Reshaping of Ancient Israelite History*, 11.
4. For a review of selected studies on the Deuteronomic History, see Person, *Deuteronomic School*, 34–50.
5. Emanuel Tov, *Textual Criticism of the Hebrew Bible* (Minneapolis: Fortress Press, 1992), 339. See also idem, "Some Sequence Differences between the MT and LXX and Their

Thus, Graeme Auld could conclude the following concerning source-redactional issues:

> The greatest variation between the different ancient texts of Kings is mostly within the material which I am suggesting was added to the common source of Kings and Chronicles to make the book of Kings as we know it. I suspect that, just because it was being added to an existing corpus of traditions, there were different views about where it should be placed—and these are reflected in the different ancient witnesses. [6]

Here we can plainly see where Auld took a principle from text criticism and applied it to source and redactional questions concerning the relationship of Kings and Chronicles. David Carr recently reached similar conclusions, when he argued for a "trend towards expansion" based on "empirical" evidence, especially text-critical studies, from a variety of ancient Near Eastern texts (for example, Gilgamesh, Atrahasis, and the Sumerian King List), biblical texts (for example, Jeremiah, Ezra/Esdras), and extrabiblical texts (for example, the *Temple Scroll*). Carr concluded that "Chronicles did not use a version of Samuel–Kings identical to proto-MT or indeed any version witnessed to in our current manuscripts."[7] When Carr then compared Samuel–Kings and Chronicles to pentateuchal sources for another type of redactional control, he observed that "links to the Pentateuch are far less common in material shared between Chronicles and Samuel–Kings than they are in material specific to Chronicles on the one hand and Samuel–Kings on the other."[8] This disparity between synoptic and nonsynoptic texts supported his contention of a "trend towards expansion," in that the expansive, later material contains more intertextual references. Carr, therefore, has used empirical evidence to lend qualified support for Auld's thesis of a common source behind Samuel–Kings and Chronicles.[9]

Ramifications for the Literary Criticism of the Bible," *JNSL* 13 (1987): 151–60; and Julio C. Trebolle, "Samuel/Kings and Chronicles: Book Divisions and Textual Composition," in *Studies in the Hebrew Bible, Qumran, and the Septuagint Presented to Eugene Ulrich* (ed. Peter W. Flint, Emanuel Tov, and James C. VanderKam; VTSup 101; Leiden: Brill, 2006), 97.

6. Auld, *Kings without Privilege*, 6.

7. David M. Carr, "'Empirical' Comparison and the Analysis of the Relationship of the Pentateuch and the Former Prophets," in *The Pentateuch and the Former Prophets: Overarching Perspectives for Composition and Theology* (ed. Konrad Schmid and Thomas Dozeman; Ancient Israel and Its Literature; Atlanta: Society of Biblical Literature, forthcoming in 2011), 19. Page references here and below are to author's prepublication manuscript.

8. Ibid., 27. See n. 7 above.

9. In his 2006 essay, Carr's support of Auld's thesis lacked the same nuances of qualification as his 2011 essay. Compare David M. Carr, "Empirische Perspektiven auf das Deuteronomistische Geschichtswerk," in *Die deuteronomistischen Geschichtswerke. Redaktions- und religionsgeschichtliche Perspektiven zur "Deuteronomismus"-Diskussion in Tora und Vorderen Propheten* (ed. Markus Witte et al.; BZAW 365; Berlin: Walter de Gruyter,

This chapter and the next draw on the work of some of these scholars who have applied this text-critical approach to the study of the relationship between the Deuteronomic History and the book of Chronicles, especially that of Julio Trebolle, Adrian Schenker, Graeme Auld, and Robert Rezetko. However, although their use of text-critical controls has advanced the discussion, their own arguments require further revision on the basis of the characteristic of multiformity as understood in oral traditions and in the use of texts in primarily oral societies.

I divide my discussion into two parts: one concerning the parallels between Samuel and Chronicles and one concerning the parallels between Kings and Chronicles. This not only represents a discussion of the material in its canonical order but also represents a difference of opinion concerning the text-critical evidence in the book of Samuel and that in the book of Kings. Even many scholars who argue for the consensus model of the Deuteronomic History as the source for Chronicles also argue that MT Samuel represents a later expansive textual tradition and that other textual traditions (especially LXX Samuel, 4QSam^a) more accurately reflect the *Vorlage* used by the Chronicler. However, fewer are willing to conclude the same concerning MT Kings. For example, Steven McKenzie concluded:

> The 4QSam^a fragments have made it clear that [the Chronicler] used a text of [Samuel] that was different from [MT Samuel]. However, the situation in regard to [the Chronicler's] *Vorlage* of [Kings] is not necessarily the same as it is for his *Vorlage* of [Samuel]. . . . There can be little doubt that [MT Kings] and [MT Chronicles] reflect a single text type of [Kings], i.e., [the Chronicler's] *Vorlage* of [Kings] was proto-Rabbinic. [10]

McKenzie's conclusion continues to have its supporters;[11] however, some recent text-critical work—for example, that of Trebolle and Schenker—challenges this conclusion concerning the relationship between Kings and Chronicles.

In "Samuel/Kings and Chronicles: Book Divisions and Textual Compositions," Trebolle argued that a common source for the David material was later expanded in both Samuel–Kings and Chronicles.[12] His reconstruction is based

---

2006), 1–17; and idem, "'Empirical' Comparison" (see esp. 16 n. 33 [see p. 88 n. 7 above], where he specifically noted this shift in his own evaluation of Auld's thesis).

10. McKenzie, *Chronicler's Use of the Deuteronomistic History*, 119, 155. See also idem, "1 Kings 8: A Sample Study into the Texts of Kings Used by the Chronicler and Translated by the Old Greek," *BIOSCS* 19 (1986): 31.

11. For example, Knoppers, *I Chronicles 1–9*, 66–71.

12. Trebolle, "Samuel/Kings and Chronicles." Diana Edelman also discussed Auld's proposal in relationship to 2 Samuel 5–24//1 Chronicles 11–24 and reached some similar conclusions; however, Edelman did not reference any of the text-critical evidence. She concluded that Auld's Shared Text thesis was possible, but further study was necessary. See

on his analysis of Samuel–Kings//Chronicles and the delimitation of the *kaige* and non-*kaige* recensions of the LXX for this material.

The non-*kaige* recension of the LXX is found in 1 Sam 1:1–2 Sam 11:1. This section is then followed by the *kaige* recension in 2 Sam 11:2–1 Kgs 2:11. Trebolle argued that these recensional sections may represent a different, ancient division of the books—that is, the early forms behind both 1 Sam 1:1–2 Sam 11:1 and 2 Sam 11:2–1 Kgs 2:11 may have each been on separate scrolls—especially when one takes seriously the evidence of the relationship between Samuel–Kings and Chronicles.[13]

Trebolle noted the literary relationship between Samuel–Kings and Chronicles as follows. In the different portrayals of the David narrative, Samuel and Chronicles have a sequence of events from the time David became king of all of Israel (2 Sam 5:1–5//1 Chr 11:1–3) that is very similar to the brief report of Joab besieging Rabbah (2 Sam 11:1//1 Chr 20:1a). What follows this block in Chronicles parallels materials in the so-called Appendix in 2 Samuel (1 Chr 20:4–8 = 2 Sam 21:18–22; 1 Chronicles 21 = 2 Samuel 24), whereas the material in Samuel–Kings is unique to Samuel–Kings—that is, the story of David and Bathsheba (2 Sam 11:2–12:25) and the succession narrative (2 Samuel 13–20; 1 Kings 1–2).[14]

Trebolle demonstrated how the relationship between Samuel–Kings and Chronicles, on the one hand, and the divisions between the non-*kaige* recension and the *kaige* recension, on the other hand, collate well to provide strong evidence of where the ancient texts of Samuel–Kings were divided. Thus, Trebolle identified a common source for 2 Sam 5:1–11:1//1 Chr 11:1–20:1a that narrated from when David became king of all of Israel (2 Sam 5:1–5//1 Chr 11:1–3) to the brief report of Joab besieging Rabbah (2 Sam 11:1//1 Chr 20:1a), the ending of which corresponds to the ending of the non-*kaige* recension. This common source was later expanded into both Samuel–Kings and Chronicles. Trebolle noted that "the redactional texts, especially the Deuteronomistic ones, are located especially at the beginning and end of these books, where editorial activity is more obvious from duplicate passages and transpositions that give rise to different textual forms attested by the manuscript tradition."[15] Trebolle's primary interest concerned the material following 2 Sam 11:1//1 Chr 20:1a, and thus he did not elaborate much on the beginning of this common source and the additions made at the front end of it. Therefore, some of what

---

Diana Edelman, "The Deuteronomist's David and the Chronicler's David: Competing or Contrasting Ideologies," in *The Future of the Deuteronomistic History* (ed. Thomas Römer; BETL 147; Leuven: Leuven University Press, 2000), 67–83.

13. Trebolle, "Samuel/Kings and Chronicles," 97–100. See also, Trebolle, "Kings (MT/LXX) and Chronicles," 499.

14. Trebolle, "Samuel/Kings and Chronicles," 100.

15. Ibid., 97.

follows is my extension of his argument in adherence to the methods and principles he laid out.

Trebolle did not discuss his reasons for identifying the beginning of the
common source; however, when he referred to his reconstructed source he
began with the report of David's becoming king of all of Israel (2 Sam 5:1–
5//1 Chr 11:1–3).[16] Although this would be an excellent beginning to a source
concerning David, I think it is just as possible that the source began with the
report of the death of Saul and some of his sons (1 Chr 10//1 Sam 31). At least
the fact that this is where Chronicles begins immediately following the genealogies (1 Chr 1–9) strongly recommends the possibility.

I have attempted to summarize Trebolle's approach to the David story (or
maybe more appropriately my extension of his approach) in a chart show-
ing the common source and additions in both Samuel–Kings and Chronicles.
The chart helps to illustrate the expansive character of both Samuel–Kings and
Chronicles, especially with regards to their unique material. For an example
from Samuel–Kings, four additional chapters begin David's story, describing
his struggle with the remaining sons of Saul (2 Sam 1–4), placed between the
report of Saul's death (1 Sam 31//1 Chr 10) and the report of David as king
over all of Israel (2 Sam 5:1–5//1 Chr 11:1–3).[17] For an example from Chronicles, following the list of David's mighty men (1 Chr 11:10–47//2 Sam 23:8–39)
there is unique material concerning David's early supporters coming from a
variety of tribes, emphasizing his support throughout Israel (1 Chr 12) (see
chart on following page).[18]

Also on the chart are those passages that are not unique in Samuel–Kings
or Chronicles but for which Trebolle had redactional reasons for excluding
them from the common source other than their occurrence after the ending of
the non-*kaige* recension (2 Sam 11:1//1 Chr 20:1a). The first synoptic material
following the end of his reconstructed common source is the passage concerning David's capture of Rabbah (2 Sam 12:26–31//1 Chr 20:1b–3), which
Trebolle rejected as dependent on the ending of the common source—that is,
the report of Joab besieging Rabbah (1 Chr 20:1a//2 Sam 11:1)—but this passage elevates David by displacing Joab.[19] In addition, Trebolle considered those
passages that occur in different locations to be redactional additions (2 Sam
23:8–39//1 Chr 11:10–47 and either 2 Sam 5:11–25//1 Chr 14:1–17 or 2 Sam
6:1–11//1 Chr 13:5–14).[20]

---

16. Ibid., 100.

17. For my discussion of this passage, see chapter 5 below, pp. 132–34.

18. For my discussion of this passage, see chapter 5 below, pp. 145–50.

19. Trebolle, "Samuel/Kings and Chronicles," 101–2.

20. Although Trebolle commented on the different sequences of the material in
2 Sam 5:11–6:11//1 Chr 13:5–14:17, he did not reconstruct the common source here ("Sam-
uel/Kings and Chronicles," 102–5). He concluded, however, that "Chronicles follows a text

Hypothetical Common Source Based Significantly
on the Work of Julio Trebolle[21]

Common Source	Additions in Samuel–Kings	Additions in Chronicles
1 Chr 10:1–14//1 Sam 31:1–13		
	2 Sam 1:1–4:12	
1 Chr 11:1–9//2 Sam 5:1–10		
	2 Sam 23:8–39	1 Chr 11:10–47
		1 Chr 12:1–13:4
	2 Sam 6:1–11	1 Chr 13:5–14
1 Chr 14:1–17//2 Sam 5:11–25		
		1 Chr 15:1–24
1 Chr 15:25–16:3//2 Sam 6:12–19a		
		1 Chr 16:4–42
1 Chr 16:43//2 Sam 6:19b–20a		
	2 Sam 6:20b–23	
1 Chr 17:1–18:17//2 Sam 7:1–8:18		
	2 Sam 9:1–13	
1 Chr 19:1–20:1a//2 Sam 10:1–11:1		
	2 Sam 11:2–12:25	
	2 Sam 12:26–31	1 Chr 20:1b–3
	2 Sam 13:1–21:17	
	2 Sam 21:18–22	1 Chr 20:4–8
	2 Sam 22:1–23:7	
	2 Sam 24:1–25	1 Chr 21:1–27
		1 Chr 21:28–29:19
	1 Kgs 1:1–2:9	
	1 Kgs 2:10–12	1 Chr 29:20–30

---

of Samuel in which the materials of the Appendix were closely connected to those prior to 2 Sam 11:1" (104–5). In this case, the chart represents the opposite decision to that suggested by Rezetko (*Source and Redaction*, 27), simply to illustrate how both options seem reasonable. That is, a common order of the material in Samuel and Chronicles could be restored no matter which of these two passages (2 Sam 5:11–25//1 Chr 14:1–17 or 2 Sam 6:1–11//1 Chr 13:5–14) one removes as a later addition.

21. Trebolle, "Samuel/Kings and Chronicles." The section of the chart on 1 Chr 11:1–16:43//2 Sam 23:8–39; 5:11–6:23 is influenced significantly by the chart for this material in Rezetko, *Source and Redaction*, 27. The order given for parallels found in different locations (considered additions) follows that of Chronicles. For a full summary of Rezetko's discussion of this material, see below, pp. 94–105.

As noted above, the chart actually contains some decisions that Trebolle himself did not make. For example, he devoted little discussion to where the common source began and in some cases chose not to reconstruct portions of it, most likely because the textual data supported both options for the reconstruction—such as deciding which of the two sections was the later addition that created a different arrangement of the material, 2 Sam 5:11–25//1 Chr 14:1–17 or 2 Sam 6:1–11//1 Chr 13:5–14.[22] In fact, even though I think that the chart helps one to understand his argument better, it is actually misleading to some extent, because Trebolle explicitly resisted reconstructing the text of what might be imagined as the "original" common source. Rather, as is evident in the following quotation, he insisted that we accept the multiformity of the texts:

> When studying the historical books, alongside the analytical model that assigns various texts to successive redactions another analytical model has to be used that accepts the co-existence of parallel editions. The final process of composition and redaction of a work can give rise to several editions that can co-exist and even intermix. [23]

The common scholarly preoccupation with reconstructing the one "original" text of Samuel or exactly what the Chronicler's *Vorlage* may have been or discerning individual layers when assuming a unilinear redactional process all run counter to Trebolle's understanding of the textual diversity in ancient Israel, such that a different model is necessary. This different model is one that accepts the fluidity and multiformity of the textual tradition—that is, a model that is consistent with the understanding developed in the previous chapters of how literature may have been composed and transmitted in a culture that was primarily oral in nature. In fact, the following quotation from Albert Lord's work on oral tradition illustrates the close connection between Trebolle's understanding of textual plurality and the multiformity found in oral traditions: "In oral tradition the idea of an original is illogical."[24] John Miles Foley has argued an analogous textual plurality for the orally derived Homeric epics over an eight-hundred-year period. He wrote that "up to the

---

22. Trebolle, "Samuel/Kings and Chronicles," 102–5.

23. Ibid., 98. Sidnie White Crawford provided an excellent example of the ancient acceptance of a multiplicity of texts when she concluded the following concerning the author of 4QTestimonia: "The scribe chose what we would identify as two different text-types for his anthology of Scripture passages. These textual choices demonstrate that the scribal composer did not discriminate between text-types; evidently all these variants texts were equally authoritative to him" (*Rewriting Scripture in Second Temple Times* [Studies in the Dead Sea Scrolls and Related Literature; Grand Rapids: Eerdmans, 2008], 35).

24. Lord, *Singer of Tales*, 101.

time of Aristarchus, Homer's poems existed not in one exclusive version but rather in many versions of different but—from the perspective of the tradition—equal authority."[25]

In the following, we will see that this model of textual multiplicity can inform the discussion of the relationship between Samuel–Kings and Chronicles as we explore further the possibility that MT Samuel–Kings and MT Chronicles descended from a common source.

PARALLELS BETWEEN THE BOOK OF SAMUEL AND THE BOOK OF CHRONICLES

As noted in the introduction to this chapter, the consensus model allows that MT Samuel has undergone some later recensional activity since Samuel served as the *Vorlage* for portions of Chronicles and that the *Vorlage* is preserved better in LXX Samuel and 4QSam[a].[26] However, the acceptance of this observation by those who support the consensus model has generally not led to the reassessment of the consensus model itself, since the differences between MT Samuel and the other versions are often not taken seriously in the redactional study of Samuel and in discussions of how Samuel and Chronicles are related. That is, many continue simply to compare MT Samuel and MT Chronicles.

Below I will discuss some of the synoptic passages in 2 Sam 5–6; 23//1 Chr 11–16 as well as some representative secondary literature on these passages. We will see that, although the consensus model accepts the fact that MT Samuel underwent recensional activity after an earlier form of Samuel was the *Vorlage* for Chronicles, the full force of this process has not yet been taken seriously. When one follows the implications of this development to their logical conclusion, one concludes that Samuel as preserved in all of the extant versions underwent recensional activity after its use as the *Vorlage* of Chronicles. In other words, the current forms of Samuel and Chronicles are descended from a common source, which was an early, no longer extant form of Samuel.

2 SAMUEL 5–6; 23//1 CHRONICLES 11–16

The most thorough recent study of 2 Sam 5–6; 23//1 Chr 11–16 is Robert Rezetko's monograph *Source and Revision in the Narratives of David's Transfer of the Ark*. Rezetko depended significantly on text-critical approaches to Samuel//Chronicles and drew on recent discussions of the late date of the Deuteronomistic History and the relationship between the Deuteronomistic History

---

25. Foley, *Traditional Oral Epic*, 30.

26. See Rezetko's summary of the history of text criticism and its implication for research on Samuel (*Source and Revision*, 55–68).

and the book of Chronicles as well as his own critique of the consensus model regarding preexilic Early Biblical Hebrew (EBH) and postexilic Late Biblical Hebrew (LBH). He stated his concluding thesis as follows:

> Samuel's editors in the period of the Second Temple considerably reshaped an earlier version of the story of David's ark transfer. Consequently, many textual and linguistic details attested in MT 2 Sam 6 are secondary and often later than details in the parallel texts of MT 1 Chron 13,15–16. [27]

His conclusions led him to qualified support of Auld's thesis of a Shared Text— that is, support for a common source behind Samuel–Kings//Chronicles with an understanding that both MT Samuel and MT Chronicles include additions to this common source.

> [W]hen we compare the details of the alternative formulations of David's ark transfer in Samuel and Chronicles in the extant witnesses to these books (Hebrew, Greek, etc.), we conclude that Samuel developed beyond the point in time when Chronicles made use of Samuel (and Kings), whenever that was. In short, compared with Chronicles, Samuel (and Kings) cannot be seen as earlier source-material only, since this book also displays its own separate editorial shaping, which advanced independently and even beyond Chronicles.[28]

Rezetko's qualified support of Auld's thesis closely parallels my own, in that he understood that the common source was an earlier version of Samuel–Kings.

Although his emphasis is clearly on 2 Sam 6 and 1 Chr 13; 15–16, he sets his discussion of these passages in the broader context of 2 Sam 5–6; 23//2 Chr 11–16. He summarizes the relationship between these two complexes as shown in the chart on the following page. As Rezetko's chart clearly demonstrates, here Samuel//Chronicles have five parallel passages in the same order (2 Sam 5:1–5//1 Chr 11:1–3; 2 Sam 5:6–10//1 Chr 11:4–9; 2 Sam 6:1–11//1 Chr 13:5–14; 2 Sam 6:12–19a//1 Chr 15:25–16:3; 2 Sam 6:19b–20a//1 Chr 16:43), two parallel passages in a different order (2 Sam 5:11–25//1 Chr 14:1–17; 2 Sam 23:8–39//1 Chr 11:10–12:41), one passage unique to Samuel (2 Sam 6:20b–23), and three passages unique to Chronicles (1 Chr 13:1–4; 1 Chr 15:1–24; 1 Chr 16:4–42).

---

27. Rezetko, *Source and Revision*, 3. When discussing his "textual-exegetical" method, Rezetko explicitly stated that he depended on the approach of Trebolle, among others (ibid., 55–57); therefore, it is no accident that in his brief study of this same material Trebolle independently reached some of the same conclusions as Rezetko. See Trebolle, "Samuel/Kings and Chronicles," 102–4.

28. Rezetko, *Source and Revision*, 3.

Relationship of 2 Samuel 5–6; 23 and 1 Chronicles 11–16
Based on the Work of Robert Rezetko[29]

2 Samuel 5–6; 23	1 Chronicles 11–16
David is made king over Israel at Hebron (2 Sam 5:1–5)	David is made king over Israel at Hebron (1 Chr 11:1–3)
David captures Jerusalem (2 Sam 5:6–10)	David captures Jerusalem (1 Chr 11:4–9)
David consolidates his kingdom (2 Sam 5:11–25)	[see below, 1 Chr 14:1–17]
[see below, 2 Sam 23:8–39]	The role of David's mighty warriors (1 Chr 11:10–12:41)
	David proposes to bring the ark to Jerusalem (1 Chr 13:1–4)
David goes to fetch the ark and Uzzah is slaughtered (2 Sam 6:1–11)	David goes to fetch the ark and Uzzah is slaughtered (1 Chr 13:5–14)
[see above, 2 Sam 5:11–25]	David consolidates his kingdom (1 Chr 14:1–17)
	David prepares to bring the ark to Jerusalem (1 Chr 15:1–24)
David brings the ark to Jerusalem and blesses the people (2 Sam 6:12–19a)	David brings the ark to Jerusalem and blesses the people (1 Chr 15:25–16:3)
	David prepares for Yahweh's cultic service (1 Chr 16:4–42)
The people return home and David returns to bless his house (2 Sam 6:19b–20a)	The people return home and David returns to bless his house (1 Chr 16:43)
Michal the daughter of Saul chides David (2 Sam 6:20b–23)	
The role of David's mighty warriors (2 Sam 23:8–39)	[see above, 1 Chr 11:10–12:41]

The consensus model would explain these variations quite simply as two rearrangements, one omission, and three additions by the Chronicler to the text of Samuel. Rezetko challenges this consensus, for example, by concluding that 2 Sam 6:20b–23 is an addition to a common source and that MT 2 Sam

---

6:20b–23 shows even further development when compared to the other versions of Samuel.[30] In this section, I will analyze two of the parallel passages in these complexes (2 Sam 6:12–19a//1 Chr 15:25–16:3 and 2 Sam 23:8–39//1 Chr 11:10–47) in dialogue with Rezetko and others. In chapter 5, I will analyze two of the unique passages as well (2 Sam 6:20b–23; 1 Chr 15:1–24).

My analysis below of 2 Sam 6:12–19a//1 Chr 15:25–16:3 and 2 Sam 23:8–39//1 Chr 11:10–47 leads to two conclusions. First, Rezetko provided further text-critical support for a common source behind Samuel//Chronicles in ways that strengthen my own thesis—that is, the common source is an earlier, no longer extant form of Samuel (and Kings). Second, Rezetko provided further evidence of multiformity in the Samuel//Chronicles tradition. However, his interpretation of this multiformity is sometimes problematic in that he over-emphasized what from our modern perspective appear to be differences in meaning, but from the perspective of the ancients were probably read as synonymous interpretations of the ongoing tradition.

2 SAMUEL 6:12–19A//1 CHRONICLES 15:25–16:3

Consistent with many earlier studies, Rezetko made a variety of good arguments for often accepting a non-MT reading as the earliest reading with secondary expansion in both MT Samuel and MT Chronicles. As such, his text-critical analysis of these parallel passages did not differ significantly from the consensus model, which allows for the superiority of LXX Samuel over MT Samuel in many cases and a *Vorlage* similar to that of LXX Samuel as the basis of MT Chronicles' *Vorlage*. However, his interpretation of the text-critical variants challenged the consensus model in terms of the overarching themes in MT Samuel as compared to those of MT Chronicles concerning how Samuel and Chronicles differ from each other, especially since he was somewhat amenable to Auld's hypothesis of a common source. This challenge occurred in his discussion of two themes: (1) David's royal-sacral role (that is, David as king-priest) and (2) Michal's despising of David (2 Sam 6:16//1 Chr 15:29).

Rezetko reviewed the secondary literature and noted that "[s]cholars tend to assume that editors updated Chronicles according to a corporate-levitical thrust."[31] This tendency is based on a variety of readings, for example, MT 2 Sam 6:13 reads "he [David] sacrificed an ox and a fatling" whereas MT 1 Chr 15:26 reads "they [the Levites] sacrificed seven bulls and seven rams" and MT 2 Sam 6:17 reads "David presented burnt offerings" whereas MT 1 Chr 16:1 reads "they [the Levites] offered burnt offerings." On MT 2 Sam 6:13//MT 1 Chr 15:26,

---

Rezetko noted that "[m]ost believe David alone makes the sacrifices in 2 Sam 6:13 whereas the Levites, and in all probability apart from David's participation, make the sacrifices in 1 Chr 15:26."[32] Since the consensus model assumes that the Chronicler is using Samuel for his source, the Chronicler must have intentionally changed the singular verb form in 2 Sam 6:13 to the plural verb form in 1 Chr 15:26 to emphasize what Rezetko called "the corporate-levitical thrust."

Rezetko, however, has convincingly argued against this interpretation. First, he reconstructed the history of the text on the basis of LXX 2 Sam 6:13 with both MT 2 Sam 6:13 and MT 1 Chr 15:26 containing secondary material. The LXX 2 Sam 6:13 reading refers to the sacrifice with a noun, "a sacrifice: calf and lamb," thereby leaving ambiguous who and how many performed the sacrifice. The MT 2 Sam 6:13 reading ("he sacrificed") and the MT 1 Chr 15:26 reading ("they sacrificed") are both secondary readings that remove the ambiguity. Second and most convincingly, Rezetko noted that those who strive to make an argument for the "corporate-levitical thrust" of the Chronicler must conclude that the Chronicler's methodology was, in the words of Sara Japhet, "incomplete" and "inconsistent" because of material in Chronicles that poses problems for this argument.[33] Rezetko noted that in all of Samuel–Kings

> there are only five synoptic passages relating a king's (licit) participation in cultic activity.... In view of the paucity of related material in his *Vorlage*, and in view of his ideological bent, it is doubtful that the Chronicler is guilty of such oversights and shortcomings.[34]

Rather, in 1 Chr 15:25–16:3 the Chronicler's use of his source continues to portray David in ways that have cultic implications. David wears an ephod (1 Chr 15:27//2 Sam 6:14), blesses the people (1 Chr 16:2//2 Sam 6:18), and distributes food immediately following the sacrifice (1 Chr 16:3//2 Sam 6:19). Thus, Rezetko concluded that "the [plural] verb form in Chronicles does not aim to attenuate David's 'priestly' activity."[35]

Rezetko's criticism of the generally accepted interpretation of the Chronicler's use of his *Vorlage* in relationship to what he called the "corporate-levitical thrust" has merit, at least on the basis of his analysis of 2 Sam 5–6; 23//1 Chr 11–16. His criticism points to the methodological problem of focusing too

---

32. Ibid., 207.

33. Ibid., 208, citing Sara Japhet, *The Ideology of the Book of Chronicles and Its Place in Biblical Thought* (trans. Anna Barber; BEATAJ 9; Frankfurt: Peter Lang, 1989), 442–44.

34. Rezetko, *Source and Redaction*, 208. The five passages are (1) 2 Sam 6:13, 17–18//1 Chr 15:26; 16:1–2; (2) 2 Sam 24:18–25//1 Chr 21:18–26; (3) 1 Kgs 8:5, 62–64//2 Chr 5:6; 7:4–5, 7; (4) 1 Kgs 9:25//2 Chr 8:12; and (5) 1 Kgs 10:5//2 Chr 9:4.

35. Rezetko, *Source and Redaction*, 209.

much on the variations between MT Samuel and MT Chronicles without a thorough analysis of the common material and without adequate reference to the other text-types (especially LXX Samuel). Thus, Rezetko has brought a needed correction to the discussion. Unfortunately, he then made an analogous mistake when he proposed a similar conclusion about the nature of the secondary material of MT Samuel:

> Scholars tend to assume that editors updated Chronicles according to a corporate-levitical thrust, but this chapter [concerning 2 Samuel 6:11–15, 17–20a//1 Chronicles 13:14; 15:25–28; 16:1–3, 43] has shown that they may equally or more probably have revised Samuel with an interest in David's royal-sacral status.[36]

That is, the ideological differences between Samuel and Chronicles should be explained not primarily on the basis of changes the Chronicler made to the *Vorlage* but on the basis of changes the tradents behind MT Samuel made to its *Vorlage*. His conclusion about MT Samuel's heightened interest in "David's royal-sacral status" is based on what he considers to be ten secondary readings in MT 2 Samuel.[37] One of these variants concerns the sacrifice, which was discussed above. He argued that the MT-2 Sam 6:13 reading ("he sacrificed") is a heightening of David's "royal-sacral status" when compared to the ambiguous reading of the *Vorlage* (LXX 2 Sam 6:13: "a sacrifice"). Another one of these variants concerns David's cultic dress ("a linen ephod"), which Rezetko understood as a cultic upgrade in MT 2 Sam 6:14 from the more neutral "garment" (בגד) behind LXX 2 Sam 6:14. However, the broader context of David's sacral status in the passage that is shared by all of the extant texts undercuts Rezetko's argument. In fact, he seemed to recognize this when he wrote the following:

> The variant readings in synoptic MT Samuel . . . enhance these three themes [one of which is David's cultic status] beyond their presence in the shared material in Samuel and Chronicles. For example, the theme of cultic practice is evident already in references to "before Yahweh/God" (2 Sam 6:5, 17//1 Chron 13:8; 16:1; cf. 13:10), David's sacrifice (*shared* in 2 Sam 6:18//1 Chron 16:2), David's blessing (2 Sam 6:18//1 Chron 16:2), and perhaps עגלה חדשה (2 Sam 6:3 [cf. v. 4]//1 Chron 13:7).[38]

---

36. Ibid., 233.

37. Ibid., 289–90. Although Rezetko listed ten variants in his conclusion (289–90), the conclusion quoted here was based on only the five variants that occur in 2 Sam 6:11–15, 17–20a//1 Chr 13:14; 15:25–28; 16:1–3, 43, which he discussed in "this chapter" (that is, his chapter 5).

38. Rezetko, *Source and Revision*, 290.

As Rezetko himself demonstrated, those who argue that the Chronicler strives to attenuate David's royal-sacral status in favor of the Levites have necessarily overemphasized the difference between Chronicles and MT Samuel by overlooking the shared material. Rezetko has likewise overemphasized the difference between his reconstructed original (often based on LXX Samuel) and MT Samuel in order to argue an opposing position as a corrective—that is, that MT Samuel heightens David's royal-sacral status. When one considers that these differences are often not any greater in degree than what one might expect in a tradition that values multiformity and fluidity, they seem insignificant. This is especially the case, since, as Rezetko himself pointed out, the theme of David as a cultic figure, as a king-priest, is present in his reconstructed common source and in material found in all of the extant textual traditions. Therefore, it is difficult to conclude on the basis of so few variations that this theme is either attenuated or heightened in any of the traditions for 2 Sam 6:12–19a//1 Chr 15:25–16:3. Thus, for example, the ancient tradents may very well have understood all three expressions of the sacrifice—that is, "a sacrifice" (LXX 2 Sam 6:13), "he sacrificed" (MT 2 Sam 6:13), and "they sacrificed" (MT 1 Chr 15:26)—as related to David as a king-priest, since all of the extant texts portray David in cultic roles (for example, 2 Sam 6:18//1 Chr 16:2). At the same time, we cannot easily conclude, on the one hand, that the ancient tradents always understood David himself as actively performing the sacrifice in the role of a priest/Levite or, on the other hand, that they never understood him in this role but simply were referring to the king's role of providing financial support for the priests/Levites. An ancient scribe who had a theological predisposition toward David himself offering sacrifices would understand the text's references to the Levites as those assisting David in the ceremony. An ancient scribe who had a theological predisposition toward David being a figurehead for the work of the Levites, would understand the text's references to David as the major sponsor of the work of the Levites who perform their service on behalf of David and the people. To draw from Carr's work on memory again, if the scribes already knew what the tradition taught and they assumed that the text faithfully re-presented the tradition, they would most likely have read the text to be consistent with the tradition. In the process of copying, they very well might have produced a text with a few variants here and there that from our modern perspective might be a heightening of their own interpretation but from their perspective would simply be a continuation of the tradition as expressed in their understanding of the *Vorlage*. That is, what we see as variants they may have understood as readings in which nothing had changed in terms of meaning. Therefore, although I allow the possibility of a scribe producing a text that has changes that might have some theological motivation, I think that it is quite difficult to conclude that any particular text has undergone that type of change as a result of an intentional decision, because our notion of a variant would differ so much from the ancients' definition and because the text has undergone so many gradual changes over the years that it is extremely difficult to isolate the work of any particular scribe or even in many cases the work of a specific scribal school.

The reference to Michal's despising David's celebration in 2 Sam 6:16//1 Chr 15:29 provides further evidence of the tradition allowing such multiformity. The verbs used to refer to David's celebration differ significantly among the versions. Rezetko provides an excellent chart summarizing the variance of these verbs among the Hebrew, Aramaic, Syriac, Greek, and Latin versions of 2 Sam 6:16//1 Chr 15:29.[39] The English translations he gives include the following: leaping, whirling, dancing, praising, rejoicing, making merry, playing music, shaking, skipping, laughing, and jumping. As Rezetko notes, it is extremely difficult to retrovert the versions into Hebrew when one is dealing with such a variety of synonyms; however, even if his English translations have exaggerated the evidence somewhat, it is clear that the tradition preserved various ways of describing David's joyous celebration. Because of this diversity, we can surmise that, in a real sense, none of the particular selections of verbs describing David's behavior is sufficient to describe the breadth and depth of the traditional understanding of David's celebration. Because of this multiformity, one should not speculate on which specific group of verbs represents the earlier or later formulation of verbs, at least on the basis of the verbs themselves.[40] Rather they should be treated as synonymous readings with their various connotations mutually influencing each other.

The description of Michal despising David in 2 Sam 6:16//1 Chr 15:29 occurs in what many understand as an unexpected location in the narrative— that is, in the middle of the account of David bringing the ark to Jerusalem and blessing the people. This is even more the case in Chronicles, since this is the only reference to Michal.[41] Rezetko provided an excellent statement of the problem:

> [T]he storyteller's brief comment relates neither Michal's affiliation *to David*, nor the location of "the window," nor the reason for her disdain. Does silence in these

---

39. Ibid., 240.

40. Contra Rezetko, *Source and Revision*, 241: "MT Samuel may reflect revision." Of course, if one has strong evidence elsewhere that a particular text is a later revision, then one may state that that text's particular formulation of verbs may be later. In that sense, Rezetko may be justified in his conclusion.

41. This observation is used by critics of Auld's Shared Text hypothesis—that is, the reference to Michal in 1 Chr 15:29 requires knowledge of the other texts in Samuel (1 Sam 14:49; 18:20, 27, 28; 19:11–13, 17; 25:44; 2 Sam 3:13–14; 6:16, 20b–23; 21:8). See, for example, McKenzie, "Chronicler as Redactor," 82. For my discussion of this issue, see my treatment of 2 Sam 6:20b–23 below in chapter 5, pp. 134–38.

matters presuppose earlier canonical accounts regarding Michal or did it suggest their addition? Does previous information concerning Saul sufficiently prepare for *his daughter's* reaction to King David? If so, are the depiction of Saul's death in 1 Sam 31//1 Chron 10 and the brief statement in 2 Sam 5:2//1 Chron 11:1 adequate for making sense of Michal's antipathy?[42]

Reflecting tendencies in most of the recent scholarship, Rezetko imagined only two options, both of which assume a unilinear direction of literary influence. Either (1) the reference to Michal in 2 Sam 6:16//1 Chr 15:29 is later than and dependent on (some of) the other Michal accounts or (2) it is earlier than (some of) the others and they are dependent on it. Rezetko concluded the latter. We are exploring a third option that is rarely even entertained. Although some modern literature may have such a unilinear development, ancient literature should be understood more from a perspective of oral traditions, which allow for multiformity and in which the function of the literary text is as a mnemonic device that represents the broader oral tradition. Therefore, if any text represents only a variety of selections from the broader oral tradition, then any text is necessarily an incomplete bearer of the tradition. Furthermore, an ancient reader would interpret the reference to Michal in 2 Sam 6:16//1 Chr 15:29 (or anywhere else for that matter) as referring to all that that reader already knows about Michal from the broader tradition, rather than interpreting the text in a linear fashion based on the order of events as given in the any particular text.[43] This, however, does not necessarily suggest that the broader tradition does not value some chronological sequences for the material. Rather, even within any standard chronological sequences that may exist, cross-references to, for example, individual characters like Michal are not constructed in a unilinear fashion, because any segment of the broader traditional sequence can

---

42. Rezetko, *Source and Revision*, 234–35. See similarly Gary N. Knoppers, *I Chronicles 10–29: A New Translation with Introduction and Commentary* (AB 12A; New York: Doubleday, 2004), 626; and Japhet, *I & II Chronicles*, 307.

43. Rezetko's different response to this criticism of Auld's work should also be noted: "The assertion is unproven that 1 Chron 15:29 requires prior knowledge of Michal in order to make sense of the Chronicler's statement, and the same can be said for claims about 2 Sam 6:16" (*Source and Revision*, 282). For example, he noted that the Chronicler has already reported the death of Saul and his sons (1 Chr 10:1–12//1 Sam 31:1–13), thereby effectively preparing "the reader for comprehending the role of 'Michal, the daughter of Saul' as a foil in 1 Chron 15:29" (ibid.; see similarly A. Graeme Auld, "What Was the Main Source of the Books of Chronicles?" in *The Chronicler as Author: Studies in Text and Texture* [ed. M. Patrick Graham and Steven L. McKenzie; JSOTSup 263; Sheffield: Sheffield Academic Press, 1999], 94). Although I think Rezetko (and Auld) is correct that prior knowledge of Michal is not required, I have argued that it nevertheless would have been available in the broader tradition to the ancient readers. See also my discussion of 2 Sam 6:20b–23 below in chapter 5, pp. 134–38.

be presented as a selection of the tradition that nevertheless represents the whole tradition through various associations made through the characters, events, wording, and so on. Thus, to address Rezetko's representative question, in a real sense there is no "silence in these matters," because the broader tradition originally spoke through this reference to Michal, even though it did so without explicit references to Michal as David's wife in this particular occurrence. Even if the "previous information concerning Saul" itself may not "sufficiently prepare" readers for Michal's despising, the audience's knowledge of the broader tradition would have. Even if "the depiction of Saul's death in 1 Sam 31//1 Chr 10 and the brief statement in 2 Sam 5:2//1 Chr 11:1" alone are judged to have been inadequate "for making sense of Michal's antipathy," the audience's knowledge of the broader tradition would have adequately prepared the readers for Michal's motivation.

2 SAMUEL 23:8–39//1 CHRONICLES 11:10–47

Above I have presented a careful critique of Rezetko's interpretation of one of the parallel passages that occurs in the same order in 2 Sam 5–6; 23//1 Chr 11–16—that is, 2 Sam 6:12–19a//1 Chr 15:25–16:3. I could make a similar critique of the other parallel passages, both those that occur in the same order and those that occur in different orders. Rather than doing that again for 2 Sam 23:8–39//1 Chr 11:10–47, I want briefly to note how the different arrangement of a passage in Samuel//Chronicles may bear on Rezetko's thesis.

Since his monograph emphasizes 2 Sam 6//1 Chr 13; 15–16, Rezetko does not provide a thorough discussion of 2 Sam 23:8–39//1 Chr 11:10–47. In fact, he does not thoroughly discuss the only other parallel passage that occurs in a different order (2 Sam 5:11–25//1 Chr 14:1–17) probably for the same reason.[44] Therefore, the following discussion is my extension of Rezetko's discussion of 2 Sam 5–6; 23//1 Chr 11–16.

---

44. As noted above (pp. 91–92 n. 20) in my discussion of Trebolle, "Samuel/Kings and Chronicles," a common sequence of narrative events can be restored by removing either 2 Sam 5:11–25//1 Chr 14:1–17 or 2 Sam 6:1–11//1 Chr 13:5–14 as a redactional addition denoted by its variant location. The graphic representation of these passages on Rezetko's chart privileges 2 Sam 6:1–11//1 Chr 13:5–14 over 2 Sam 5:11–25//1 Chr 14:1–17 as belonging to the common source without explanation. When asked about this issue in personal correspondence, Rezetko stated that the chart communicates more than he had intended, because he was attempting simply to be descriptive of the relationship between MT 2 Sam 5–6; 23//MT 1 Chr 11–16 without favoring any particular decision concerning the reconstruction of the common source. Since I am not discussing either of these texts further, this problem can be set aside as irrelevant for my purposes, especially when one takes Trebolle's insistence on textual plurality seriously.

As noted in the introduction to this chapter, Tov stated that differences in sequence often denote a later addition to the text, and Auld included this principle as one of his criteria for reconstructing his Shared Text.[45] When one applies this criterion to these parallel passages, the conclusion is obvious: these parallel passages were additions to a common source.

However, the consensus model starts with the priority of Samuel and then interprets Chronicles in light of this priority. Therefore, according to this view, the Chronicler rearranged the material here. For example, Gary Knoppers argued that 1 Chr 11:10–47 is based primarily on 2 Sam 23:8–39 (//1 Chr 11:11–41a), including some additions by the Chronicler (11:10, 41b–47).[46] Knoppers noted that 1 Chr 11:10 was probably an addition by the "technique of repetitive resumption" in that the insertion is bracketed by "Now these are the commanders of David's warriors" (11:10) and "This is the muster of David's mighty warriors" (11:11).[47] Because of the "obscurity of several names" Knoppers argued that 11:41b–47 probably was the Chronicler's addition to Samuel based on an older source that the Chronicler did not significantly alter. However, he noted that he could not rule out the possibility that 11:41b–47 was originally part of the Samuel passage.[48]

Knoppers's analysis of 2 Sam 23:8–39//1 Chr 11:10–47 and related passages demonstrates that, even in the consensus model, there is often an assumption of multiplicity in the tradition. First, Knoppers (and others) argued that, because of the obscure names in 11:41b–47, this addition must not be original to the Chronicler; rather, the Chronicler has an extrabiblical source from which he is drawing material, especially lists such as this one. Second, Knoppers argued that an early form of 2 Sam 23:8–39 was the source for 1 Chr 11:10–47, which

---

45. Tov, *Textual Criticism*, 339; Auld, *Kings without Privilege*, 6. Rezetko also referred to Tov's work (*Source and Revision*, 69).

46. Knoppers, *I Chronicles 10–29*, 547–55. Some critics of Samuel do not include any of the Miscellany (that is, 2 Sam 20:23–24:25) in the Deuteronomistic edition of Samuel. For example, P. Kyle McCarter Jr. rejected the Deuteronomistic character of 2 Sam 20:23–24:25, but maintained the antiquity of 2 Sam 23:8–39 since, in his opinion, it "derives from an early point in David's career" (*II Samuel: A New Translation with Introduction and Commentary* [AB 9; New York: Doubleday, 1984], 501; see also 16–19). If, as McCarter argued, 2 Sam 23:8–39 is a post-Deuteronomistic addition to Samuel, then this could support a shorter *Vorlage* of Samuel for Chronicles, thereby explaining the different position of 2 Sam 23:8–39 and 1 Chr 11:10–47.

47. Knoppers, *I Chronicles 10–29*, 547. The translation is Knoppers's (532). See also Kalimi, *Reshaping of Ancient Israelite History*, 292.

48. Knoppers, *I Chronicles 10–29*, 555. See similarly Peter B. Dirksen, *1 Chronicles* (trans. Antony P. Runia; Historical Commentary on the Old Testament; Leuven/Dudley, Mass.: Peeters, 2005), 174–75; Japhet, *I & II Chronicles*, 236; and H. G. M. Williamson, *1 and 2 Chronicles* (NCB; Grand Rapids: Eerdmans, 1982), 104.

in turn was a source for 1 Chr 27:2–15.[49] Since all three of these lists have discrepancies as well as similarities, this is certainly an argument for multiplicity within the tradition, even within the book of Chronicles itself.

Therefore, I argue that both 2 Sam 23:8–39 and 1 Chr 11:10–47 are additions to a common source, which explains the different arrangements of the passages as well as the different content in the lists. The multiplicity of the broader oral tradition can be seen in the addition of these two passages.

Rezetko's analysis of 2 Sam 6:12–19a//1 Chr 15:25–16:3 and my extension of his analysis of 2 Sam 23:8–39//1 Chr 11:10–47 provide additional support for the consensus model's understanding that LXX Samuel preserves a version of Samuel earlier than MT Samuel and closer to the *Vorlage* of Chronicles. In other words, both MT Samuel and MT Chronicles represent different expansions of their common *Vorlage*, an earlier form of Samuel often preserved in LXX Samuel. However, Rezetko took this conclusion a step further by providing qualified support for Auld's thesis of a Shared Text—in his opinion, an earlier version of a Deuteronomistic Samuel–Kings than is preserved in any of the extant texts. He argued against the common interpretation that the Chronicler's revision of the *Vorlage* resulted in a corporate-levitical thrust by minimizing David's sacral role and against some of the criticisms of Auld's thesis. His discussion highlights some of the multiplicity in the textual tradition; however, his interpretation of this multiplicity is sometimes problematic in that he overemphasized what from our modern perspective appear to be differences in meaning but from the perspective of the ancients were probably read as synonymous interpretations of the ongoing tradition. For example, although his critique of the commonly held theme of the corporate-levitical thrust in Chronicles is well founded, his counterproposal that Samuel represents a revision emphasizing David's royal-sacral status overemphasizes the variations between Samuel and Chronicles in anachronistic ways and in ways that do not adequately take into account the common material in Samuel//Chronicles. Therefore, Rezetko's text-redactional work provides some support for my own thesis, even though some of his conclusions need to be revised on the basis of a better understanding of the use of texts in primarily oral societies.

PARALLELS BETWEEN THE BOOK OF KINGS AND THE BOOK OF CHRONICLES

As noted in the introduction to this chapter, although many of those who accept the consensus model allow that MT Samuel has undergone some

---

49. Knoppers, *I Chronicles 10–29*, 548–52, 895, 899–900. See my discussion of 1 Chronicles 27 below in chapter 5, pp. 150–52.

recensional additions since an earlier form of Samuel was used as a *Vorlage* for Chronicles, few conclude the same concerning the relationship between Kings and Chronicles. Rather, they maintain that the *Vorlage* of Kings used by the Chronicler is quite similar to MT Kings.[50]

Some recent text critics, however, have challenged the consensus model's understanding of the text history of MT Kings.[51] For example, in a series of publications, Adrian Schenker has argued that MT Kings represents a new edition of Kings (post-LXX) that was produced during the time of John Hyrcanus (129/128 B.C.E.).[52] However, probably the most influential text-critical scholar in these discussions is Julio Trebolle, who has convincingly argued that for some sections of the book of Kings the *Vorlage* of the Old Greek text (sometimes as preserved in the Old Latin) preserves an earlier Hebrew text-type than the MT.[53] Below I discuss 1 Kgs 3–10//2 Chr 1–9 and then 1 Kgs 22//2 Chr

---

50. For example, McKenzie, *Chronicler's Use of the Deuteronomistic History*, 119, 155; Knoppers, *I Chronicles 1–9*, 66–71; Klein, *1 Chronicles*, 32; Williamson, *1 and 2 Chronicles*, 19.

51. In *Kings–Isaiah and Kings–Jeremiah Recensions*, I also concluded that MT 2 Kgs 18–20 and MT 2 Kgs 24:18–25:30 preserve a later, expansive text when compared to LXX Kings and the parallels in Isaiah (Isa 36–39) and Jeremiah (Jer 52), especially in the LXX versions of the parallels.

52. Adrian Schenker, "Die Textgeschichte der Königsbücher und ihre Konsequenzen für die Textgeschichte der hebräischen Bibel, illustriert am Beispiel von 2 Kön 23:1–3," in *Congress Volume: Leiden 2004* (ed. André Lemaire; VTSup 109; Leiden: Brill, 2006), 65–79; idem, *Septante et texte massorétique dans l'histoire la plus ancienne du texts de 1 Rois 2–14* (CahRB 48; Paris: J. Gabalda, 2000); idem, *Älteste Textgeschichte der Königsbücher: Die hebräischen Vorlage der ursprunglichen Septuaginta als älteste Textform der Königsbucher* (OBO 199; Fribourg: Academic Press, 2004); and idem, "Junge Garden oder akrobatische Tänzer? Das Verhältnis zwischen 1 Kön 20 MT und 2 Regn 21 LXX," in *The Earliest Text of the Hebrew Bible: The Relationship between the Masoretic Text and the Hebrew Base of the Septuagint Reconsidered* (ed. Adrian Schenker; SBLSCS 52; Atlanta: Society of Biblical Literature, 2003), 17–34. Although I concur with Schenker's text-critical arguments that LXX Kings often preserves an earlier text than MT Kings, I am not yet convinced of his historical arguments for the setting of MT Kings. Furthermore, I find the arguments of Julio Trebolle more nuanced, so that they probably more accurately reflect the textual history of Kings. Therefore, although I draw from the work of Schenker, my discussion below is indebted first and foremost to Trebolle.

53. Julio C. Trebolle, "From the 'Old Latin' through the 'Old Greek' to the 'Old Hebrew' (2 Kings 10:23–25)," *Textus* 11 (1984): 17–36; idem, "Kings (MT/LXX) and Chronicles"; idem, "Light from 4QJudgᵃ and 4QKgs on the Text of Judges and Kings," in *The Dead Sea Scrolls: Forty Years of Research* (ed. Devorah Dimant and Uriel Rappaport; STDJ 10; Leiden: Brill, 1992), 315–24; idem, "Old Latin, Old Greek and Old Hebrew in the Book of Kings (1 Ki. 18:25 and 2 Ki. 20:11)," *Textus* 13 (1986): 85–94; idem, "Samuel/Kings and Chronicles"; idem, "Redaction, Recension, and Midrash in the Books of Kings"; idem, *Salomón y Jeroboán: Historia de la recensión y redacción de 1 Reyes, 2–12, 14* (Bibliotheca

17–20, drawing extensively from the work of Trebolle, and then provide a brief discussion of 2 Kgs 22–23//2 Chr 33–34.

1 Kings 3–10//2 Chronicles 1–9

In some of his more recent works, Trebolle has applied his conclusions concerning the relationship of the Old Greek and MT Kings to the relationship between Kings and Chronicles.[54] For example, based on his analysis of the Solomon narrative (1 Kgs 3–10//2 Chr 1–9), he concluded as follows:

> The text of LXX 3 Kingdoms represents an older textual form than that which was transmitted by MT Kings and Chronicles. Proof of this is that it does not include additions of Chronicles which have made their way in MT Kings, like those present in 1 Kgs 8.16. The LXX version reflects a Hebrew text of Kings which did not know such influence of Chronicles.[55]

Trebolle provides an excellent chart comparing MT Chronicles, the main text of LXX Kings, MT Kings, and the LXX Kings Supplement in columns.[56] He notes that the most stable and oldest passages are found in all three traditions—that is, LXX Kings, MT Kings, and Chronicles—with the next level of stability represented by the passages common to both LXX Kings and MT Kings.[57] Because of his understanding of the text-critical evidence and its relationship to Chron-

---

Salmanticensis: Dissertationes 3; Salamanca: Universidad Pontificia, 1980); and idem, "The Text-Critical Use of the Septuagint in the Books of Kings," in *VII Congress of the International Organization for Septuagint and Cognate Studies, Leuven, 1989* (ed. Claude E. Cox; SBLSCS 31; Atlanta: Scholars Press, 1991), 285–99.

54. Trebolle, "Kings (MT/LXX) and Chronicles"; and idem, "Samuel/Kings and Chronicles."

55. Trebolle, "Kings (MT/LXX) and Chronicles," 493. Trebolle has certainly noted exceptions—for example, he argued that the reading להיות נגיד על in the first line of 4QKgs (= 1 Kgs 8:16), which corresponds to the reading in 1 Chr 6:6, is earlier and was omitted from both MT 1 Kgs 8:16 and the Old Greek (= LXX 1 Kgs 8:16) ("Light from 4QJudgᵃ and 4QKgs," 315–16). Schenker also concluded that LXX 1 Kings 2–14 preserves an earlier version than MT 1 Kings 2–14. See Schenker, *Septante et texte massorétique*. Frank Polak concluded that both the LXX and the MT of the Solomon narrative "contain a secondary recension of the ancient Solomon account" ("The Septuagint Account of Solomon's Reign: Revision and Ancient Recension," in *X Congress of the International Organization for Septuagint and Cognate Studies, Oslo 1998* [ed. Bernard A. Taylor; SBLSCS 51; Atlanta: Society of Biblical Literature, 2001], 149). Contra Percy S. F. van Keulen, *Two Versions of the Solomon Narrative: An Inquiry into the Relationship between MT 1 Kgs. 2–11 and LXX 3 Reg. 2–11* (VTSup 104; Leiden: Brill, 2005).

56. Trebolle, "Kings (MT/LXX) and Chronicles," 494–95.

57. Trebolle, "Kings (MT/LXX) and Chronicles," 495–97.

icles, Trebolle concluded that, with some modifications, Auld's argument for a Shared Text may be valid for 1 Kgs 3–10//2 Chr 1–9.[58] Below I examine two passages in the Solomon narrative—that is, 1 Kgs 3:1–28//2 Chr 1:3–13 and 1 Kgs 9:10–28//2 Chr 8:1–18—drawing on the work of Trebolle and others.

1 KINGS 3:1–28//2 CHRONICLES 1:3–13

Trebolle's analysis of these parallel texts is summarized in his chart for the reign of Solomon as follows:[59]

2 Chronicles	LXX Kings Main Text	MT Kings	LXX Kings Supplement
			2:47l
	lacking	3:1a	
		3:1b	2.35c
	3:2–3	3:2–3	
1:3–13	**3:4–15**	**3:4–15**	
	3:16–28	3:16–28	
	...		
	3:1b [after 5:14]		

What Trebolle referred to as the "triple textual tradition"—that is, Chronicles, MT Kings, and LXX Kings agreeing in content and order—is in boldface. The "double textual tradition" (MT Kings//LXX Kings) is underlined. Those verses that are found in both LXX Kings and MT Kings but in different orders are italicized.

If one were to assume a unilinear development, the text-redactional history of 1 Kgs 3:1–28//2 Chr 1:3–13 would be as follows. The earliest core is found in 1 Kgs 3:4–15//2 Chr 1:3–13. Chronicles would generally be the more conservative text in comparison to Kings, because Kings includes the additions of 1 Kgs 3:2–3 and 3:16–28 (in both LXX and MT) and the later additions in MT 1 Kgs 3:1a (lacking in LXX) and 1 Kgs 3:1b (located differently in LXX and MT) whereas in Chronicles the addition is only 2 Chr 1:1–2.[60] Although this

---

58. Ibid., 498.

59. Ibid., 494.

60. Trebolle does not include 2 Chr 1:1–2 in his chart; however, they do not have parallels in Kings. Other critics also have argued for the secondary character of some of these verses on other bases. For example, Volkmar Fritz asserted that 1 Kgs 3:1–3 is secondary and that 3:4–28 is from "the Deuteronomistic Historian" (*1 & 2 Kings: A Continental Commentary* [trans. Anselm Hagedorn; Minneapolis: Fortress Press, 2003], 33–43). Simi-

reconstruction matches that proposed by Auld quite well,[61] Trebolle resisted such simplification of the process. Although he agreed that the "triple textual tradition" would be the most original, he nevertheless concluded: "The texts common to LXX and MT Kings, missing in 2 Chronicles, are not necessarily more recent. . . . They can also be ancient, although of a different provenance."[62] That is, although they may also be ancient and have been preserved in the textual tradition behind LXX Kings and MT Kings, one should not assume that they were in the *Vorlage* on which Chronicles is based. Furthermore, he noted that the texts in MT Kings that are lacking in the main text of LXX Kings "correspond in a large proportion with materials present in the supplements of LXX."[63] Rather than imagining a unilinear development of these texts, Trebolle allowed for a multiplicity of texts, or in his own words, "several editions that can co-exist and even intermix."[64]

This multiformity is evident even within the "triple textual tradition"—for example, within 2 Chr 1:3–13//1 Kgs 3:4–15 are the pluses in 2 Chr 1:4–5 and 1 Kgs 3:10. Furthermore, multiplicity exists in other forms even when much the same vocabulary is being used in the parallels. In a recent essay, David Carr discussed what he termed "memory variants" and provided examples from 1 Kgs 3:2–15//2 Chr 1:1–13:[65]

MT 1 Kings 3	MT 2 Chronicles 1
4b a thousand offerings Solomon offered	6 he [Solomon] offered on it a thousand of offerings
5a At Gideon the LORD appeared to Solomon in a dream at night	7a On that night God appeared to Solomon
8 a great people, who cannot be numbered or counted	9 a great people, as much as the dust of the earth

In the first of these two examples, the variations are fairly minor. In 1 Kgs 3:4b//2 Chr 1:6 and in 1 Kgs 3:5a//2 Chr 1:7a we see a simple inversion of word order. In 1 Kgs 3:5a//2 Chr 1:7a the variation between "God" and "the

larly, John Gray assigned 1 Kgs 3:1–3 as secondary material (*I & II Kings: A Commentary* [OTL; Philadelphia: Westminster, 1963], 114–16).

61. Auld, *Kings without Privilege*, 26, 34, 54, 64, 150.

62. Trebolle, "Kings (MT/LXX) and Chronicles," 496.

63. Ibid., 496.

64. Trebolle, "Samuel/Kings and Chronicles," 98.

65. Carr, "'Empirical' Comparison," 6–7 [see p. 88 n. 7 above]. Carr provided the examples in Hebrew; I provide them here in English translation. He also provided a Hebrew synopsis of the texts (ibid., 27–28).

LORD" occurs. Although the difference in 1 Kgs 3:8//2 Chr 1:9 is greater, it is still what is often referred to as a "synonymous reading."[66] Carr has argued that scribes, when reproducing an older tradition, often worked on the basis of their memories rather than written texts. When reproducing texts from memory, the scribes introduced what he has termed "memory variants" into the texts, which he defined as follows: "variants that show up in parallel versions of texts: exchanges of words with similar meanings, meaningless shifts in word order, variation in syntactically equivalent expressions, etc."[67] Carr noted that evidence for "memory variants" comes also from studies in other literature, including Homer, Old English, Middle English, medieval French, and Sumerian.[68] He concluded that the presence of "memory variants" is a strong indication of the transmission of texts by memory. As illustrated in his analysis of 1 Kgs 3:2–15//2 Chr 1:1–13, Carr concluded that

> these memory variants are evidence that early versions of Chronicles and Sam-uel–Kings were transmitted in an environment where written texts were memo-rized and often accessed by means of memory. . . . As a result, minor variations of this sort—typical of memory slips and switches—between Samuel–Kings and Chronicles may not point to subtle exegesis on the part of the author(s) of Chron-icles but to the sorts of oral-written dynamics typical of the transmission of many ancient texts.[69]

Carr also discussed how his conclusions have led him to appreciate some of the strengths of Auld's Shared Text hypothesis.[70] Above we have seen how both Trebolle's text-redactional arguments and Carr's arguments for the role of memory in text reproduction challenge the consensus model's interpretation of 1 Kgs 3:1–28//2 Chr 1:3–13, thereby providing greater room for the possibility of Samuel–Kings and Chronicles being based on a common source. Now I will review the arguments of Zipora Talshir, one of the critics of Auld's hypothesis, who used the Solomon narrative in her discussion.[71]

---

66. For my discussion of synonymous readings in the context of an argument similar to that of Carr, see Person, "Ancient Israelite Scribe as Performer," 604–5.

67. Carr, "'Empirical' Comparison," 4. See p. 88 n. 7 above.

68. Ibid., 5 n. 9. See p. 88 n. 7 above.

69. Ibid., 7. See p. 88 n. 7 above.

70. Ibid., 12–19. See p. 88 n. 7 above.

71. Zipora Talshir, "The Reign of Solomon in the Making: Pseudo-Connections between 3 Kingdoms and Chronicles," *VT* 50 (2000): 233–49. For her earlier discussion of the text-critical evidence comparing 3 Kingdoms and Chronicles, see Zipora Talshir, "The Contribution of Diverging Traditions Preserved in the Septuagint to Literary Criticism of the Bible," in *VIII Congress of the International Organization for Septuagint and Cognate Studies* (ed. Leonard Greenspoon and Olivier Munnich; SBLSCS 41; Atlanta: Scholars Press, 1995), 21–41.

Talshir's criticism of Auld's hypothesis included a discussion of Solomon's marriage to Pharaoh's daughter (1 Kgs 3:1b; 9:24//2 Chr 8:11).[72] Auld excluded 1 Kgs 3:1b from his Shared Text because of its different placement in the LXX but included 1 Kgs 9:24//2 Chr 8:11.[73] Talshir insisted that, since the Chronicler later referred to the marriage, the reference to the marriage in 1 Kgs 3:1b must have been in his *Vorlage*: "In the Chronicler's Books of Kings, then, the marriage must have been mentioned, including the chronological reference to the building of Temple and palace. Without it the later reference makes no sense."[74] Talshir claimed that Auld's scenario required the redactor of the LXX *Vorlage* to introduce 1 Kgs 3:1b (although following 5:14), "which he found floating in the air."[75] I suspect that her wording here is meant to be dismissive of something that she thought was highly unlikely. However, if "floating in the air" can mean existing in the memory of the tradents as opposed to being written down, then the broader oral tradition very well may have been the source. Furthermore, if Solomon's marriage to Pharaoh's daughter is preserved in the tradition although not necessarily in a written text, the reference to the marriage in 1 Kgs 3:1b is not necessary for the ancient audience to understand the reference in 1 Kgs 9:24//2 Chr 8:11. When they hear or read "But the daughter of Pharaoh went up from the city of David to her house that he [Solomon] had built for her" (1 Kgs 9:24)//"Solomon brought the daughter of Pharaoh from the city of David to the house he had built for her, for he said, 'My wife shall not live in the house of David king of Israel'" (2 Chr 8:11), they would already know that the Pharaoh's daughter was Solomon's wife. Even if they did not, however, the content would be sufficient for them to assume that fact, since Solomon built her a house. Certainly Solomon's own identification of Pharaoh's daughter as his wife (2 Chr 8:11) would be sufficient. Therefore, Talshir's conclusion that 2 Chr 8:11 without 1 Kgs 3:1b "makes no sense" itself makes no sense.[76]

---

72. Talshir, "Reign of Solomon," 236–38. Talshir based her criticism also on the consensus model of linguistic development of Biblical Hebrew (248 n. 31).

73. Auld, *Kings without Privilege*, 26, 54, 64.

74. Talshir, "Reign of Solomon," 237.

75. Ibid., 236.

76. Some other redaction critics have suggested that 1 Kgs 3:1 is a late addition on the basis of criteria not related to text-critical evidence. For example, Mordechai Cogan wrote, "The placement of this verse in its present position is not immediately clear, because it is poorly connected to its context" (*I Kings: A New Translation with Introduction and Commentary* [AB 10; New York: Doubleday, 2001], 184).

1 KINGS 9:10–28//2 CHRONICLES 8:1–18

Trebolle's analysis of these parallel texts is summarized in his chart for the reign of Solomon as follows:[77]

2 Chronicles	LXX Kings Main Text	MT Kings	LXX Kings Supplement
	9:16–17a [before 5:15]		
	. . .		
	9:24a [after 9:9]		
8:1–2	9:10–14	9:10–14	
		9:15a	2:35k
		9:15b	2:35i
8:3–6*		9:16–17a*	
8:6*–9		9:17b–18*	2:35i
		9:19–22	
8:10	lacking	9:23 (5:30)	2:35h
8:11		9:24a	2:35f
	lacking	9:24b	2:35f
8:12	lacking	9:25	2:35g
8:17–18	**9:26–28**	**9:26–28**	
	. . .		
	9:15a,b [after 10:22]		
	9:17b–18		
	9:19–22		

What Trebolle called the "triple textual tradition"—that is, Chronicles, MT Kings, and LXX Kings agreeing in content and order—is in boldface. Those verses that are found in both LXX Kings and MT Kings but in different orders are italicized.

Although Trebolle correctly concluded that "several editions . . . can co-exist and even intermix,"[78] it may be helpful to imagine what the redactional development may have been of this material. A common source concerning Solomon's interaction with Hiram (2 Chr 8:1–2, 17–18//1 Kgs 9:10–14, 26–28) may have been expanded in all three traditions. In LXX Kings, the common

---

77. Trebolle, "Kings (MT/LXX) and Chronicles," 495.
78. Trebolle, "Samuel/Kings and Chronicles," 98.

source remained together with all of the additions occurring either before and after this material (given in order of occurrence: 9:16–17a, 24a, 15, 17b–18, 19–22) or in the Supplement (2:35). In MT Kings and Chronicles, the additional material was added within the common source (2 Chr 8:3–12; MT 1 Kgs 9:15–25).[79]

However, if we are allowing for a multiplicity of texts as Trebolle has argued, the above description of the redactional development of these texts may be too simplistic. Another way of explaining the relationship between these texts is that the broader oral tradition preserved most (if not all) of the material now preserved in 1 Kgs 9:10–28//2 Chr 8:1–18. Any written text was understood to be an imperfect representation of the broader oral tradition. The first text may have been what is preserved in all three texts in the same order (2 Chr 8:1–2, 17–18//1 Kgs 9:10–14, 26–28), but that would not deny the existence of the other material within the broader tradition. Later, when the first text was expanded in order to include more of the tradition, the additional material was added in different locations, because, as is common in oral traditions, the sequence of narrated events is not fixed in a linear text but exists in the multiplicity of the tradition. These later expansive texts would not necessarily need to agree in what additions were made or where the additions were made, because the broader tradition allowed for multiformity and each of them could still be understood as an imperfect representation of the broader tradition that existed in the memory of the tradents. If this is the case, then each of the extant texts can be judged as equally representing the broader oral tradition, especially since every verse has a parallel in at least one of the other texts when you include the LXX Supplement.

Trebolle's chart above gives a helpful summary of the relationship between the three texts and, therefore, demonstrates the multiplicity among the three texts in terms of the arrangement of verses. However, one could possibly misread the chart in ways that would minimize the multiformity of this material if one does not carefully compare even the material within the "triple textual tradition." Therefore, as an example, I briefly analyze the common material in 1 Kgs 9:10–14//2 Chr 8:1–2. Below I provide an English synopsis of this material based on MT Kings and MT Chronicles.

---

79. Some older critical studies have suggested that some of these verses are redactional additions. For example, Gray assigned the following to late additions: 1 Kgs 9:11a, 12–13, 20–22, 25 (*I & II Kings*, 222). Note, however, that Gray's redactional reconstruction diverges from the text-critical evidence—that is, some of his "late" material is common to MT Kings, LXX Kings, and MT Chronicles (11a, 12–13).

MT 1 Kings 9:10–14	MT 2 Chronicles 8:1–2
¹⁰At the end of twenty years when Solomon built the two houses, the house of the LORD and the house of the king, ¹¹Hiram, king of Tyre, supplied Solomon with wood of cedar and cypress and with gold, all that he desired. Then King Solomon gave to Hiram twenty cities in the land of the Galilee. ¹²But when Hiram came from Tyre to see the cities that Solomon had given him, they did not please him. ¹³He said, "What are these cities that you have given to me, my brother?" He called them, "the land of Cabul," as it is until this day. ¹⁴But Hiram had sent to the king a hundred and twenty talents of gold.	¹At the end of twenty years when Solomon built the house of the LORD and his house, ²Solomon rebuilt the cities that Huram had given to Solomon and he settled there the sons of Israel.

These parallel texts describe a period of Solomon's building projects. Both texts contain a mention of Solomon's building of the temple and the palace during a twenty-year period. They include references to Hiram/Huram, who provided wood, gold, and workers for both projects (see 2 Chr 2:3–18). Both contain references to the twenty cities that changed hands between Solomon and Hiram/Huram, although there may be some variation in the tradition about these twenty cities. Kings explicitly notes that Solomon gave the twenty cities to Hiram as a gift that Hiram possibly returned to Solomon as unworthy cities; Chronicles could be assuming knowledge of the same tradition, but that is not clear. Thus, Trebolle's insistence on the multiformity behind these texts should be viewed at both a macro- and micro-level. These texts display variety in the order of narrated events, and even in the common material they differ in their wording.[80]

In my discussion of 1 Kgs 3:1–28//2 Chr 1:3–13 above, I rejected Talshir's criticism of Auld's hypothesis of a Shared Text that lacks the reference of Solomon's marriage to Pharaoh's daughter in 1 Kgs 3:1b. She argued that 1 Kgs 3:1b was necessary, in order for the later reference in 2 Chr 8:11 (// 1 Kgs 9:24) to be meaningful. I countered that the audience's knowledge of this marriage may simply be assumed without reference to a specific text. The above summary of Trebolle's work provides yet another possible response to Talshir's criticism—that is, because of the different location of 1 Kgs 9:24 in the MT and the LXX,

---

80. Williamson argued that the Chronicler's *Vorlage* was corrupt here, so that he made the "best reconstruction he could make" (*1 and 2 Chronicles*, 228–29).

maybe Auld should not have included any reference to Pharaoh's daughter in his Shared Text.[81] Whether or not the earliest text representing the tradition had a reference to Pharaoh's daughter, the source for any material concerning Solomon's marriage to Pharaoh's daughter could have been from the broader oral tradition whenever it entered into the written text(s).

Talshir's criticism of Auld's hypothesis of a Shared Text also included other references to 1 Kgs 9:10–28//2 Chr 8:1–18. Explicitly following Trebolle's earlier text-critical work, Auld excluded the account of the building of the royal palace (1 Kgs 7:1–12) from his Shared Text because it is lacking in Chronicles and is found in different locations in LXX Kings and MT Kings.[82] Talshir insisted that the Chronicler must have known the text in 1 Kgs 7:1–12 and omitted it, because, on the one hand, the Chronicler began his discussion of Solomon's building activities with a reference to both the temple and the palace (2 Chr 2:1, 12) and, on the other hand, *"the Chronicler mentions later on the palace alongside the Temple in several back-references which he borrows from 1 Kgs"*—that is, 2 Chr 7:11//1 Kgs 9:1; 2 Chr 8:1//1 Kgs 9:10; and 2 Chr 9:11//1 Kgs 10:12.[83] Since these "back-references" to Solomon's building both the temple and the palace are found in what Trebolle later called the "triple textual tradition," Auld included them in his Shared Text.[84] To Talshir, this seemed to be an inconsistency—that is, these back-references must be referring to something that appeared earlier in the Chronicler's *Vorlage* that was omitted. Furthermore, when one compares the references to both temple and palace in 2 Chr 2:1 and 2:12 to their respective parallels in Kings (1 Kgs 5:1 and 5:7), the presumed *Vorlage* does not mention Solomon's building of both temple and palace. For Talshir, the Chronicler must have used a *Vorlage* with 1 Kgs 7:1–12 to add these earlier references and for the back-references to make any sense. However, such knowledge of Solomon's building the palace is, as Talshir observed, already present in Chronicles, and any other knowledge of Solomon's palace building could have come from the broader oral tradition.

1 KINGS 22//2 CHRONICLES 17–20

2 Chronicles 17–20 contains much more information concerning the reign of Jehoshaphat than is found in 1 Kgs 22. They share two accounts: (1) Micaiah's prophecy of the defeat of Ahab and Jehoshaphat's military alliance against Ramoth-gilead (2 Chr 18:1–34//1 Kgs 22:1–40) and (2) the summary of

---

81. Again, Auld was inconsistent with his own stated methodology; see Auld, *Kings without Privilege*, 6.

82. Auld, *Kings without Privilege*, 22–29, 57.

83. Talshir, "Reign of Solomon," 239 (emphasis hers).

84. Auld, *Kings without Privilege*, 62–65.

Jehoshaphat's reign (2 Chr 20:31–21:1//MT 1 Kgs 22:41–51//LXX 1 Kgs 16:28a–h). Chronicles, however, contains unique material concerning Jehoshaphat's rise to power (17:2–19), the rebuke by the prophet Jehu (19:1–3), his appointment of judges (19:4–11), and his victory over Moab and Ammon (20:1–30).[85] Because of this relationship, Auld included only 1 Kgs 22:2–35a//2 Chr 18:1–34 and 1 Kgs 22:41–44, 46, 49, 51//2 Chr 20:31–37 in his Shared Text.[86]

In "The Trouble with King Jehoshaphat," Steven McKenzie argued against Auld's interpretation of the Jehoshaphat account in Chronicles.[87] He began his critique with the assertion that the Chronicler's version of the Jehoshaphat account is unique in his ambivalence toward the king, especially because of the conflicting notices of his removing (17:6) or not removing (20:33) the "high places." He then attempted an answer to the question of why this narrative is unique in its ambivalence. He evaluated the possibility that the Chronicler used a no longer extant source, such as Auld's Shared Text, and concluded that "the Chronicler, far from preserving some older source also behind the Deuteronomistic History, makes use of Kings in essentially its latest textual version!"[88] As we will see, however, McKenzie's arguments are problematic at a variety of levels.

First, McKenzie began with an assertion of the uniqueness of the Chronistic account based on the ambivalent evaluation of Jehoshaphat present in the narrative. In fact, McKenzie's own words hint at the difficulty with this interpretation:

> While the evaluation of Jehoshaphat in the book of Kings is positive overall with no explicit reservations *except perhaps for the notice that the high places were not removed*, features of its narrative seem ready-made for the Chronicler's interpretation.[89]

Recently Ehud Ben Zvi has convincingly argued that modern scholars too often overemphasize the differences between Chronicles and its sources because we ignore the multivocality of both the Deuteronomistic History

---

85. For my discussion of this unique material, see chapter 5 below, pp. 152–54.

86. Auld, *Kings without Privilege*, 109–12.

87. Steven L. McKenzie, "The Trouble with King Jehoshaphat," in *Reflection and Refraction: Studies in Biblical Historiography in Honour of A. Graeme Auld* (ed. Robert Rezetko, Timothy H. Lim, and W. Brian Aucker; VTSup 113; Leiden: Brill, 2007), 299–314.

88. Ibid., 306.

89. Ibid., 313 (emphasis mine). Klein similarly concludes that even the Chronicler's revisions of the synoptic passage of 1 Kings 22 give "an entirely new orientation" to the account. See Ralph W. Klein, "Reflections on Historiography in the Account of Jehoshaphat," in *Pomegranates and Golden Bells: Studies in Biblical, Jewish, and Near Eastern Ritual, Law, and Literature in Honor of Jacob Milgrom* (ed. David P. Wright, David Noel Freedman, and Avi Hurvitz; Winona Lake, Ind.: Eisenbrauns, 1995), 649.

and Chronicles.[90] After reviewing various themes such as deferred and non-deferred judgment, prophecy, all Israel, and the Davidic monarchy, Ben Zvi concluded the following:

> The converging lines mentioned here draw attention to the fact that, particularly at the level of ground ideas, core ideological concepts, and basic communicative (rhetorical) grammar as well as general historiographical tendencies, the gap between Chronicles and the Deuteronomistic History (in its present form) was not as large as often claimed.[91]

Ben Zvi specifically discussed a pertinent example of what McKenzie called ambivalence—that is, Chronicles contains conflicting reports of whether Asa removed (2 Chr 14:2–4) or did not remove (2 Chr 15:17) the "high places" and how Asa's son Jehoshaphat is likewise characterized.[92] Thus, the portrayal of this ambivalence toward Jehoshaphat is not unique in Chronicles.

Although McKenzie is correct that this ambivalence toward Jehoshaphat is not explicit in Kings—his removing the high places in 2 Chr 17:6 has no parallel in Kings—this ambivalence related to Asa is at least implicit in both Kings and Chronicles (2 Chr 14:3//1 Kgs 15:12 and 2 Chr 15:17//1 Kgs 15:14), although there is some difference in wording. In both accounts Asa is judged to have done what was good in God's sight (2 Chr 14:2//1 Kgs 15:11), and in both this is clearly related to religious reforms. The question concerns how extensive the religious reforms relating to the high places must be, and Chronicles and Kings have somewhat different answers to this question. Here are the most pertinent verses:

2 Chronicles 14	1 Kings 15
[3]He removed the foreign altars and the high places, broke down the pillars, hewed down the sacred poles, [4]and commanded Judah to seek the LORD, the God of their fathers, and to keep the law and the commandment. [5]He removed from all the cities of Judah the high places and the incense altars.	[12]He put away the male temple prostitutes out of the land, and removed all the idols that his fathers had made.

90. On the Jehoshaphat account in Chronicles, Williamson made a similar point but one based on his reconstruction of earlier sources. He concluded that the Chronicler's own evaluation of Jehoshaphat did not differ from his Kings *Vorlage* here; the ambivalence occurred when the Chronicler used other sources for his Jehoshaphat account that had a more positive view (*1 and 2 Chronicles*, 277–80).

91. Ben Zvi, "Are There Any Bridges Out There?" 85.

92. Ben Zvi, *History, Literature and Theology*, 50.

2 Chronicles 15	1 Kings 15
[16]Asa the king even removed Maacah his mother from being queen mother, because she had made to Asherah an abominable image. Asa cut down her image, crushed it, and burned it in the Wadi Kidron. [17]But the high places were not removed from Israel. Nevertheless the heart of Asa was true all his days.	[13]He even removed Maacah his mother from being queen mother, because she had made an abominable image to Asherah. Asa cut down her image and burned it in the Wadi Kidron. [14]But the high places were not removed. Nevertheless the heart of Asa was true to the LORD all his days.

Clearly both accounts portray Asa as undertaking significant cultic reforms, which included even disciplining his own mother. Because of the different wording, however, we can see that Kings and Chronicles interpret the failure to remove the high places differently. In Chronicles, Asa removed the high places in Judah, not in the northern kingdom of Israel. In Kings, Asa removed none of the high places. Despite this difference, both accounts contain some ambivalence toward Asa and his reforms. Therefore, the ambivalence McKenzie identified in the Chronicles account of Jehoshaphat is not unique in Chronicles itself, and similar ambivalence can be found in Kings in accounts of other kings.

Second, McKenzie rejected the possibility that the Chronicler used a no longer extant source because the Jehoshaphat narratives have "the mark of the Chronicler's hand" and because "the Chronicler's composition [is] based on other parts of Chronicles and of the Hebrew Bible."[93] However, these are not mutually exclusive, especially if the tradition behind both Kings and Chronicles continued to develop independently for an extended period of time. In fact, I would expect that any community of tradents would over time revise and reword any source so that it takes on the unique linguistic qualities of the community within their own traditional context, including some influence from its authoritative traditions, both written and oral.

Finally, McKenzie's conclusions concerning the text-critical evidence and the relationship between Kings and Chronicles are problematic. With Auld and others, McKenzie accepted the validity of the widely held conclusion that the chronology preserved in LXX Kings is earlier than that of MT Kings.[94]

---

93. McKenzie, "Trouble with King Jehoshaphat," 302, 304.

94. Ibid., 306; Auld, "What Was the Main Source," 95; J. Maxwell Miller, "The Elisha Cycle and the Accounts of the Omride Wars," *JBL* 85 (1966) 441–54; James Donald Shenkel, *Chronology and Recensional Development in the Greek Text of Kings* (HSM 1; Cambridge, Mass.: Harvard University Press, 1968); Julio C. Trebolle, "The Different Textual Forms of MT and LXX in Kings and the History of the Deuteronomistic Composition and Redaction

However, he nevertheless concluded as follows: "The shift in the MT chronology was probably caused by the occurrence of Jehoshaphat's name in the story in 2 Kgs 3.4–27, which also led to his addition to the story in 1 Kings 22//2 Chronicles 18."[95] That is, an earlier version of Kings had the chronology as preserved in LXX Kings. This version included the Elisha narratives, including 2 Kgs 3:4–27, that mentioned both Ahab and Jehoshaphat. Because the Elisha narrative with its reference to Jehoshaphat created a chronological problem in this earlier version, the tradition represented by MT Kings revised the chronological framework, also adding Jehoshaphat to an earlier version of the narrative about Ahab in 1 Kgs 22. When the Chronicler used this later version of 1 Kgs 22 (very similar to MT Kings), he revised his *Vorlage* further so that the earlier addition of Jehoshaphat to this story was even less obvious—that is, the use of singular verbs and pronouns originally referring to Ahab alone still preserved in the Kings account were changed to plurals in the Chronicles account.[96] Here McKenzie overemphasized the significance of this grammatical difference between Kings and Chronicles. Since all of the extant texts clearly include both Ahab and Jehoshaphat, I would not make much of this type of variation. For example, in both "Shall *we* go up to Ramoth-gilead?" (2 Chr 18:5) and "Shall *I* go up to Ramoth-gilead" (1 Kgs 22:6) Ahab is speaking to the prophets in response to Jehoshaphat's request for prophetic consultation (2 Chr 18:4//1 Kgs 22:5); therefore, in both versions Ahab is speaking on behalf of both Jehoshaphat and himself and the grammatical difference is insignficant.

Trebolle offered a different understanding of the textual history of the Jehoshaphat accounts based on the text-critical evidence of MT Kings versus LXX Kings and how Kings compares to Chronicles.[97] Trebolle's study concerns 1 Kgs 16:23–2 Kgs 14:16; however, I will discuss only those portions of his argument that relate to the question of the relationship of 2 Chr 17–20 to Kings as summarized in the chart on the following page.[98] Trebolle observed that the placement of the formulae concerning Jehoshaphat differs between MT Kings (22:41–51) and LXX Kings (16:28a–h) and agreed with Shenkel and others (including McKenzie) that the chronological framework in LXX Kings is earlier than that of MT Kings. He then noted that the Chronicles account agrees with the LXX order—that is, unlike MT Kings, the regnal formulae in both 2 Chr 17:1–19 and LXX 1 Kgs 16:28a–h occur before the narratives of

of These Books," paper presented at the annual meeting of the Society of Biblical Literature, New Orleans, November 2009, p. 2.

95. McKenzie, "Trouble with King Jehoshaphat," 306.

96. Ibid., 305–6.

97. Trebolle, "Different Textual Forms of Kings."

98. Ibid., 9.

MT 1 Kings	LXX 1 Kings	Inserted Narratives in Kings (MT and LXX)
Omri 16:23–28	Omri 16:23–28	
lacking	Jehoshaphat 16:28a–h	
Ahab 16:29–34	Ahab 16:29–34	
		Elijah 17–19; 21
		Aramean wars 20; 22:1–38
Ahab 22:39–40	Ahab 22:39–40	
Jehoshaphat 22:41–51	lacking	
Ahaziah 22:52–54	Ahaziah 22:52–54	

Ahab (2 Chr 18:1–34 and LXX 1 Kgs 16:29–34; 22:1–40).[99] He argued also that the prophetic narratives of Elijah and Elisha, as well as the material concerning the Aramean wars (1 Kgs 17–22), were later additions to an earlier synchronic history, based primarily on the observation that these narratives are lacking in Chronicles.[100]

Trebolle concluded that "Chronicles allows us to access . . . a stage of the composition of Kings prior to those two editions"—that is, before MT Kings and LXX Kings.[101] His analysis therefore lends support to a thesis of a common source for both Kings and Chronicles and suggests a response to McKenzie's criticism of Auld in relation to the Jehoshaphat accounts. If, as McKenzie concluded, the secondary MT chronological order is due to the reference to Jehoshaphat in the Elisha material of 2 Kgs 3:4–27, then why not conclude with Trebolle that the Elijah and Elisha material is also secondary, especially since it is not paralleled in Chronicles and Chronicles agrees with LXX Kings in the placement of the regnal formula for Jehoshaphat before the Ahab account? Because of the different orders of the regnal formula preserved in MT Kings and LXX Kings, the regnal formulae in MT 1 Kgs 22:41–51//2 Chr 20:31–21:1 may be secondary additions to the common source—that is, in this instance

---

99. Contra McKenzie, "Trouble with King Jehoshaphat," 306. McKenzie argued that the placement of 2 Chr 18:1–19:3 agrees with the MT order, because the regnal formulae follow this account (MT 1 Kgs 22:41–51//2 Chr 20:31–21:1). The difference between Trebolle and McKenzie concerns which of the two formulae in Chronicles (2 Chr 17:1–19; 20:31–21:1) they are discussing. Trebolle referred to the initial regnal formula in Chronicles; McKenzie to the concluding one. However, note that McKenzie stated that the Chronicles account differs significantly, with the exception of 18:1–34 and the regnal formula in 17:1a (301).

100. Trebolle did not state why he included 1 Kgs 22:1–38 in this secondary material, even though Chronicles has a parallel account (2 Chr 18:1–34).

101. Trebolle, "Different Textual Forms of Kings," 1.

Chronicles has a second regnal formula for Jehoshaphat, which agrees with the later MT Kings order in addition to the initial regnal formula as found in the common source and also preserved in LXX Kings.

2 KINGS 22–23//2 CHRONICLES 34–35

The reign of Josiah plays an especially important role in most discussions of the Deuteronomistic History. The law book that was discovered and read to Josiah is identified as an early form of Deuteronomy, and the resulting reforms are often understood as the circumstances for the first redaction of the Deuteronomistic History. Comparatively, however, the reign of Josiah in Chronicles receives little discussion, most likely because it is considered secondary and, therefore, of little historical value.[102] However, if both 2 Kgs 22–23 and 2 Chr 34–35 are based on a common source, the preferential treatment given the account in Kings must be corrected.[103]

Despite this privileging of Kings, the consensus model nevertheless must acknowledge that this approach requires some explanation of various inconsistencies as illustrated in Sara Japhet's analysis of these passages. First, the account of Josiah's reform in Chronicles is, in her words, "more plausible."[104] According to Kings, Josiah's reform was "a one-time, all embracing event, which took place at Josiah's eighteenth year as a result of the 'finding of the book.'"[105] According to Chronicles, the reform spanned ten years of Josiah's reign, culminating in the covenant renewal and Passover celebration. Second, when one assumes that the Chronicler's *Vorlage* is Kings, one must reach an inconsistent conclusion concerning the Chronicler's tendency in the portrayal

---

102. Recent exceptions to this tendency are the following: Ben Zvi, "Observations on Josiah's Account in Chronicles"; Louis C. Jonker, *Reflections of King Josiah in Chronicles: Late Stages of the Josiah Reception in II Chr. 34f.* (Textpragmatische Studien zur Literatur- und Kulturgeschichte der Hebräischen Bibel 2; Gütersloh: Gütersloher Verlagshaus, 2003); and Kenneth A. Ristau, "Reading and Rereading Josiah: The Chronicler's Representation of Josiah for the Postexilic Community," in *Community Identity in Judean Historiography: Biblical and Comparative Perspectives* (ed. Gary N. Knoppers and Kenneth A. Ristau; Winona Lake, Ind.: Eisenbrauns, 2009), 219–22.

103. Although in previous sections I have discussed the text-critical evidence relating to the passages under review, I have chosen not to in this case, primarily out of a concern for the length of the work. However, for an excellent discussion of 2 Kgs 23:1–3 (MT, LXX, VL) and 2 Chr 34:29–32 (MT, LXX) that provides some text-critical support for the arguments made here, see Schenker, "Die Textgeschichte der Königsbücher." Schenker concluded that MT Kings is a post-LXX Kings edition produced during the time of John Hyrcanus 129/128 B.C.E.

104. Japhet, *I & II Chronicles*, 1020.

105. Ibid., 1017.

of Josiah. Thus, Japhet concluded that the Chronicler was theologically motivated to enhance the portrayal of Josiah by not having him wait until his eighteenth year for the reform and by the motivation for the reform being his own,
which was later confirmed by the finding of the law book.[106] However, Japhet
must then conclude, "At the same time, the Chronicler tempers the praise of
Josiah."[107] The problem of these inconsistencies can be minimized when we
consider a common source for the account in both Kings and Chronicles and
understand their particular representations of the tradition within the context
of multiformity.

The relationship between the Kings and Chronicles accounts can be summarized in the following chart:

2 Kings 22–23:	*2 Chronicles 34–35:*
Introductory regnal formula (2 Kgs 22:1–2)	Introductory regnal formula (2 Chr 34:1–2)
Temple restoration; book find-ing; covenant renewal (2 Kgs 22:3–23:3)	Josiah's reforms (2 Chr 34:3–7)
Josiah's reforms (2 Kgs 23:4–20)	Temple restoration; book find-ing covenant renewal (2 Chr 34:8–33)
Passover celebration (2 Kgs 23:21–23)	Passover celebration (2 Chr 35:1–19)
The LORD's anger persists (2 Kgs 23:24–27)	
The death of Josiah (2 Kgs 23:28–30)	The death of Josiah (2 Chr 35:20–36:1)

As this chart demonstrates, both accounts contain very similar elements; the
two differences are the order of Josiah's reforms and the book finding and the
plus in Kings concerning the LORD's anger at Judah because of Manasseh's sins
despite Josiah's righteousness. Of course, within each of these elements we find
additional variations—for example, the Passover celebration in Chronicles is
more elaborate.

In my discussion of earlier synoptic material I have often followed the
principle of considering a difference in the sequence of events as indication
of a secondary addition. In this case, I do not for three reasons. First, it is not
clear which element was secondary—that is, if we remove either the passages

---

106. Ibid., 1019–20.
107. Ibid., 1020.

of Josiah's reforms or the passages of the temple restoration and book finding, we have a consistent order. Second, I allow that what from our perspective may be considered variant texts could have coexisted and nevertheless carried equal authority, because the ancients may not have considered them to be different. Third, I find Katherine Stott's discussion of the comparative evidence for the story of the finding of the law book compelling.

Stott surveyed parallels of this story in the ancient world, including Philo's *Phoenician History*, Dictys's *The Trojan War*, Pausanias's *Description of Greece*, Plutarch's *De genio Socratis*, and Livy's *History of Rome*. She concluded that "this story [2 Kgs 22–23] was constructed according to literary conventions that circulated in both Near Eastern and classical antiquity."[108] Stott did not discuss her conclusions in relation to the Chronicles account. However, her comparative evidence actually helps emphasize how similar the accounts are in Kings and Chronicles, in that both share in what she considered the literary conventions of the time. She provided evidence of the following common themes: "the book is authored by an important figure of antiquity," "the book is deposited in a temple," "the book is 'lost' or 'forgotten' for a period of time," "the book is discovered (in a temple)," "the book is discovered by a priest," "the book is presented to a king," "the book requires interpretation," and "the book provides the basis for reform."[109]

In two recent studies, Ben Zvi also noted this commonality between the Josiah accounts in Kings and Chronicles.[110] Concerning the Chronicles account, he concluded that "the structure of the narrative, the positive depiction of the king, well-known discourses about building and restoring temples, and the common motif of finding texts in temple and holy places all converge in creating a familiar expectation."[111] This familiar expectation would not have clashed as sharply with the Josiah account in Kings in the minds of the ancients as is generally posited in modern scholarship. In fact, in his later essay on the Josiah account in Kings, Ben Zvi explicitly stated that some of his remarks concerning the Chronicles account "apply also to the Kings account."[112]

---

108. Stott, *Why Did They Write This Way*, 109. Thomas Römer also discussed the comparative material, including the Egyptian Book of the Dead and a royal inscription of Nabonidus, so that he too concluded, "the authors or the redactors of 2 Kgs 22 resort to the same literary convention" (*So-Called Deuteronomistic History*, 53).

109. Each of these elements is a subheading in Stott's fourth chapter (*Why Did They Write This Way*, 104–8).

110. Ben Zvi, "Observations on Josiah's Account in Chronicles"; idem, "Imagining Josiah's Book." Ben Zvi and Stott have obviously been in dialogue concerning these issues. Ben Zvi explicitly thanked Stott ("Imagining Josiah's Book," 208 n. 64) and Stott acknowledged him (*Why Did They Write This Way*, xi).

111. Ben Zvi, "Observations on Josiah's Account in Chronicles," 95.

112. Ben Zvi, "Imagining Josiah's Book," 199 n. 30.

Stott's conclusions have helped us see the similarities between the Kings and Chronicles accounts, especially in light of common literary conventions of the time. Now I want to show how even the two elements that appear to differ in terms of the larger outline of the accounts—the report of Josiah's reforms and the plus in Kings concerning God's continuing wrath—draw from the broader tradition as a common source and, therefore, differ much less than is often supposed, especially when we consider the role of multiformity.

From our modern literate perspective, Kings and Chronicles differ concerning the order of Josiah's reforms in relation to the finding of the law book; therefore, we typically determine that a different theology must be involved. However, we must ask the question: Is this how these texts would have been heard or read by their ancient audiences? Both accounts, as is typical, begin with the summary judgment of the king: "He did what was right in the eyes of the LORD and walked in [all] the ways of David his father and did not turn aside to the right or the left" (2 Kgs 22:2//2 Chr 34:2). Therefore, the ancient audience probably already knew of the book finding and the reforms, and, if Stott's analysis is correct, the ancient audience would associate these two elements into one larger story of finding the law book. If this is the case, then the order in which Kings and Chronicles recounts the two events may be somewhat insignificant.[113] Certainly both accounts combine these two elements. Furthermore, both accounts contain similar elements. Josiah destroyed the "high places" and their altars (2 Kgs 23:5, 8, 9, 13, 15; 2 Chr 34:3), the asherim and ritual items associated with them (2 Kgs 23:4, 6, 7, 14; 2 Chr 34:3,

---

113. The consensus model asserts that the significance of the changes made to the Kings account by the Chronicler are theological in nature. This has been challenged recently by Thomas Römer, who used the difference between Kings and Chronicles as a control on his redaction-critical analysis of Kings. That is, he concluded that the finding of the law book in Kings is a late Persian addition because of the different locations of this theme in relation to the reform (*So-Called Deuteronomistic History*, 49–56, 176–77; see also idem, "Response," 38–41). Although there are aspects of Römer's argument that I find attractive, I nevertheless think he has made some unnecessary conclusions. First, he concluded, "The double account in Chronicles shows that the reform and the book-finding were not considered related to each other" ("Response," 39). Again, I find Stott's analysis compelling that the literary conventions of finding a law book are often related to a legal reform. Second, I think that Römer places too much trust in our ability to apply redaction criticism to a text and obtain valid results without the type of empirical evidence provided by, for example, text criticism (see further Person, review of Thomas Römer, *The So-Called Deuteronomistic History*). Therefore, even though he has the comparative evidence of Chronicles for his reconstruction of the redaction history of Kings in this case, I think he has not adequately understood the role of multiformity in the tradition and how this understanding suggests that the differences between the Kings and Chronicles accounts are not as significant as is commonly held.

4, 7), and the incense altars (2 Kgs 23:5, 8; 2 Chr 34:4, 7). Josiah killed the priests and used their bones to pollute the altars (2 Kgs 23:14, 20; 2 Chr 34:5) and similarly placed the pieces of the destroyed ritual items over tombs (2 Kgs 23:6; 2 Chr 34:4). Josiah's reforms began in Jerusalem and Judah (2 Kgs 23:4; 2 Chr 34:3–5) and then spread out to other parts of his realm (2 Kgs 23:15–20; 2 Chr 34:6–7). Thus, even though the order of events as narrated in Kings and Chronicles differs, the two reform accounts have striking similarities, and both are clearly related to the story of the finding of the law book.

The additional material in Kings concerning God's persistence in punishing Judah for past sins (2 Kgs 23:24–27) does not have a parallel in the Chronicles account between the Passover celebration and the death of Josiah. This account, however, simply repeats the theme found in the synoptic material in Huldah's prophecy (2 Kgs 22:18–20//2 Chr 34:26–28)—that is, despite Josiah's proper response, God will destroy Jerusalem and Judah as punishment for its past pagan practices.

As we have just seen, some of what is often understood from our modern perspective as inconsistent may not have been so viewed by the ancient audience. Both accounts of Josiah's reign contain similar elements, and the differences have too often been exaggerated. What we understand as inconsistencies exist between the Kings and Chronicles account, but these inconsistencies may have been viewed as inconsequential by the ancients. In fact, we should remember that even within the synoptic material an inconsistency exists—that is, despite Huldah's prophecy of Josiah's peaceful death (2 Kgs 22:20//2 Chr 34:28), Josiah is killed on the battlefield by Pharaoh Necho in both accounts (2 Kgs 23:28–30//2 Chr 35:20–24). Thus, we can use the words of Ben Zvi to conclude that, when reading these two accounts with a new perspective allowing multiformity, "[t]he messages are not contradictory, but complementary."[114]

CONCLUSION: MULTIFORMITY IN THE SYNOPTIC PASSAGES

Before discussing the role of multiformity in the synoptic passages, it may be helpful to recall Auld's thesis of the Shared Text and the arguments of his critics. Auld drew from text-critical principles to reconstruct a *Vorlage* of the material common to Samuel–Kings and Chronicles and insisted that both Samuel–Kings and Chronicles are expansions of this Shared Text. He also insisted that the Shared Text was not Deuteronomistic; in fact, he rejected the very notion

---

114. Ben Zvi, *History, Literature and Theology*, 60. Ben Zvi's conclusion was in the context of the multiformity within Chronicles; however, he noted similar multiformity within Samuel–Kings (58–59) as well as between Samuel–Kings and Chronicles. He also concluded that too often modern scholarship emphasizes the differences between Samuel–Kings and Chronicles and minimizes the similarities ("Are There Any Bridges Out There?").

of a Deuteronomistic History as applied to Deuteronomy–Kings at any level of its history. Auld's thesis has drawn some needed criticism. For example, some critics have correctly pointed out that some of the passages in Auld's Shared Text, in McKenzie's words, "remain replete with deuteronomistic vocabulary and ideology" or, in Knoppers's words, contain a "preponderance of Deuteronomistic expressions and themes."[115] I share this criticism, which is why my own position is somewhat closer to the consensus model in that the common source was an early form of Samuel–Kings, which was (or at least became) a part of the Deuteronomic History. Where I differ with McKenzie, Knoppers, and others is that I do not think that any of the extant texts of Samuel–Kings closely represents this *Vorlage*, because with Auld I think they all are expansive. However, I must disagree with what has been another emphasis in the criticism of Auld's thesis—that is, the Chronicler necessarily assumed that his readers were familiar with the written text of his *Vorlage*. For example, Knoppers wrote, "[S]ome passages in the Chronicler's narration of Judahite history presuppose texts known from Kings dealing with the northern kingdom, even though the Chronicler does not include these texts within his own narration."[116] We have seen in two examples—the reference to Michal (1 Chr 15:29//2 Sam 6:16) and the reference to Pharaoh's daughter (2 Chr 8:11//1 Kgs 9:24a)—how the text of Chronicles alone provides enough information for its readers to interpret adequately the references without knowledge of the additional material found in Samuel–Kings. However, even if this were not the case, Chronicles would not necessarily have to assume knowledge of a specific written text, its *Vorlage*, but could simply assume knowledge of Michal and Pharaoh's daughter from the broader tradition. Therefore, although Auld's critics correctly point out that the Chronistic school probably assumes more knowledge of, for example, Pharaoh's daughter than Chronicles provides, this knowledge does not necessarily have to come from the version of Samuel–Kings that served as its written *Vorlage*.[117] In fact, since the reference to Pha-

---

115. McKenzie, "Chronicler as Redactor," 86; Knoppers, *I Chronicles 1–9*, 67.

116. Knoppers, *I Chronicles 1–9*, 67. See similarly McKenzie, "Chronicler as Redactor," 81–85; Klein, *1 Chronicles*, 37; Talshir, "Reign of Solomon," 236–39. In *1–2 Chronicles*, McKenzie seemingly moderated his position somewhat. On the one hand, he insisted that the Chronicler "clearly anticipates his audience's familiarity with the content of Samuel-Kings," but then concluded that "the Chronicler probably did not expect his audience to make the kinds of detailed comparisons of his work with Samuel and Kings that modern scholars make" (36). Thus he concluded, "At most, the readers of Chronicles were likely generally familiar with the stories he borrowed. It was the general familiarity that allowed the Chronicler to reshape the stories for his own purposes" (36).

If this "general familiarity" can come from the broader tradition (contained in both written and oral forms), then my position is not that far from McKenzie's later position.

117. See similarly A. Graeme Auld, "Prophets Shared—But Recycled," in *The Future*

raoh's daughter in 1 Kgs 9:24 (//2 Chr 8:11) is found in different locations in MT Kings and LXX Kings, another response to Talshir's criticism could be that Auld should not have included even this reference to Pharaoh's daughter in his Shared Text. The text-critical evidence for the references to Pharaoh's daughter can serve as evidence that the broader oral tradition later inserted these references into the written texts in various locations as the parallel texts expanded to represent the broader tradition more fully.

Although I structured this chapter to discuss Samuel//Chronicles and Kings//Chronicles separately as the consensus model would require, we have seen that this was not necessary. The text-critical evidence, especially as presented by Trebolle, demonstrates that not only is the Samuel *Vorlage* of Chronicles (often with the support of LXX Samuel) a version earlier than MT Samuel, but also that the Kings *Vorlage* of Chronicles (often with the support of LXX Kings) is a version earlier than MT Kings. In fact, when the text-critical evidence of the extant versions of Samuel–Kings (especially that of different location of common material) is compared to Chronicles, the result can be a common written source even smaller than that reconstructed by Auld. For example, assuming Trebolle's argument combining the evidence of MT Samuel–Kings, LXX Samuel–Kings, and MT Chronicles, a reconstructed common text becomes even smaller when one considers the following as secondary, all of which Auld included in his Shared Text: 2 Sam 23:8–39//1 Chr 11:10–47; 2 Sam 6:1–11//1 Chr 13:5–14; 2 Sam 12:26–31//1 Chr 20:1b–3; 2 Sam 21:18–22//1 Chr 20:4–8; 2 Sam 24:1–25//1 Chr 21:1–27; and 1 Kgs 2:10–12//1 Chr 29:20–30.[118]

Although the text-critical evidence can be used to reconstruct a common source behind Samuel–Kings and Chronicles, with Trebolle I have cautioned that our modern notions of a unilinear process of textual development that began with one original text that then became the *Vorlage* for all of the extant texts is anachronistic, based on our modern notions of how texts function in

---

of the Deuteronomistic History (ed. Thomas Römer; BETL 147; Leuven: Leuven University Press, 2000), 27–28; Rodney K. Duke, *The Persuasive Appeal of the Chronicler* (JSOTSup 88; Sheffield: Almond, 1990), 36–37. Rolf Rendtorff reached a similar conclusion in his study of two texts in Chronicles that include references to sacrifice (2 Chr 8; 29–31) and how they compare to pentateuchal texts, especially the Priestly source. He concluded that "the authors of the books of Chronicles knew a great deal about their people's national and religious traditions without having constantly to consult written documents" ("Chronicles and the Priestly Torah," in *Text, Temples, and Traditions: A Tribute to Menahem Haran* [ed. Michael V. Fox et al.; Winona Lake, Ind.: Eisenbrauns, 1996], 259). Thus, it is better to "understand the Chronicler not in terms of literary dependence but in terms of personal knowledge and experience within the cultic reality of his own time" (266).

118. Trebolle, "Samuel/Kings and Chronicles." See my revision of this work by Trebolle above, pp. 89–94. Auld, *Kings without Privilege*, 51, 44, 50, 50–51, 52–53, 54–55.

a highly literate society. Based on his knowledge of the diversity of Hebrew text-types in ancient Israel, Trebolle resisted reconstructing the one common source and insisted that we consider how the "co-existence of parallel editions" was the norm.[119] Furthermore, these coexisting parallel texts could be understood as equally representative of the broader textual tradition. Trebolle's insights parallel remarkably well the insights about the role of multiformity in oral traditions. In oral traditions no single performance is considered wholly authoritative; each performance is authoritative in that it points to the broader oral tradition but remains a selective, imperfect representation of the tradition in its fullness. Similarly, none of the coexisting texts would be considered to represent the tradition in its totality (including what is written down and that which remains in the mind of the community), even though each is an instantiation of the broader tradition. Therefore, the search for the *original* text of Samuel, Kings, or Chronicles or the *one* common source behind Samuel–Kings and Chronicles is a search for something that never existed. Of course, there must have been a first written text behind the extant written texts; however, this text did not necessarily have the determinative authority for all its textual descendants as the search for the original text purports. If any one written text was understood to be an imperfect representation of the broader tradition, then a plurality of such imperfect texts was not only allowed but necessary, because only in their multiformity would they begin to approach the fullness of the broader tradition. Furthermore, whenever one of these imperfect texts was copied, the scribe would not necessarily be bound to copy the *Vorlage* word for word, because the text itself was merely a limited representation of the broader tradition in the mind of the community. Therefore, the scribe could make what from our perspective may be changes to the text that nevertheless still faithfully re-present the tradition that the *Vorlage* also represented. Based on what we know about textual traditions in the ancient world, I agree with Carr that there was a "trend towards expansion." As the written text became more valued as a means of preserving verbal art, later texts incorporated more material from the broader oral tradition. When the first texts were expanded in order to include more of the tradition, the additional material was added in different locations, because, as is common in oral traditions, the sequence of narrated events is not fixed in a linear text but exists in the multiformity of the tradition. These later expansive texts would not necessarily need to agree in what additions were made or where the additions were made, because the broader tradition allowed for multiplicity and each of them could still be understood as an imperfect representation of the broader tradition that existed in the memory of the tradents. If this is the case,

---

119. Trebolle, "Samuel/Kings and Chronicles," 98.

then each of the extant texts, despite whatever variations we may observe, can be judged as equally representing the broader oral tradition. This is not to deny that theological differences of opinion existed in the ancient world; however, if this portrayal of the composition and transmission of ancient texts such as Samuel–Kings and Chronicles is accurate, it greatly complicates our ability to tease out these theological differences from the texts we have in all of their multiformity.

Given this reconstruction of the process of the interaction of texts and the broader oral tradition in ancient Israel, Auld's thesis of a smaller common source behind Samuel–Kings//Chronicles has some validity. However, Auld's attempt to reconstruct this one source must be corrected with the idea that this common source existed in multiple forms from the beginning of its history, none of which would have been understood as so authoritative as to dismiss the authority of the others. As a consequence, our exegetical methods do not enable us to reconstruct what the multiformity of coexisting parallel editions was. Furthermore, this reconstruction of the process (not the specific texts or the content of the tradition in its totality) should caution us not to overemphasize what we perceive as differences between texts, when these differences may have been inconsequential from an ancient perspective.[120] This overemphasis on variations is behind the criticisms of Auld's Shared Text that insist that the readers of Chronicles must have known the written text of Samuel–Kings in a form very close to the MT in order to understand, for example, the reference to Michal (1 Chr 15:29//2 Sam 6:16) rather than allowing the possibility that the source for such given or known background information could come from the broader tradition. This overemphasis results in conclusions such as what Rezetko called the consensus model's identification of the "corporate-levitical thrust" as a theological theme of the Chronicler and what he proposed as the alternative, the theme of "David's royal-sacral status" in Samuel. Because of this danger I may have erred on the side of minimizing such consequential differences, those variations that are intentional and theologically motivated. My minimizing of such consequential differences is not because I doubt that theologically motivated changes were made; rather, it is because recognition of the important role of multiformity in the tradition greatly disadvantages our ability to tease out which variations are consequential. However, as one who is still learning to take seriously the full implications of both the textual plurality evident in our extant texts and the important role of multiformity in primarily oral societies as well as the function of texts in these societies, I prefer to err on this side rather than the other.

---

120. Ben Zvi has also recently cautioned against overemphasizing the differences between Samuel–Kings and Chronicles ("Are There Any Bridges Out There?").

5

MULTIFORMITY AND THE NONSYNOPTIC PASSAGES

In the previous chapter on selected synoptic passages I argued that the text-critical evidence strongly suggests that MT Samuel–Kings and MT Chronicles are expansions of a common source—that is, earlier, no longer extant versions of Samuel–Kings that existed in various parallel editions. Over time, as the tradition increasingly valued preserving verbal art in written texts, the texts expanded in order to preserve more of the tradition in written form. These expansions occurred in a variety of ways, continuing the multiformity of texts representing the broader tradition.

In this chapter I examine the nonsynoptic material in Samuel–Kings and Chronicles. According to the consensus model, based on a comparison between the current versions of Samuel–Kings and Chronicles, the material lacking in Chronicles represents "omissions," and the material lacking in Samuel–Kings represents "additions" in Chronicles. These "omissions" and "additions" are generally considered to be the result of the Chronicler's theologically motivated changes to the *Vorlage* of Samuel–Kings. However, given the arguments above, we will explore the possibility that most, if not all, of the material unique to each literary work consists of additions to a written common source, which may have been motivated not by theological differences but by the multiformity of the broader tradition that is preserved in expanding written texts. In other words, this unique material is unique only in that the other literary work does not contain the same verses; however, the content of these unique texts is not that anomalous when compared with material found elsewhere in the same literary work and, in fact, in the other as well, especially in their common material. This unique material typically fits quite well into its immediate literary context as well as into the broader tradition represented by both Samuel–Kings and Chronicles.

MATERIAL UNIQUE TO THE BOOKS OF SAMUEL AND KINGS (THE SO-CALLED OMISSIONS IN CHRONICLES)

The consensus model generally proposes that the material in Samuel–Kings that is lacking in Chronicles came, on the one hand, from the hand of the

Deuteronomist(s) because it fits well within its literary context and, on the other hand, was omitted by the Chronicler because of some theological motivation. Below I review these propositions as they apply to 2 Sam 1–4; 2 Sam 6:20b–23; 1 Kgs 4:20–26; and 1 Kgs 14:1–20. With the consensus model, I conclude that the unique material in Samuel–Kings was produced by the Deuteronomic school, because I discern clear traces of Deuteronomic phraseology and themes so much so that these passages generally fit into their literary contexts. However, rather than explaining that these texts are unique to Samuel–Kings because the Chronicler omitted them, I can account for their uniqueness on the basis of the continuing Deuteronomic tradition's expansion of a common source—that is, earlier, no longer extant versions of Samuel–Kings. Against the consensus model, I also conclude that the Chronistic school would not necessarily be theologically motivated to omit these passages, even if they had them in their *Vorlagen*. Even though there are differences in terms of what material is preserved in the written texts, the unique material in Samuel–Kings remains within the realm of theological possibility for the Chronistic school, especially when we take seriously the role of multiformity within the broader tradition. In fact, just because these passages are not in Chronicles does not preclude that the Chronistic school might have known of some of this material and might even have accepted it as authoritative. The observation that this material is lacking in Chronicles does not require a conclusion that the Chronistic school rejected it for theological reasons. Furthermore, in two cases (1 Kgs 4:20–26; 14:1–20) the text-critical evidence undercuts the consensus model's argument in that the material is lacking in LXX Kings in addition to Chronicles, suggesting that it was added to MT Kings as the tradition strove to preserve more traditional material in a written text.

2 SAMUEL 1–4

In her essay "The Dialogism of Chronicles," Christine Mitchell insisted on reading 1 Chr 10:1–11:9 on its own terms—that is, without viewing it as a rereading of 1 Sam 31:1–2 Sam 5:10.[1] She concluded that the passage has its own literary logic and demonstrates how the death of Saul, the unfit king, prepares the way for David, God's chosen. She thus emphasized how the Chronicler's interpretation of this material does not necessarily represent a strong variation from that of Samuel:

> The Chronicler's text can be read as simply showing another position while accepting that Samuel had a valid position as well; it does not have to be a

1. Christine Mitchell, "The Dialogism of Chronicles," in *The Chronicler as Author: Studies in Text and Texture* (ed. M. Patrick Graham and Steven L. McKenzie; JSOTSup 263; Sheffield: Sheffield Academic Press, 1999), 311–26.

correction or a replacement for Samuel; it is more of a "yes, but . . ." . . . . The reader of Chronicles does not have to know Samuel–Kings in order to get the messages of Chronicles. But the reader of Chronicles who also knows Samuel–Kings can appreciate the dialogue between the two, as well as the little ironies and playfulness that Chronicles has built into its text. [2]

She noted that her way of reading Chronicles did not necessarily depend on which one was given priority in terms of literary influence or even if they descended from a common source.[3]

In this section I want to turn Mitchell's argument on its head—that is, that one can read 2 Sam 1–4 without reference to Chronicles, but when one reads it in dialogue with Chronicles, one can better "appreciate the dialogue between the two." Just as Chronicles is not necessarily a correction or a replacement of Samuel, Samuel is not necessarily a correction or replacement of Chronicles. Both are descended from a common source, such that the different positions that each takes on the end of Saul and his sons and David's succession are not necessarily conflicting versions but can be understood as simply extensions of a shared tradition based on a common written source.

The material in 2 Sam 1–4 is unique to Samuel. On the basis of his analysis of both the relationship between Samuel–Kings and Chronicles, on the one hand, and his analysis of the transitions between the non-*kaige* and *kaige* recensions in LXX Samuel–Kings, Julio Trebolle concluded that 2 Sam 1–4 is an addition to a common source.[4] Here I reproduce the relevant portion of the chart I gave above in chapter 4, summarizing Trebolle's reconstruction.

Common Source	*Additions in Samuel–Kings*
Saul's death (1 Chr 10//1 Sam 31)	
	Elaborations upon the end of Saul's dynasty and David's rise to power (2 Sam 1–4)
David becomes king over all Israel (1 Chr 11:1–9//2 Sam 5:1–10)	

2. Ibid., 326. Contra Yairah Amit, "The Saul Polemic in the Persian Period," in *Judah and the Judeans in the Persian Period* (ed. Oded Lipschits and Manfred Oeming; Winona Lake, Ind.: Eisenbrauns, 2006), 649–53.

3. Mitchell, "Dialogism of Chronicles," 326. Although she asserted that the direction of literary influence had no bearing on her conclusion, she nevertheless seems to accept the consensus model's assumption that the Chronicler used Samuel–Kings as its *Vorlage* rather than that they both used a common source.

4. For my more complete discussion of 1 Sam 31:1–1 Kgs 2:12//1 Chr 10–29 as reconstructed by Trebolle, see chapter 4 above, pp. 89–94.

The common source contained the report of Saul's death followed by David being made king. The additions of 2 Sam 1–4 contain a variety of narratives that emphasize the theme that Mitchell identified for 1 Chr 10:1–11:9, "the unfitness of Saul and the fitness of David":[5] David's grief at the news of Saul's death (2 Sam 1:1–16), David being proclaimed king over Judah (2:1–7), the war between the house of Saul and the house of David (2:8–3:1), a short genealogy of David's sons born at Hebron (3:2–5; see 1 Chr 3:1–4a), the agreement between Abner and David (3:6–21), Joab's murder of Abner (3:22–39), and the assassination of Ish-bosheth, Saul's son who was king of Israel (4:1–12). In other words, this additional material is simply an elaboration on the theme of how unfit Saul was and how David should become king over all of Israel, both north and south. In this elaboration, we learn more about how David overcame the resistance of the sons of Saul (and their allies), who wanted to retain the throne for themselves and who controlled the northern tribes for a period of time before David gained control of all of Israel. In this sense, the account in Samuel does not differ significantly from the account in Chronicles; they both portray the transition of power from Saul (and his sons) to David.[6] In fact, the observation that the genealogy of David's sons born at Hebron is found also in the opening genealogy of Chronicles (1 Chr 3:1–4a) suggests that the tradents responsible for Chronicles may even have known of some of these narratives from the broader tradition.[7] If so, not including these narratives would not necessarily suggest a theologically motivated rejection of them, since no one text can possibly represent the broader tradition in its fullness.

2 SAMUEL 6:20B–23

As we saw in the previous chapter, Robert Rezetko has argued that 2 Sam 5–6; 23//1 Chr 11–16 have a common source and that both MT 2 Sam 6 and MT 1 Chr 13; 15–16 show clear expansion from that common source. One part of his argument is that 2 Sam 6:20b–23, which is unique to Samuel, is an

---

5. Mitchell, "Dialogism of Chronicles," 324

6. For my discussion of the subtle differences between Samuel and Chronicles, see my comments on 1 Chr 12 below, pp. 145–50.

7. Auld noted that the common list of David's sons in 2 Sam 5:14–16//1 Chr 3:5–8 contains theophoric names using El forms and none with YHWH forms. In contrast, 2 Sam 3:2–5 contains theophoric names using YHWH forms and none with El forms. When combined with his argument that MT Samuel changed Elohim (preserved in LXX Samuel and MT Chronicles) to YHWH, he concluded that the common list in 2 Sam 5:14–16//1 Chr 3:5–8 preserves a tradition earlier than the unique material in 2 Sam 3:2–5. See Auld, "Deuteronomists between History and Theology," 356–58. Although Auld's observation is quite interesting, it is not clear how he accounted for the parallel between 2 Sam 3:2–5 and 1 Chr 3:1–4a, especially since 1 Chr 3:1–4a also has YHWH form.

addition to this common source.[8] Since this is a passage that is often referred to by critics of Auld's Shared Text hypothesis, I will look carefully at these arguments.

Auld excluded 2 Sam 6:20b–23 from his Shared Text quite simply because it was unique to Samuel.[9] However, some of Auld's critics have argued that 2 Sam 6:20b–23 was necessarily part of a series of passages concerning Michal in the Chronicler's *Vorlage*, without which the reference to Michal in 2 Sam 6:16 (//1 Chr 15:29) would be meaningless. For example, Steven McKenzie wrote: "Since Chronicles does not elsewhere mention Michal or David's marriage to her, the reader has to know Samuel in order to make sense of Chronicles at this point."[10] Thus, according to McKenzie and many others, the Chronicler omitted this material for various possible ideological reasons.[11]

Rezetko responded to this criticism with three arguments.[12] First, his own literary analysis led him to the conclusion that "6:20b–23 is an expansionary supplement of the brief reference to Michal in v. 16" that parallels the supplements in the nonsynoptic material in 1 Samuel concerning Saul and David, especially concerning the references to Michal.[13] He noted that 2 Sam 6:1–20a is a literary unity that fits well into the plot structure of the synoptic material. In contrast, 2 Sam 6:20b–23 disrupts the plot structure and appears to draw from both the reference to Michal in 2 Sam 6:16//1 Chr 15:29 and the following explicitly pro-Davidic/anti-Saulide passage of God's covenant with David (2 Sam 7:8–9, 11b–16//1 Chr 17:7–8, 10b–14).[14] Furthermore, Rezetko concluded that MT 2 Sam 6:1–20a provides evidence of expansion that includes the theme of the Davidic displacement of the Saulide dynasty, thereby paralleling the addition of 2 Sam 6:20b–23.

Second, one of the ideological reasons generally given for the omission concerns the Chronicler's tendency to give a more idealized portrayal of David. Rezetko challenged this view by noting that the Chronicler's David is not an

---

8. Rezetko, *Source and Revision*, 292. Trebolle independently also concluded that 2 Sam 6:20b–23 is probably an addition to a common source ("Samuel/Kings and Chronicles," 107).

9. Auld, *Kings without Privilege*, 14; idem, "What Was the Main Source?" 93–94.

10. McKenzie, "Chronicler as Redactor," 82. See also Klein, *1 Chronicles*, 31.

11. Rezetko has provided a thorough summary of the various reasons usually given for the Chronicler's omission of this material (*Source and Revision*, 281–82).

12. Rezetko's response builds on the earlier response by Auld himself. See Auld, "What Was the Main Source?" 93–94.

13. Rezetko, *Source and Revision*, 279; for his supporting arguments, see 278–79.

14. Similarly, McCarter concluded that "the Michal materials in vv. 14–16, 20–23 were probably secondary" (*II Samuel*, 184).

ideal character.[15] Even many who have argued that the Chronicler omitted
2 Sam 6:20b–23 have acknowledged this. For example, Sara Japhet wrote:

> Not all the shadows in David's career were in fact omitted: his rejection from
> building the Temple is justified by the fact that "he shed blood" (I Chron. 22.7–8;
> 28.3), and he is twice described as committing a sin: during the transfer of the ark
> from Kiriath-jearim (I Chron. 15.13), and by undertaking the census (I Chron.
> 21.1, 3, 8). [16]

Therefore, the Chronicler would not necessarily be motivated to omit this passage from his *Vorlage*, since he includes other passages that similarly portray
David in an unfavorable light.

Third, the critics' assertion that the reference to Michal in 1 Chr 15:29
requires knowledge of the other Michal material in Samuel is, in Rezetko's
words, "unproven."[17] Rezetko noted that the Chronicler has already provided
enough information for readers to understand the reference:

> The Chronicler has already related Saul's lineage (1 Chron 8:33; 9:39), Saul's and
> his sons' death (1 Chron 10:1–12//1 Sam 31:1–13), David's control of Saul's army
> (1 Chron 11:2//2 Sam 5:2), David's battles with Saul and the desertion of some of
> Saul's warriors to David (1 Chron 12:1–2, 19, 23, 29), and he has pointedly articu-
> lated Saul's cultic unfaithfulness (1 Chron 10:13–14; 13:3), and he has reported
> the coronation of David as king over Israel (1 Chron 11:1–3//2 Sam 5:1–3).
> This information efficiently prepares the reader for comprehending the role of
> "Michal, the daughter of Saul" as a foil in 1 Chron 15:29. Furthermore, *exactly
> what* in 1 Sam 14:49; 18:20–28; 19:11–17; 25:44; 2 Sam 3:13–14, is required for
> understanding 2 Sam 6:16? What difference does it make here whether or not she
> is even David's wife? The contrast is between David and Saul, and she is unmis-
> takably one of Saul's. [18]

In my opinion, Rezetko has made a strong argument for his conclusion:
"the burden of proof rests on scholars who assert that the statement in 2 Sam
6:16//1 Chron 15:29 requires prior knowledge of Michal and they should also
show that this prior knowledge must be literary in form."[19] However, I think
he should have made much more of the last point in the wording of this conclusion, questioning whether this "prior knowledge must be literary in form."
All literary texts assume a certain amount of knowledge on the part of their

15. Rezekto, *Source and Revision*, 282.

16. Japhet, *I & II Chronicles*, 48. Rezetko provided additional examples (*Source and
Revision*, 282 n. 212).

17. Rezetko, *Source and Revision*, 282.

18. Ibid.

19. Ibid., 283.

audience, but we are arguing that it is even more so the case with texts written in a primarily oral society such as ancient Israel, because the texts act more as mnemonic devices that selectively point to the broader oral tradition rather than as the primary depository of knowledge itself. For example, the references to Daniel and Job in the book of Ezekiel (14:14, 20; 28:3) do not necessarily require knowledge of these biblical books. Further, references to the patriarchs in the Deuteronomic History (for example, Abraham in Deut 1:8; 6:10; 9:5, 27; 29:12; 30:20; 34:4; Josh 24:2–3; 1 Kgs 18:36; 2 Kgs 13:23) do not necessarily require knowledge of the canonical book of Genesis.[20] Moreover, as Auld has suggested, the references to the prophet Jeremiah in Chronicles (2 Chr 16:10; 36:21) require knowledge of the tradition but not necessarily a particular text-type of the book of Jeremiah.[21] That is, it is quite possible that these references are from the broader oral tradition that influenced all of these texts, no matter when any of the traditions were first written down. If any written text is necessarily only a selection from a broader oral tradition, then a reference to Michal does not necessarily need to include that she is David's wife or Saul's daughter. This information can simply be understood as a significant part of the tradition well known to the reading/hearing audience, even though only Samuel contains most of this information in an extant written form. Therefore, even in 2 Chr 15:29, the ancient audience would have likely interpreted Michal as David's wife and as standing in a palace window, despising her husband because he has displaced her father.

If this is the case, then Rezetko has overstated the contrast between MT 2 Sam 6, on the one hand, and the other versions of 2 Sam 6 and 1 Chr 13; 15–16, on the other, in order to conclude that some of the secondary material in MT 2 Sam 6 is "related to the theme *apology of Davidic kingship. David is appropriately and rightfully king rather than Saul.*"[22] In addition to the plus in 2 Sam 6:20b–23, Rezetko identified twelve secondary readings in MT 2 Samuel 6 related to this theme.[23] The argument I have given above undercuts the assumed theological motivation for adding 2 Sam 6:20b–23 or any of the variants related to this theme, since the theme clearly exists in all of the extant texts, an observation

---

20. Although he often assumed that the rereaders of Chronicles were aware of Samuel–Kings as authoritative texts, Ehud Ben Zvi still made the argument that Chronicles assumes knowledge of a variety of stories not included in its narrative, including the exodus, Sinai/Horeb, Joshua, the judges, and Samuel (*History, Literature and Theology*, 31, 92). Even though Ben Zvi approached Chronicles as representing a text-centered community, he nevertheless argued that Chronicles assumed that its readers had knowledge of the broader tradition and, therefore, did not have to include everything that was considered important.

21. Auld, "Prophets Shared—But Recycled," 27.

22. Rezetko, *Source and Revision*, 287 (emphasis his).

23. Ibid., 287–88.

that Rezetko himself made.[24] Therefore, although from our perspective one text might heighten or diminish this theme, the ancients could have understood all of the extant texts as supporting the theme of the Davidic displacement of the Saulide dynasty as an expression of God's will without necessarily concluding that one text emphasizes the theme more than another.

1 KINGS 4:20–26

This passage describes the glory of Solomon's empire in terms of the vastness of land area, of the submission of all of the kings in Beyond the River, and of the peace and prosperity Judah and Israel experienced. The consensus model assumes that the Chronicler omitted this passage,[25] but the fact that it is lacking in LXX 1 Kings undercuts this assumption.

Trebolle's analysis of these parallel texts is summarized in his chart for the reign of Solomon as follows:[26]

2 Chronicles	LXX 1 Kings Main Text	MT 1 Kings	LXX 1 Kings Supplement
	lacking	4:20	2:46a
9:26		4:21a	2:46b*/k
	lacking	4:21b	
		4:22–24	2:46efg^a
	lacking	4:25	2:46g^b
1:14; 9:25	lacking	4:26 = 10:26	2:46i
	...		
	4:22–24 (after 4:28)		
...	...		
9:26	4:21a (after 10:26)		

As we can see from Trebolle's chart, all of MT 1 Kgs 4:20–26 is lacking in the parallel text of LXX Kings—that is, between 4:1–19 and 4:27–28. Critics have long suspected that 4:20–26 may be secondary.[27] First, MT 1 Kgs 4:20–26 divides what appears to be a literary unit; the reference to "those officials" that begins 4:27–28 seems to refer to the list of officials in 4:7–19. Second, the duplication

---

24. See esp. ibid., 290.

25. For example, see Japhet, *I & II Chronicles*, 643.

26. Trebolle, "Kings (MT/LXX) and Chronicles," 494.

27. For example, Fritz, *1 & 2 Kings*, 53; Gray, *I & II Kings*, 135. In fact, Gray concluded that here the LXX is "a better text than MT, reproducing more closely and without so much late redactional interpolation the archival source" (135).

of MT 1 Kgs 4:26 = 1 Kgs 10:26 (both MT and LXX) betrays the secondary character of 1 Kgs 4:20–26. Most of MT Kgs 4:20–26 is found either elsewhere in the main text of LXX Kings (4:22–24; 4:21a) or in the supplementary material following 2:46. Furthermore, Chronicles contains only small portions of the tradition (2 Chr 9:26; 1:14; 9:25). Despite the difference in order between MT Kings and LXX Kings, 2 Chronicles agrees with LXX Kings in the placement of the description of Solomon's reign from the Euphrates to the Egyptian border—that is, 2 Chr 9:26 and LXX 1 Kgs 4:21a follow the description of the size of Solomon's army, including the "twelve thousand horsemen" (2 Chr 9:25//1 Kgs 10:26 [both MT and LXX]). Thus, Trebolle concluded that Chronicles used a *Vorlage* similar to that of LXX Kings.[28]

Nevertheless, 1 Kgs 4:20–26 may have come from the broader tradition, because it contains close parallels with the supplementary material in LXX 1 Kgs 2:46a–i. Below I provide an English synopsis for these two texts.

MT 1 Kings 4:20–26	LXX 1 Kings 2:46a–i
	ᵃKing Solomon was very prudent and wise, and Judah and Israel were as numerous as the sands of the sea; eating and drinking and rejoicing.
²⁰Judah and Israel were as numerous as the sands of the sea; eating and drinking and rejoicing.	
²¹Solomon was ruling over all the kingdoms from the river to the land of the Philistines, even until the border of Egypt;	ᵇSolomon was ruling over all the kingdoms;
they brought tribute and served Solomon all the days of his life.	they brought tribute and served Solomon all the days of his life.
	ᶜSolomon began to open the resources of Lebanon, ᵈand he built Thermai in the wilderness.
²²Solomon's provisions for one day were 30 cors of flour and 60 cors of meal, ²³10 fattened cattle, 20 pasture-fed cattle, and 100 sheep/goats, besides deer, gazelles, roebucks, and fattened fowl. ²⁴For he ruled over all the Beyond the River, from Tiphsah to Gaza, over all the kings of Beyond the River; and he had peace on all his surrounding borders.	ᵉSolomon's provisions for one day were 30 cors of flour and 60 cors of meal, 10 fattened cattle, 20 pasture-fed cattle, and 100 sheep/goats, besides deer, gazelles, and fattened fowl. ᶠFor he ruled over all the Beyond the River, from Raphi to Gaza, over all the kings of Beyond the River; ᵍand he had peace on all his surrounding borders.
²⁵Judah and Israel dwelt in safety, each under his own vine and under	Judah and Israel dwelt in safety, each under his own vine and under

28. Trebolle, "Kings (MT/LXX) and Chronicles," 496.

his own fig tree, from Dan to Beersheba, all the days of Solomon.	his own fig tree, from Dan to Beersheba, all the days of Solomon.
	ʰAnd these were the officials of Solomon: Azariah, son of Zadok, the priest; Orniou, son of Nathan, chief of the officers; Edram, over his house; Souba, the scribe; Basa, son of Achithalam, the recorder; Abi, son of Joab, commander in chief; Achire, son of Edrai, over the levies; Banaia, son of Iodae, over the main court and over the brickworks; and Zachour, son of Nathan, the counselor.
[see 4:2–6]	
²⁶Solomon had 40,000 stalls of horses for his chariots and 12,000 horsemen.	ⁱSolomon had 40,000 stalls of horses for his chariots and 12,000 horsemen.

The similarities between MT 1 Kgs 4:20–26 and LXX 1 Kgs 2:46a–i are substantial, including the wording and order of their common material. Nevertheless, the subtle differences in wording, the pluses, and their different placements point toward the multiformity of the tradition. The different placements of these parallel texts suggest that they were added later to a common source— that is, an earlier, no longer extant form of Kings. This common source itself probably assumed knowledge of this material, since LXX Kings and Chronicles contain brief references to this material in the same order (2 Chr 9:26; LXX 1 Kgs 4:21a), even though a common source may not have contained a written account. In any event, these additions (MT 1 Kgs 4:20–26 and LXX 1 Kgs 2:46a–i) do not diverge significantly in terms of content from the common source. For example, 1 Kgs 10:14–29//2 Chr 9:13–28 contain a shared account similarly describing Solomon's wisdom and wealth.²⁹

1 KINGS 14:1–20

The prophecy of Ahijah against Jeroboam I (MT 1 Kgs 14:1–20) is lacking in the parallel account of LXX Kings but is found in a shorter form in LXX 1 Kgs 12:24g–n. Many commentators on Chronicles overlook this fact and assume that the Chronicler omitted this account. For example, Japhet wrote the following:

> A comparison of the new composition with I Kings 12–14 reveals a surprising literary fact: II Chron. 11 fills the space originally created by the omission of the

---

29. Trebolle ("Kings [MT/LXX] and Chronicles," 495) included 1 Kgs 10:14–29//2 Chr 9:13–28 in his triple textual tradition, which preserves the common source.

story of Jeroboam (I Kings 12.25–14.20). It is the commonly accepted view that the placing of this chapter in its present position was due exclusively to theological considerations. [30]

She then criticized the exclusive focus on theological considerations, suggesting that "literary-compositional aspects also play a role."[31] However, nowhere does she acknowledge that the text-critical evidence in Kings suggests that 1 Kgs 12:25–14:20 should not be treated as one monolithic complex with the same textual history. Below I will summarize the work of Adrian Schenker and Gary Knoppers, both of whom concluded that LXX 1 Kgs 12:24g–n preserves an earlier version of the tradition and that MT 1 Kgs 14:1–20 is a later, expansive version based on an earlier source. We will then examine the implications of their text-critical conclusions for the thesis of a common source behind Samuel–Kings and Chronicles.

In a variety of related studies concerning MT Kings and LXX Kings Schenker has concluded that MT Kings is a late expansive text based on the Hebrew *Vorlage* of LXX Kings and produced during the time of John Hyrcanus.[32] Although I am not yet convinced of his dating of MT Kings to about 140 B.C.E., I find his conclusions concerning the relationship between LXX Kings and MT Kings convincing. Although his discussion concerned 1 Kgs 2–14 in its entirety, here I will focus only on his analysis of MT 1 Kgs 14:1–20 and LXX 1 Kgs 12:24g–n.

Schenker noted that 1 Kgs 14:1–20 is lacking in the Old Greek with a similar account occurring in LXX 1 Kgs 12:24g–n.[33] He concluded that the Old Greek represents a different, earlier Hebrew version of Kings and that MT 1 Kgs 14:1–20 is an expansion based on this earlier version, drawing material from other biblical sources, especially elsewhere in the Deuteronomistic History. For example, MT 1 Kgs 14:7–10 is completely lacking in the LXX—that is, LXX 1 Kgs 12:24:g–n also has no corresponding verses. However, MT 1 Kgs 14:7–10 clearly fits within the tradition of the Deuteronomistic History as the following chart demonstrates:[34]

30. Japhet, *I & II Chronicles*, 663.

31. Ibid.

32. Schenker, "Die Textgeschichte der Königsbücher"; idem, *Septante et texte massorétique;* idem, Älteste Textgeschichte der Königsbücher; and idem, "Junge Garden oder akrobatische Tänzer?" See also idem, "Jeroboam and the Division of the Kingdom in the Ancient Septuagint: LXX 3 Kingdoms 12:24a–z, MT 1 Kings 11–12; 14 and the Deuteronomistic History," in *Israel Constructs Its History: Deuteronomistic Historiography in Recent Research* (ed. Albert de Pury, Thomas Römer, and Jean-Daniel Macchi; JSOTSup 306; Sheffield: Sheffield Academic Press, 2000), 214–57.

33. Schenker, *Septante et texte massorétique*, 155–57.

34. This chart is based on Schenker's discussion (*Septante et texte massorétique*, 156). See similarly Gary N. Knoppers, *Two Nations under God: The Deuteronomistic History of*

MT 1 Kings 14:7–10	Other Deuteronomistic material
[7]made you leader over my people Israel	1 Sam 9:16: to be ruler over my people Israel 1 Sam 13:14: to be ruler over his people 2 Sam 7:8: to be ruler over my people, over Israel 1 Kgs 16:2: made you leader over my people Israel etc.
[8]and tore the kingdom away from the house of David and I gave it to you	1 Kgs 11:31: Behold, I am tearing the kingdom from the hand of Solomon, and I will give you ten tribes.
yet you have not been like my servant David	1 Kgs 11:32: my servant David
who kept my commandments and followed me with all his heart, doing only that which was right in my sight	1 Kgs 11:34: David my servant whom I chose and who kept my commandments and my statutes 1 Kgs 15:5: David did what was right in the sight of the LORD, and did not turn aside from anything that he commanded him
[9]but you have done evil more than all those who were before you	Jer 16:12: and you have done evil more than your fathers
and you have gone and made for yourself other gods, and molten images, provoking me to anger, and have thrust me behind your back;	1 Kgs 15:30: because of his anger which he provoked the LORD 1 Kgs 16:2: provoking me to anger with their sins (see also 1 Kgs 16:7, 13, 26, 33)
[10]therefore, behold, I will bring evil upon the house of Jeroboam.	2 Kgs 21:12: therefore . . . behold, I am bringing evil upon Jerusalem and Judah
I will cut off from Jeroboam every male, both bond and free in Israel,	1 Sam 25:22: if by morning I leave a single male of all who belong to him
and will consume the house of Jeroboam, just as one burns up dung until it is all gone.	1 Kgs 21:21: I will consume you 2 Kgs 9:37: like dung on the field

---

Solomon and the Dual Monarchies, vol. 2, *The Reign of Jeroboam, the Fall of Israel, and the Reign of Josiah* (HSM 53; Atlanta: Scholars Press, 1994), 97–100, and my discussion of Knoppers below.

Thus, Schenker concluded that MT 1 Kgs 14:1–20 is an expansion of the earlier material found in LXX 1 Kgs 12:24g–n based on phraseology largely attested in other Deuteronomistic material.

In his work *Two Nations under God*, Knoppers devoted an entire chapter to his discussion of Jeroboam's fall and reached conclusions similar to those of Schenker.[35] Drawing on earlier work by Trebolle,[36] Knoppers concluded that both MT 1 Kgs 14:1–20 and LXX 1 Kgs 12:24g–n are expansions of an earlier common source.[37] Although in his opinion LXX 1 Kgs 12:24g–n shows no influence of Deuteronomistic editing,[38] Knoppers concluded that the MT version was the result of the Deuteronomist because "some sixteen deuteronomistic clichés permeate 1 Kgs 14:7–11,15a,16."[39] Since none of these Deuteronomistic clichés is in the LXX version—that is, they are all found in MT pluses—Knoppers concluded that this confirmed that MT 1 Kgs 14:1–20 is a later expansion of an early pre-Deuteronomistic source and that the LXX version more closely preserves this source.[40] Thus, like Schenker, Knoppers con-

---

35. Knoppers, *Two Nations under God*, chapter 4.

36. Trebolle, *Salomón y Jeroboán*.

37. Knoppers, *Two Nations under God*, 91.

38. Contra Schenker, "Jeroboam and the Division of the Kingdom," 256. Schenker noted that the Deuteronomistic influence is the greatest in MT 1 Kgs 11–12; 14 (215); however, he nevertheless concluded that the LXX version "shows some Deuteronomistic signs" (256).

39. Knoppers, *Two Nations under God*, 97. See similarly Schenker, *Septante et texte massorétique*, 156, and the chart above based on Schenker for examples in 1 Kgs 14:7–10.

40. Contra Steven L. McKenzie, *The Trouble with Kings: The Composition of the Book of Kings in the Deuteronomistic History* (VTSup 42; Leiden: Brill, 1991), chapter 1. McKenzie concluded that the supplement in LXX 1 Kgs 12:24a–z is an abbreviation of the MT version, omitting information in the earlier account (MT 1 Kgs 14:7-10) that is necessary in order to understand the LXX account. McKenzie's explanation for why Deuteronomistic language is lacking in the LXX account is that it is simply a coincidence of the later redactor abbreviating the account: "It is not that he deliberately excluded that [Deuteronomistic] language" (*Trouble with Kings*, 30).

McKenzie's argument concerning necessary background information here is the same form of argument that he makes concerning the reference to Michal in 1 Chr 15:29 (//2 Sam 6:16) ("Chronicler as Redactor," 82). As discussed above in the sections on 2 Sam 6:12–19a//1 Chr 15:25–16:3 (pp. 97–103) and 2 Sam 6:20b-23 (pp. 134–38), such background information does not necessarily have to come from an earlier written text but could come from knowledge of the broader oral tradition. Furthermore, the coincidence that the Deuteronomistic language was removed in the later text seems more improbable than that it reflects a later redaction. Responding to arguments like McKenzie's, Schenker wrote: "If the latter [LXX 1 Kgs 12:24a–z] is later than the MT, the question comes up of knowing precisely why the Deuteronomistic marks have been eliminated from it. If, on the contrary, the [LXX version] precedes the account of the MT or is parallel to it, with the two being derived from a common source, another question comes up: how is it that this earlier or parallel

cluded that the LXX version more closely preserves the earliest tradition and that MT 1 Kgs 14:1–20 is a later expansive text that draws phraseology from other biblical texts, especially the Deuteronomistic History. The difference is that Knoppers associated the redaction of MT 1 Kgs 14:1–20 with his Josianic redactor (Dtr[1]) and Schenker with his much later redactor during the second century B.C.E.

Knoppers has not yet stated what the implications of his conclusions are for the question of the Chronicler's *Vorlage*. He has concluded that in general the Chronicler was using a *Vorlage* very similar to MT Kings;[41] however, his commentary on this portion of Chronicles is not yet published. On the other hand, Schenker has concluded that the LXX version of 1 Kings 11–12; 14 was the source for both MT Kings and MT Chronicles.[42] Schenker's conclusion concerning the Chronicler's *Vorlage* refers to the relationship between MT 1 Kgs 11–12; 14 and LXX 1 Kgs 12:24a–z as a whole; therefore, it is not certain how he might address this issue for specific passages such as MT 1 Kgs 14:1–20 and LXX 1 Kgs 12:24g–n. However, given the arguments above concerning the significance of the different locations of parallel texts, I propose the following. Since both MT 1 Kgs 14:1–20 and LXX 1 Kgs 12:24g–n are lacking a parallel account in Chronicles, the different locations of these parallel accounts indicate that the written common source behind Samuel–Kings and Chronicles probably lacked this account. The account was then later added to the Kings texts as the tradition strove to preserve more of the broader tradition in written texts.

MATERIAL UNIQUE TO THE BOOK OF CHRONICLES
(THE SO-CALLED "ADDITIONS" IN CHRONICLES)

The consensus model generally proposes that the unique materials in Chronicles are additions that are often connected to the theologically motivated changes evident in the synoptic material and the omissions made by the Chronicler—that is, the Chronicler's theological agenda thoroughly affected his use of his *Vorlage* so as to become evident in his so-called omissions, additions, and substitutions. Some scholars have also argued that some of these additions come from the hand of later redactors, reflecting their own theological perspectives. Furthermore, because some of the so-called additions seem to be more historically plausible than accounts in Samuel–Kings, some scholars

---

form alone would be lacking the Dtr elements?" ("Jeroboam and the Division of the Kingdom," 215). With both Schenker and Knoppers, I think it is much more probable that the Deuteronom(ist)ic language was added in the later MT version.

41. Knoppers, *I Chronicles 1–9*, 66–71.

42. Schenker, "Jeroboam and the Division of the Kingdom," 253, 256–57.

have argued that in some cases the Chronicler's additions may not reflect the Chronicler's theological agenda but may result from the Chronicler's use of earlier, extrabiblical sources that were superior to the historical information in Samuel–Kings.

In this section I critically review the consensus arguments on the so-called additions in Chronicles in four select texts: 1 Chr 12; 1 Chr 27; 2 Chr 17–20; and 2 Chr 36:22–23. I conclude that the unique material in Chronicles does not reflect a significantly different theological position, especially when we allow for the type of multiformity found in oral traditions and orally derived literature. The unique material often contains themes and phrases found elsewhere in biblical literature, including Samuel–Kings, so much so that the Chronistic account can be understood as complementary to the account in Samuel–Kings, not contradictory. This does not deny certain differences in details and emphases between the Chronistic accounts and the Deuteronomic account, but these differences nevertheless seem to fall within the realm of acceptability by the broader tradition represented by Samuel–Kings and Chronicles as well as other biblical books. Thus, although these passages can be understood as additions to a shorter common written source, they should not necessarily be understood as additions to the broader tradition itself.

1 CHRONICLES 12

Above I drew heavily from the work of Robert Rezetko on 2 Sam 5–6; 23//1 Chr 11–16. I argued that this material demonstrates that both MT Samuel and MT Chronicles are expansions based on a common source (sometimes preserved in LXX Samuel). An example of such expansion was given in a discussion of the synoptic material in 2 Sam 6:12–19a//1 Chr 15:25–16:13.[43] The variant lists of David's officers (2 Sam 23:8–39//1 Chr 11:10–47) can be understood as additions to this common source, especially since they occur in different locations in the narratives.[44] Another addition to this common source is the unique material in 2 Sam 6:20b–23.[45] In this section, I argue that 1 Chr 12:1–40 also can be understood as an addition to this common source.

In this unique passage, we are given lists of those who supported David in his quest to become king, coming from all of the tribes of Israel. The following tribes are explicitly mentioned here: Benjamin (12:2–7, 16–18), Gad (12:8–15), Judah (12:16–17), and Manasseh (12:19–21); however, the reference to "the Thirty" (12:18) connects this passage to 1 Chr 11:10–47 (//1 Sam

---

43. See chapter 4, pp. 97–103.
44. See chapter 4, pp. 103–5. In addition, see the similar argument for the list of David's officers found in 1 Chr 27 in the following section.
45. See above, pp. 134–38.

23:8–39), which includes mighty men from all of Israel. Thus, these lists are all-inclusive, in that "all the rest of Israel were of one mind to make David king" (12:38).

Knoppers's discussion of 1 Chr 11:10–47 and 1 Chr 12:1–40 actually lends itself quite well to the thesis of a common source. Knoppers noted that 11:10–47 and 12:1–40 both emphasize an all-Israel theme concerning early support for David in contrast to the portrayal of David's tumultuous rise to power in Samuel. Although I find his description of this contrast convincing, I do not share his interpretation of the literary history behind this interpretation. Below I will first summarize his position noting on the one hand, his accurate description of this contrast but emphasizing, on the other, that his interpretation of this contrast simply assumes the consensus model of the Chronicler using a version of Samuel quite similar to our extant texts of Samuel.

Knoppers argued for an all-Israel emphasis in the additions to the synoptic material in 11:10–47 and in the addition of 12:1–40. Concerning 11:10–47 he wrote:

> Most of the warriors in vv. 26–41a stem from Judah, Benjamin, Simeon, Ephraim and (old) Dan, while only a few hail from the Transjordan. Given David's place of origin, this might be expected. But the picture changes with the addition of vv. 41b–47. Many of the warriors listed in these verses stem from the Transjordan. Such a broad show of support is consistent with the Chronicler's pan-Israel interests. David attracts troops from a variety of geographical locations. [46]

Concerning 12:1–40 he wrote:

> By portraying the arrival of Gadites (12:9–16), and Benjaminites (along with Judahites) at David's stronghold (12:17–19), and subsequently the arrival of Benjaminites (12:1–7) and soldiers from Manasseh at Ziqlag (12:20–23), the author narrates early support for David from a variety of tribes outside of his own. In the Chronicler's presentation, northerners do not acquiesce to David's kingship only after the house of Saul comes to a humiliating end (2 Sam 2:10). Northerners are already supporting David in tremendous numbers while Saul is king. [47]

Because of this additional material, Knoppers correctly concluded:

> The writer goes to great lengths to promote David as a king for all Israelites. David stems from Judah, but it is the tremendous support he received from areas outside his own natural power base that consolidates his kingship so impressively. The new king draws modest support from Judah, Levi, Simeon, and Benjamin and good support from Ephraim and East Manasseh. But he draws his strongest

---

46. Knoppers, *I Chronicles 10–29*, 553.
47. Ibid., 577.

support from the far-distant tribes of Zebulun, Asher, Dan, and Napthali and
from the Transjordanian tribes of Reuben, Gad, and Half-Manasseh. [48]

Knoppers's interpretation of this material as emphasizing an all-Israel theme is
based on obvious contrasts between Chronicles and Samuel and is, therefore,
representative of the consensus model. For example, McKenzie concluded that
the Chronicler's "main point is that 'all Israel' was united in anointing David as
their king."[49] Similarly, Japhet wrote that the structure of 1 Chronicles 11–12
was "to give expression to the unity of the people of Israel at the enthronement
of David."[50]

Despite the validity of this description of the contrasting portrayals of
David's rise between Samuel and Chronicles, the consensus model's explanation of the literary relationship between these two portrayals is not a necessary
conclusion. The following description by Knoppers of this contrast is accurate:

> The Chronicler's presentation of David's rise to power is perhaps best appreciated
> by comparing it with the presentation in Samuel of David's rise to kingship. There
> David begins his long and arduous rise in the service of Saul (e.g., 1 Sam 18:5–7,
> 14–16, 30; 19:7) only to become a refugee from Saul. David gathers a band of fol-
> lowers to himself, but is repeatedly betrayed by others (1 Sam 22:9–23; 23:19–20;
> 24:1–2). Despite such setbacks, David successfully evades capture. For a time
> David escapes from Saul's troops by allying himself to the Philistines (1 Sam
> 27:1–12; 29:1–11). Eventually the threat dissipates as Saul's rule deteriorates,
> and following Saul's death, David becomes king of Judah (2 Sam 2:1–4). During
> this period Israel is riven by rivalries and internal disputes. Some seven years
> ensue in which an Israelite kingdom, headed by Saul's son Ishbaal, and a Judahite
> kingdom, headed by David, coexist (2 Sam 2:8–4:12). In the war between the
> two houses David gradually wins the support of the northern tribes only after
> Ishbaal's kingdom disintegrates and Ishbaal's own troops assassinate him (2 Sam
> 4:1–8). Only in the aftermath of this divisive struggle does David become king of
> all Israel (2 Sam 5:1–3).[51]

I quote this lengthy description because it is important to point out which
material in Samuel Knoppers uses to draw the contrast. All of the following
passages, given in the same order as in the quotation from Knoppers, are
unique to Samuel: 1 Sam 18:5–7, 14–16, 30; 19:7; 1 Sam 22:9–23; 23:19–20;
24:1–2; 1 Sam 27:1–12; 29:1–11; 2 Sam 2:1–4; 2 Sam 2:8–4:12; and 2 Sam 4:1–
8. The only reference given by Knoppers that is not unique is the last reference, 2 Sam 5:1–3//1 Chr 11:1–3, in which David becomes king over all Israel

---

48. Ibid., 578.
49. McKenzie, *1–2 Chronicles*, 130.
50. Japhet, *I & II Chronicles*, 232–33.
51. Knoppers, *I Chronicles 10–29*, 575–76.

and which can be understood not only as the culmination of a long, difficult struggle for widespread support (as in Samuel) but also as an explanation of why David became king—that is, from the beginning he had the support of all of Israel (as in Chronicles). In fact, Knoppers recognized this contrast well when he wrote, "In Chronicles one should speak not so much of a united kingdom constituted by a Davidic personal union, but of an Israelite union that establishes a Davidic monarchy."[52] Thus, although Knoppers's conclusion that "[t]he Chronicler deconstructs Samuel even as he draws heavily from it to construct his own story"[53] is possible, it is not the only valid conclusion one could draw.

I describe the literary development of these contrasting descriptions of David's rise to power as follows. The common source behind Samuel and Chronicles understood that David became king with the support of "all the tribes of Israel"//"all Israel" (2 Sam 5:1//1 Chr 11:1).[54] Later tradition interpreted this support somewhat differently. The tradition that produced Samuel with its additional material portrays David's rise to power as a prolonged struggle that clearly involved intertribal rivalries and David's questionable alliance with the Philistines. The tradition that produced Chronicles with its additional material portrays David's rise to power as a prime example of what great things can be accomplished when all of Israel is united behind one leader from the beginning. Although these accounts differ, they do not necessarily require a rejection of the other; they may simply be emphasizing different aspects of a common account that is itself multivocal.[55]

This possible literary development coincides quite well with the social setting I have proposed for the Deuteronomic school and the Chronistic school. In *The Deuteronomic School*, I proposed a sketch of the Deuteronomic school's theology both during the time of Zerubbabel and later. During the time of Zerubbabel, the Deuteronomic school could justify its scribal support of Zerubbabel and Joshua in cooperation with the Persian administration.[56] However, the failure of the rebuilt temple to lead to the full restoration of Israel produced further disillusionment within the Deuteronomic school, especially

---

52. Ibid., 576.

53. Ibid.

54. For a discussion of the similarities of the all-Israel theme in the Deuteronomic History and Chronicles, see Ben Zvi, "Are There Any Bridges Out There?" 76–78.

55. Ben Zvi ("Are There Any Bridges Out There?") asserted that both the Deuteronomistic History and Chronicles are not univocal concerning a variety of theological themes but preserve a variety of voices. Furthermore, the voices in the Deuteronomistic History and Chronicles often overlap each other, even when at first glance we may interpret a different theological tendency. Therefore, "the gap between Chronicles and the Deuteronomistic History (in its present form) was not as large as often claimed" (85).

56. Person, *Deuteronomic School*, chapter 5.

with regard to the efficacy of human institutions, including the temple cult and the hope in the Davidides.[57] The portrayal of David's rise in Samuel, including intertribal rivalries and alliances with foreign powers, fits well into this reconstruction of the Deuteronomic school's theology.

Furthermore, my reconstruction of Chronicles as related to the group of scribes who returned to Jerusalem with Ezra also provides an appropriate setting to understand the development of the portrayal of David's support coming from all of Israel, including the Transjordanian tribes. From the perspective of the Deuteronomic school, which was being displaced, Ezra and his scribal group (the Chronistic school) would have been understood as coming to Jerusalem from the Transjordan. The Chronistic school's self-understanding may have been influenced also by the Transjordanian traditions, and obviously an emphasis on all Israel would prepare the Chronistic school for asserting that, even while displacing the leaders of the Deuteronomic school, their mission was an all-Israel movement as they strove to convince those already in Jerusalem, including any Deuteronomic scribes, that they were not outsiders. The idea that the book of Chronicles emphasizes cooperation among traditionally competing groups—in my reconstruction, competing scribal guilds—is consistent with some other recent discussions of Chronicles. For example, in his article "Hierodules, Priests, or Janitors?" Knoppers studied the relationship between Levites and Aaronides and the use of Deuteronomic law and Priestly law and concluded that "[t]he Chronicler stresses cooperation and complementarity, not competition and hierarchy."[58] Similarly, Christine Mitchell has demonstrated that, although conflict with the Other is a characteristic of ancient historiography, "Chronicles is not constructed by boundary-setting and exclusion, but by inclusion, in contrast to Ezra–Nehemiah."[59] Also Ehud Ben Zvi noted that in Chronicles "Israel" included Yahwists who lived beyond

---

57. Ibid., chapter 6.

58. Gary N. Knoppers, "Hierodules, Priests, or Janitors? The Levites in Chronicles and the History of the Israelite Priesthood," *JBL* 118 (1999): 70. See also Louis C. Jonker, "David's Officials according to the Chronicler (1 Chr 23–27): A Reflection of Second Temple Self-Categorization?" in *Historiography and Identity: (Re)formulation in Second Temple Historiographical Literature* (ed. Louis Jonker; London: T&T Clark, 2010), 65–91. Jonker extended Knoppers's conclusion on cooperation by drawing from social identity theory.

59. Christine Mitchell, "Otherness and Historiography in Chronicles," in *Historiography and Identity: (Re)formulation in Second Temple Historiographical Literature* (ed. Louis C. Jonker; Library of Hebrew Bible/Old Testament Studies 534; London: T&T Clark, forthcoming in 2010), 103. Mitchell agreed with the earlier works of Japhet ("Postexilic Historiography: How and Why?" in *Israel Constructs Its History: Deuteronomistic Historiography in Recent Research* [ed. Albert de Pury, Thomas Römer, and Jean-Daniel Macchi; JSOTSup 306; Sheffield: Sheffield Academic Press, 2000], 158) and Williamson (*Israel in the Books of Chronicles* [Cambridge/New York: Cambridge University Press, 1977]).

the borders of Yehud, even though Jerusalem was clearly understood as the cultic center for all of Israel.[60]

The contrasting portrayals of David's rise in Samuel and Chronicles can be understood well from the perspective of their sharing a common written source. The common source did not specify how soon David had the support of all of Israel to become king, thereby allowing different interpretations. The tradition as preserved in Samuel portrays David's rise as involving the messy reality of intertribal rivalries and foreign alliances, possibly reflecting the political realities of the Deuteronomic school in Persian-period Jerusalem. The tradition as preserved in Chronicles portrays David's rise as a success of the unity of all of the tribes of Israel, possibly reflecting the political realities of the Chronistic school in relationship to Ezra's mission. Thus, one can conclude that "[t]he messages are not contradictory, but complementary."[61]

1 Chronicles 27

Although some scholars have argued that chapters 23–27 of 1 Chronicles are clearly redactional additions, recent scholars are more apt to accept that this material (at least most of it) was original to Chronicles.[62] For example, Japhet concluded: "An unprejudiced consideration of chs. 23–27 will reveal that they exhibit a transparent structure, integrate nicely with the literary methods of the book, voice the same views as and have close affinities with the other parts of Chronicles."[63] One of the arguments for the originality of 1 Chr 23–27 is how these chapters relate to the *Vorlage* in Samuel. For example, Japhet wrote:

> The ascription to David of the administrative organization of the kingdom of Israel is in line with the Chronicler's general tendency to transfer to David's reign actions which are otherwise attributed to Solomon. As a corollary of this tendency, the Chronicler omits from his story 1 Kings 4, which describes the Solomonic administrative system.[64]

---

60. Ben Zvi, *History, Literature and Theology*, chapter 10.

61. Ben Zvi, *History, Literature and Theology*, 60. Ben Zvi's conclusion concerned the incongruences, the multiformity, within Chronicles. However, he also noted that such multiformity exists within Samuel–Kings (58–59) and between Samuel–Kings and Chronicles. My use of his conclusion here certainly seems to be consistent with his later arguments that modern scholarship too often emphasizes the differences between Samuel–Kings and Chronicles and overlooks the similarities. See Ben Zvi, "Are There Any Bridges Out There?"

62. For a brief summary of the different positions, see Klein, *1 Chronicles*, 444–47.

63. Japhet, *I & II Chronicles*, 409. See similarly Knoppers, *I Chronicles 10–29*, 791; and Klein, *1 Chronicles*, 447. Contra Dirksen, *1 Chronicles*, 273–77.

64. Japhet, *I & II Chronicles*, 468–69. See Klein, who follows Japhet's argument (*1 Chronicles*, 501).

That is, when one assumes with the consensus model that the Chronicler is making significant changes to the *Vorlage* of Samuel–Kings, one can discern certain tendencies that can then be used to argue for the originality of other passages such as 1 Chronicles 23–27.

This consensus approach leads to a hierarchy of linear influence between the lists of David's officials with 2 Sam 23:8–39 being the source for much of 1 Chr 11:10–47, which in turn was the source for much of 1 Chr 27. Each succeeding version of the list is therefore expansive.[65] In the previous chapter I argued that the different arrangement of 2 Sam 23:8–39 and 1 Chr 11:10–47 suggests that they were both additions to a common source and that when compared to each other the additions demonstrate that multiplicity was the norm for the tradition.[66] I noted that even the consensus model requires the acceptance of such multiplicity in the tradition between the Deuteronomic History and Chronicles. Furthermore, the consensus model also allows multiformity within Chronicles itself, since 1 Chr 11:10–47 differs from 1 Chr 27:1–34.[67]

If the tradition preserved a multiplicity of lists of David's mighty men, then it is possible that these three lists (2 Sam 23:8–39; 1 Chr 11:10–47; and 1 Chr 27:1–34) are all additions to a written common source based on the broader oral tradition. As such, it remains possible that, since they were likely not added simultaneously, the first written list(s) influenced the writing down of the later list(s). However, the linear progression from the shortest to the most expansive list advocated in the consensus model is not necessary to explain the multiplicity of the three lists of David's mighty men and their different locations.

Furthermore, the observation that some of the individuals in the lists seem to come and go—or in Knoppers's words "the fact that these tribal officers never appear again (following David's reign)"[68]—does not rule out that the broader tradition contained more information about these mighty men. As we noted above, even Knoppers suggests that 1 Chr 11:41b–47 is not original to the Chronicler but reflects an extrabiblical source. Whereas Knoppers is

---

65. Japhet, *I & II Chronicles*, 470; Knoppers, *I Chronicles 10–29*, 548–52, 895; Klein, *1 Chronicles*, 296, 502; Dirksen, *1 Chronicles*, 323; and Williamson, *1 and 2 Chronicles*, 102, 174.

66. See chapter 4 above, pp. 103–5.

67. Both Knoppers and Klein provided charts summarizing the differences between 1 Chr 11:11–41 and 1 Chr 27:2–15 (Knoppers, *I Chronicles 10–29*, 899; and Klein, *1 Chronicles*, 502). As noted above, earlier scholars often argued that chapters 23–27 were redactional additions, thereby disallowing such multiplicity as the work of any one author/redactor. For example, Williamson argued that 1 Chr 27 is secondary (*1 and 2 Chronicles*, 174).

68. Knoppers, *I Chronicles 10–29*, 901.

imagining a written source, I am simply suggesting that the source may have been the broader tradition in which there is an interplay between the oral tradition and written texts that represent the oral tradition; therefore, the source may have been oral rather than written.

2 Chronicles 17–20

The Chronistic account of Jehoshaphat differs significantly from the account in Kings in that it contains unique material concerning his rise to power (17:2–19), the rebuke by the prophet Jehu (19:1–3), his appointment of judges (19:4–11), and his victory over Moab and Ammon (20:1–30).[69] However, as we will see, this unique material is consistent with the portrayal of Jehoshaphat in the synoptic passages and more broadly with the portrayal of kings in general. Therefore, we should not overemphasize this difference based simply on the amount of material in the Chronistic account of Jehoshaphat.

The account of Jehoshaphat in Chronicles begins with the regnal formula in 2 Chr 17:1a (//1 Kgs 15:24b). This formula is then followed by a unique passage further describing Jehoshaphat's rise to power (17:1b–19). Jehoshaphat's rise to power reflects that of other kings, especially Solomon: he consolidated his reign (17:1b), he walked in the ways of his father David (17:3), he had great wealth and honor (17:5), and the surrounding nations feared him and brought him tribute (17:10–11). In fact, these similarities led McKenzie to conclude that "[h]is righteousness and resulting wealth and international renown are reminiscent of Solomon—high praise indeed in Chronicles (17:1, 5)."[70] This reminiscence of Solomon applies equally well to both the Chronistic account of Solomon and the Samuel–Kings account.

The prophecy of Jehu (2 Chr 19:1–3) contains themes similar to those of the synoptic material. Although Micaiah's prophecy is primarily directed at Ahab (2 Chr 18:12–27//1 Kgs 22:13–28),[71] Ahab is seeking the prophetic word at Jehoshaphat's request (2 Chr 18:4//1 Kgs 22:5) and Jehoshaphat hears Micaiah's prophecy (2 Chr 18:17//1 Kgs 22:18). Thus, the unique material in 2 Chr 19:1–3 is simply an extension of the preceding account of Micaiah's prophecy, making explicit the LORD's message to Jehoshaphat implicitly given by Micaiah and overheard by Jehoshaphat but now reiterated by Jehu. His alliance

---

69. For my discussion of this synoptic material in 1 Kgs 22//2 Chr 17–20, see chapter 4 above, pp. 115–21.

70. McKenzie, "Trouble with King Jehoshaphat," 299. McKenzie also concluded that 17:7–19 is "based on other parts of Chronicles and of the Hebrew Bible" (304), thereby highlighting similarities with the broader tradition.

71. However, in 2 Chr 18:14 Micaiah uses the second person plural, explicitly implying both Ahab and Jehoshaphat in contrast to the singular in 1 Kgs 22:15.

with Ahab against Ramoth-gilead was against God's will, but Jehoshaphat was spared Ahab's fate because of his cultic reforms (19:3; see also 17:6).

Jehoshaphat's cultic reforms are once again mentioned in the account of his appointing judges, Levites, and the high priest Amariah (2 Chr 19:4-11). Some scholars have concluded that this unique material is based on an earlier source and is historically plausible. A piece of evidence for this argument concerns its relationship to material in Deuteronomy (see Deut 1:16-17; 10:17; 16:18-20).[72] My concern here is not about the historicity of this material, for I share McKenzie's skepticism on this issue and agree with him (and Wellhausen) that this passage may have been "an extended pun on Jehoshaphat's name, 'Yahweh judges.'"[73] However, the arguments for this passage being based on an earlier source highlight the connections between this passage and other biblical material generally considered earlier, including the references to Deuteronomy given above.[74] McKenzie also noted that the portrayal of Jehoshaphat here recalls David's justice system as portrayed in 1 Chr 26:29-32.[75] Hence, this unique passage appears to be an extension of other traditional material as applied to Jehoshaphat, probably influenced by the meaning of his name.

Jehoshaphat's victory over Moab and Ammon (20:1-30) builds on themes from the earlier Chronistic account on his reign. Although at an earlier time the surrounding nations were wise in fearing Jehoshaphat and sending him tribute (17:10-11), Moab and Ammon foolishly reverse course and provoke Jehoshaphat to respond. Of course, the tradition preserves various instances of animosity between Israel/Judah, on the one hand, and Moab and Ammon, on the other (for example, see David's victory over Ammon in 2 Sam 10:1-19//1 Chr 19:10-19). Once again with the LORD's help Judah defeats its enemies. Again some scholars have concluded that this unique material is based on an earlier, historically reliable source and have pointed to its use of earlier biblical traditions as evidence.[76] Whether or not this material reflects a historical kernel, this passage clearly draws upon common themes and phraseology found in other biblical material. For example, McKenzie noted how Jehoshaphat's prayer in 2 Chr 20:6-12 draws from other biblical passages

---

72. See McKenzie's brief review of this scholarship ("Trouble with King Jehoshaphat," 308-9).

73. McKenzie, "Trouble with King Jehoshaphat," 309.

74. Although Klein approached the question of the historicity of the Chronicles account of Jehoshaphat with skepticism, he nevertheless concluded that "the Chronicler's source [for 1 Chr 19:4-11] seems to antedate the final form of Deuteronomy and reflect the period of Jehoshaphat and the end of the Southern Kingdom in its distinction between the matters of the king and the matter for Yahweh" ("Reflections on Historiography," 651).

75. McKenzie, "Trouble with King Jehoshaphat," 309.

76. See McKenzie's brief review of this scholarship ("Trouble with King Jehoshaphat," 310-12). For an example, see Japhet, *I & II Chronicles*, 782-84.

(for example, "descendants of Abraham, your friend" in 20:7; see Isa 41:8) and common themes in Chronicles (for example, the victory procession with musical instruments to the temple in 20:27–28).[77]

The Chronistic account of Jehoshaphat contains a significant amount of additional material when compared to the Kings account; however, the amount of unique material does not necessarily indicate a different theology or historical perspective, especially in light of the role of multiformity in the broader tradition. In fact, because some of this unique material seems so historically plausible, some scholars have concluded that the Chronicler must have used an earlier source than Kings in order to explain the apparent discrepancy between the historical plausibility of the Chronistic account and the historical implausibility of the Kings account. These same scholars have sometimes pointed out that some of this unique material seems to be typologically earlier than material in Deuteronomy. Although I have agreed with McKenzie's skepticism concerning such historical claims for the Chronistic account, I suggest that these arguments nevertheless lend some credence to the thesis of a common source. Furthermore, I disagree with McKenzie's assertion that these two accounts differ significantly. In the previous chapter, I showed how the material in the synoptic passages in 1 Kgs 22//2 Chr 17–20 can be read in ways that undercut the arguments often made for how different the accounts are. Here I have argued that the unique material in Chronicles is not unique in its content and perspective but in fact simply draws from the broader tradition, some of which is preserved in the written texts of both Kings and Chronicles. When we allow for a certain degree of multiformity in the tradition, these two accounts of Jehoshaphat's reign differ in the amount of material preserved but not in any significant way in their theological portrayal of his reign.

2 CHRONICLES 36:22–23

As noted in the introduction, Martin Noth dated his Deuteronomistic History to the Babylonian exile on the basis of the release of Jehoiachin (2 Kgs 25:27–30; about 560 B.C.E.) and his Chronicler's History to the Hellenistic period because of the Chronicler's historically confused use of his sources concerning Ezra and Nehemiah. With the generally accepted division of Chronicles from Ezra-Nehemiah, Chronicles is now dated earlier during the late Persian period, primarily on the basis of two observations: (1) the passage explicitly referring to the Persians (2 Chr 36:20–23) and (2) the consensus model of historical linguistics—that is, Late Biblical Hebrew is postexilic. However, I have rejected various arguments that underlie the consensus model. The Deuteronomic school

---

77. McKenzie, "Trouble with King Jehoshaphat," 311–12.

continued to redact its literature, including the Deuteronomic History, into the postexilic period, and the consensus model for the diachronic study of Hebrew (preexilic Early Biblical Hebrew versus postexilic Late Biblical Hebrew) is problematic. When one separates Chronicles from Ezra–Nehemiah, this leaves very little with which to insist on a significant difference in the dating of the Deuteronomic History and Chronicles—that is, the few references to the Persians in 2 Chr 36. Even this is undermined further, since 2 Chr 36:22–23 is widely viewed as a secondary addition to the Chronicler's work based on Ezra 1:1–3a; the only remaining Persian reference in the Chronicler's own hand is 2 Chr 36:20: "until the establishment of the kingdom of Persia."[78]

My purpose here is not to conclude whether or not 2 Chr 36:22–23 is secondary, because with McKenzie I remain an agnostic on the topic.[79] Given the limitations of the methods of source and redaction criticism, I think that distinguishing one Deuteronomist from another or one Chronistic author/redactor from another is problematic without text-critical evidence, since they use similar phraseology and themes within their own schools.[80] Furthermore, as I have argued above, the emphasis on individual writers and their original texts is anachronistic given the role of multiformity in the tradition. Rather, my purpose is simply to show that the consensus model, as it has moved further from Noth's original thesis, has progressively cut more and more out of Noth's Chronicler's Work, such that the difference between Samuel–Kings and Chronicles has become relatively insignificant. However, few seem to acknowledge this. Noth's conclusions concerning the radical difference between his Deuteronomistic History and his Chronicler's History continue to be the foundation on which most scholars base much of their study of the relationship between these two literary works. In contrast, a close analysis of 2 Chr 36:22–23 demonstrates that the reference to Cyrus is consistent with synoptic material in Samuel–Kings and Chronicles and, therefore, should not be used to justify a conclusion about how disparate these two works are. Instead, it is simply one more case of unique material in Chronicles that nevertheless reflects the broader tradition.

The Persians are not mentioned explicitly anywhere in the Deuteronomic History and in Chronicles only in the final verses (2 Chr 36:20–23). At some level this sets off the final verses of Chronicles as unique; however, we will see that the portrayal of Cyrus is consistent with the portrayal of earlier foreign monarchs as the LORD's messenger through whom the divine will is

---

78. For a review of the secondary literature on whether 2 Chr 36:22–23 is secondary, see Kalimi, *Ancient Israelite Historian*, 145–47.

79. McKenzie, *1–2 Chronicles*, 367.

80. For a fuller argument of this position concerning Deuteronomists, see Person, *Deuteronomic School*, esp. 21–24.

manifested. Cyrus's message is the LORD's message, because "the LORD stirred up the spirit of Cyrus king of Persia" (36:22).

> Thus says Cyrus king of Persia: All the kingdoms of the earth the LORD, the God of heaven, has given to me, and he has charged me to build him a house in Jerusalem, which is in Judah. Whoever is among you of all his people, let the LORD his God be with him! Let him go up. (36:23)

According to his message, Cyrus believed in the LORD as the one true God, gave credit for his imperial success to the LORD, and understood himself as charged to rebuild the temple in Jerusalem. Furthermore, Cyrus's message and actions are confirmed by their fulfillment of the prophecy of Jeremiah (36:20–22; see Jer 25:11–12; 29:10). Thus, what the LORD began with Nebuchadnezzar's destruction of Jerusalem and the resulting exile (2 Chr 36:18–21//2 Kgs 25:8–21//Jer 52:12–30) continues in Cyrus's work.

In his essay "When a Foreign Monarch Speaks," Ehud Ben Zvi surveyed the five passages in Chronicles in which a foreign monarch's words are reported in direct speech: Huram's letter to Solomon (2 Chr 2:11–16), the Queen of Sheba's speech (2 Chr 9:5–8), Sennacherib's speech to Hezekiah (2 Chr 32:10–15), Necho's words to Josiah (2 Chr 35:21), and Cyrus's edict (2 Chr 36:22–23).[81] Ben Zvi concluded that all of these speeches support "the theological message of the narrator and of the authorial voice" and that all but one (Sennacherib's speech concerning the destruction of Jerusalem) "uphold positions (and behaviors) that are expected of 'pious' Israelites."[82] Thus he concluded:

> From the theological perspective of the postmonarchic community, this amounts to the partial (but substantial) "Israelization" of the world, which in turn reflects the broad sweep of the will of YHWH—not that foreign kings will be overthrown, but that non-Israelites accept the will and instructions of YHWH (see 2 Chron. 2.10–15; 9.5–8; 35.21; 36.23) and that Israel cooperates with them under those circumstances.[83]

Although his study concerned Chronicles, Ben Zvi noted "that some of the considerations and conclusions advanced here may resonate in future studies that address similar issues in the deuteronomistic history," because three of the five passages have parallels that support his conclusions: Huram/Hiram (2 Chr 2:11–16//1 Kgs 5:7–10, 7:13–14), the Queen of Sheba (2 Chr 9:5–8//1 Kgs 10:6–9), and Sennacherib (2 Chr 32:10–15//2 Kgs 18:19–35).[84]

---

81. Ben Zvi, *History, Literature and Theology*, 270–88.
82. Ibid., 279, 280.
83. Ibid., 282.
84. Ibid., 271, 284 n. 11.

Hence, even though Cyrus's edict in 2 Chr 36:22–23 has no corresponding parallel in Kings, the portrayal of Cyrus in this passage is consistent not only with the portrayal of foreign monarchs elsewhere in Chronicles but also with the portrayal of foreign monarchs in the broader tradition represented by both Chronicles and Samuel–Kings.

In "Identity and Empire, Reality and Hope in the Chronicler's Perspective," Mark Boda discussed the final sections of Chronicles from Josiah's death to Cyrus's edict (2 Chr 35:20–36:23). He also examined Cyrus's edict in comparison to Israel's interactions with other imperial powers in the narrative and concluded that "[t]his closing model legitimizes the present imperial reality of the Chronicler's readers, affirming the constitution (golah), activities (temple rebuilding), and polity (colony) of the Persian-period Yehudite community."[85] Although he concluded that the final sections legitimize the current reality, Boda understood that this is not the Chronicler's ideal. He wrote:

> One should not ignore the key role played by the Rehoboam account, which is designed to shape the readers' understanding of imperial domination—that is, this is not the ideal but, rather, a temporary and purposeful measure. . . . Therefore, although the Chronicler ends his account with the present reality of colony, one should not assume that this represents the Chronicler's ideal. Rather, his portrayal of Hezekiah places considerable rhetorical weight on this earlier phase of imperial interaction and suggests that there is still hope for independence.[86]

Boda's analysis built on that of Ben Zvi, especially in terms of how foreign monarchs are portrayed in Chronicles. Boda highlighted how the actions of the foreign monarchs were sometimes confirmed by one of the LORD's prophets. Not only is Jeremiah referred to concerning Cyrus, but Jeremiah is mentioned in connection with Zedekiah's reign (2 Chr 36:11–17).[87] In addition, the prophet Shemaiah proclaimed to Rehoboam that Shishak's victory was due to Rehoboam's disobediance (2 Chr 12:1–16). Hence, Boda concluded: "The Chronicler makes clear to his audience that its past loss of monarchial status at the hands of the Egyptians and Babylonians as well as its present colonial identity within the Persian Empire can be directly linked to Yahweh's will."[88]

Boda's analysis of Chronicles' final sections applies quite well to Samuel–Kings. For example, although Shemaiah's prophecy is found only in the

---

85. Mark J. Boda, "Identity and Empire, Reality and Hope in the Chronicler's Perspective," in *Community Identity in Judean Historiography: Biblical and Comparative Perspectives* (ed. Gary N. Knoppers and Kenneth A. Ristau; Winona Lake, Ind.: Eisenbrauns, 2009), 270.

86. Ibid., 271.

87. Ibid., 252.

88. Ibid., 253.

Chronistic account, the account in 1 Kgs 14:21–31 also understands Shishak's invasion as divine punishment for Rehoboam's disobedience. Furthermore, although the prophet Jeremiah is not once mentioned in the Deuteronomic History, it is obvious that 2 Kgs 24:18–25:30, which includes the parallel accounts of Nebuchadnezzar, was widely read in relation to the book of Jeremiah, since these final verses were copied into the book as Jeremiah 52.[89] Boda's conclusion that the imperial success of the Egyptians and Babylonians is due to the LORD's will applies equally well to Kings and Chronicles. Although the Persians are not explicitly mentioned in Kings, the conclusion that the Persian defeat of the Babylonians and the resulting return to Jerusalem also are due to the will of the LORD obviously follows. In fact, passages in Kings can be interpreted in light of the Persian period—for example, the release of Jehoiachin in exile (2 Kgs 25:27–30//Jer 52:31–34) can be understood as demonstrating hope in the restoration of the monarchy through Jehoiachin's grandson, Zerubbabel.[90] Therefore, Boda's conclusion concerning Chronicles that, on the one hand, the political reality of imperial domination must be accepted as the current reality but, on the other hand, there can be hope of a future indepen-

---

89. Of course, if the book of Jeremiah is also a Deuteronomic redaction (as it is in my opinion), this certainly supports the contention that Jeremiah would have been understood as active during the events portrayed in the closing sections of Kings. For my discussion of Jeremiah as Deuteronomic literature, see Person, *Second Zechariah and the Deuteronomic School*, chapter 2.

90. On 2 Kgs 25:27–30//Jer 52:31–34, see Person, *Deuteronomic School*, 119–20. Boda suggested a similar reading of Jehoiachin in Chronicles, even though he did not refer specifically to Zerubbabel: "[T]he link between Jehoiakim-Jehoiachin and the temple treasure may be identifying subtly the line of Josiah-Jehoiakim-Jehoiachin as the legitimate royal line for Judah, while also creating an inseparable link between the renewal of the temple and the renewal of the royal house" ("Identity and Empire," 254–55). Further, Kalimi compared 2 Chr 36:22–23 to similar hopeful endings of other books, including 2 Kgs 25:30–34 (*Ancient Israelite Historian*, 146). On the one hand, many scholars assume that Chronicles was written in the early Persian period in which knowledge of Zerubbabel was probable, even though Zerubbabel is not mentioned in Chronicles. On the other hand, the lack of the mention of Zerubbabel and other Persian figures in the Deuteronomic History is cause to assume that the final redaction of the Deuteronomic History must have been before the Persian period. If the restoration of Jerusalem and the rebuilding of the temple in Chronicles can be associated with the Second Temple built by Zerubbabel under Darius (not Cyrus), why not conclude the same for Kings? This question becomes even more pressing when we accept with Ben Zvi that Cyrus in 2 Chr 36:22–23 is portrayed as "the divinely chosen 'builder' of the temple . . . one of the most important roles ever allocated to the Davidic dynasty" (Ben Zvi, *History, Literature and Theology*, 279). Yet this is a task accomplished later by Zerubbabel, a Davidide, under Darius.

dence is a conclusion that can be reached also concerning the Deuteronomic school's own reading of Samuel–Kings in the Persian period.[91]

Because Cyrus is explicitly identified as the temple-builder and the people are "merely invited to 'go up' [36:23]," Boda concluded that "the implied reader is not to be associated with the community in the early Persian period, the phase in which the temple was rebuilt, but with the postconstruction community."[92] Although I am hesitant to make so much of such subtle differences in light of the importance of multiformity in the tradition, Boda's suggestion relates well to my reconstruction of the Chronistic school, especially if the Second Temple is associated closely with Cyrus by means of his son Darius, under whom the temple was completed. If the Deuteronomic school is associated with the work of the rebuilding of the temple under Zerrubabbel, then emphasizing the imperial support of the rebuilding may be a subtle way of deemphasizing the role of Zerubbabel and his supporters. If the Chronistic school returned to Jerusalem with Ezra, then deemphasizing the people's role (especially that of Zerubbabel and his supporters) in rebuilding the temple and emphasizing the people's role as simply "going up" to Jerusalem may be a subtle way of justifying the late arrival of the Chronistic school.

Conclusion: Multiformity in the Nonsynoptic Passages

In the previous chapter on the synoptic passages I concluded that too often modern scholars overemphasize differences in the texts that would be inconsequential from the ancients' perspective. If multiformity was a characteristic of the broader tradition, then no single text could possibly represent the broader tradition in its fullness—that is, no single text would be necessarily more authoritative than another, even if they preserved various instantiations of the same synoptic material. However, as the tradition increasingly valued the preserving of its traditional material more so in written texts, what Carr called a "trend towards expansion" developed. Tradents added more and more material to written texts as they copied their *Vorlagen*.

In this chapter, the nonsynoptic passages can be understood in an analogous way from the perspective of the role of multiformity in the tradition and a trend toward expansion. Although the *Vorlagen* may not have contained these

---

91. See similarly Berquist, "Identities and Empire." Analogously to Boda on Chronicles, Berquist interpreted the Deuteronomistic History in light of its colonial environment and postcolonial theory. For my interpretation of various passages in the Deuteronomic History in the context of the Persian period, see chapters 5 and 6 in Person, *Deuteronomic School*.

92. Boda, "Identity and Empire," 255 n. 21. Boda also quoted Kalimi on this same point (*Ancient Israelite Historian*, 156).

additions, this unique material is not necessarily anomalous, but rather, these additions may simply be textual expansions that draw from the broader oral tradition. The above analyses of 2 Sam 1–4; 2 Sam 6:20b–23; 1 Kgs 4:20–26; and 1 Kgs 14:1–20 as well as 1 Chr 12; 1 Chr 27; 2 Chr 17–20; and 2 Chr 36:22–23 have demonstrated close connections between these additions and both synoptic and nonsynoptic material in Samuel–Kings//Chronicles. In other words, these passages are not that unique, when we compare them to the other literature preserved in the broader tradition behind both Samuel–Kings and Chronicles. If this is the case, then we may justifiably ask how this might have arisen. I suggest that the answer lies in the tradition's trend toward expansion as two different scribal schools—the Deuteronomic school and the Chronistic school—independently expanded a common written source in ways that differ somewhat but that nevertheless remain within the theological limits of a tradition that includes a significant role for multiformity. Therefore, even though, for example, the Chronistic school did not include an account of Ahijah's prophecy against Jeroboam I (MT 1 Kgs 14:1–20) or the Deuteronomic school did not include an account of Cyrus's edict (2 Chr 36:22–23), this does not necessarily require us to conclude that each did not know of the traditional element uniquely preserved in the other literary work or that they knew it and rejected it for theological reasons. Although what both of these schools produced may have expanded over time, both literary works seem to allow that the tradition is broader than what is represented within them. For example, both literary works refer their readers to additional information found in other sources. Hence, both literary works may best be understood as limited instantiations of the broader tradition in which an interplay of texts and communal memory exists, an ancient tradition that has been lost to us except as witnessed by these two competing historiographies and the textual plurality in which they exist, especially in the various versions of Samuel–Kings.

I have cautioned against overemphasizing perceived differences between Samuel–Kings and Chronicles and advocated strongly for accepting the multivocality of both literary works in the context of the acceptance of multiformity by the broader tradition. I have explicitly criticized others for making the mistake of overemphasizing differences and drawing theological and sociological conclusions based on these overemphases. Thus I have been justifiably hesitant to reach conclusions based on such differences. Despite this hesitancy, above I have considered two arguments by other scholars that easily lend themselves to supporting my thesis of competing scribal schools producing this literature. First, in my discussion of 1 Chr 12, I suggested that the consensus model's interpretation of the theme of all Israel as portrayed in Chronicles (especially as argued by Knoppers) applies quite well to my reconstruction, although the consensus model has a different redactional explanation for the different portrayals of the all-Israel theme in Samuel versus Chronicles. The all-Israel theme in Chronicles includes support for David coming early in his career from all of the tribes, including the Transjordanian tribes. From the perspective of the displaced Deuteronomic school, Ezra and his scribes (the Chronistic school) would have come from the Transjordan. The all-Israel emphasis in Chronicles could be the Chronistic school's subtle response to a possible criticism of them as outsiders. In contrast, the portrayal of David's rise to power in Samuel, involving intertribal rivalries and foreign alliances, may reflect the more fragile political conditions faced by the Deuteronomic school in early Persian Jerusalem.

Second, in my discussion of 2 Chr 36:22–23 I reviewed Boda's interpretation that the emphasis concerning who will build the temple is on imperial power, specifically Cyrus, and the people are simply called to "go up" to Jerusalem. I suggested that his interpretation may relate to the different relationships of the Deuteronomic school and the Chronistic school to the temple. The Deuteronomic school returned to Jerusalem with Zerubbabel to rebuild the temple; the Chronistic school went up to Jerusalem much later and became involved in the temple cult and its reform. Thus, the deemphasis on the people's role in the rebuilding of the temple and the substitutive emphasis of "going up" may have been influenced by the theological conflict between the Deuteronomic school, which participated in the earlier return and temple rebuilding, and the Chronistic school, which came later.

CONCLUSION

Drawing especially from Graeme Auld's thesis of a Shared Text, I have argued that the Deuteronomic History and the book of Chronicles are Persian-period historiographies produced by two competing scribal guilds, the Deuteronomic school and the Chronistic school, but that these historiographies are nevertheless based on the same broader traditions, including a common exilic source. However, despite the institutional competition between these two schools, these competing historiographies do not necessarily represent significantly divergent theologies. When one takes seriously the role of multiformity in oral traditions and in primarily oral societies such as ancient Israel, the Deuteronomic History and Chronicles can be understood as both faithfully re-presenting the same broader tradition and its theology within the limits allowed by such multiformity. These conclusions have far-reaching implications for the study of the Hebrew Bible, especially concerning the interplay between the oral and the written in the development of biblical literature. Below I summarize the conclusions of this study and then discuss briefly the implications of these conclusions.

COMPETING CONTEMPORARY HISTORIOGRAPHIES

Scholars have noted for a long time that biblical historiographies are multivocal compositions that draw from various sources of different genres. As a result, tensions exist in the works. This applies well to both the Deuteronomic History and the book of Chronicles, where both contain, for example, genealogical lists, regnal formulae, prophetic stories, and prayers, all of whose sources probably come from a variety of historical periods. Above we have explored some of the apparent tensions in these historiographies and especially between the two works. Although the consensus model generally understands the tension between these two works to result from changes the Chronicler made to his *Vorlage* primarily for theological reasons, we have explored another explanation. The tradition itself allowed such a degree of multiformity that the variation between the Deuteronomic History and Chronicles may simply be two different expressions of the same tradition without the type of theological diversion often imputed to these different expressions. Furthermore, these two different expressions may have even been contemporary to one another.

Auld reached back into earlier scholarship concerning the relationship between Samuel–Kings and Chronicles and reasserted the thesis that these two literary works were descended from a common source, his Shared Text. Auld's thesis is timely, given other conclusions being reached concerning the Deuteronomic History and Chronicles. Increasingly scholars are dating the final redaction of the Deuteronomic History later into the Persian period, bringing the Deuteronomic History closer in time to Chronicles. Meanwhile, more scholars are arguing that Chronicles was independent of Ezra–Nehemiah such that Chronicles is considered Persian-period literature, bringing Chronicles closer in time to the Deuteronomic History. Hence, the Deuteronomic History and the book of Chronicles can be reasonably understood as competing contemporary historiographies descended from a common source.

As can be expected when someone challenges the consensus model, Auld's thesis drew criticism. The primary challenges to Auld's thesis came in the form of two arguments. First, many quickly dismissed his argument for failure to consider adequately the consensus model's understanding of historical linguistics—that is, Early Biblical Hebrew (EBH) versus Late Biblical Hebrew (LBH). Of course, this was really a criticism not only of Auld but also of others who were dating the Deuteronom(ist)ic History later into the Persian period. If the Deuteronom(ist)ic History was written in the pre-exilic language of EBH and Chronicles was written in the postexilic language of LBH, then the chronological sequence of the consensus model remained valid—that is, the postexilic Chronicler used the preexilic (or mostly preexilic) source of the Deuteronom(ist)ic History as his *Vorlage*, updated it with references to the Persian period, and adapted it to the new linguistic environment. Auld expected this criticism and "summarily answered" it, but the task of a more complete response remained for others.[1] One of Auld's students, Robert Rezetko, began a more detailed response that reached its fruition when his work was combined with that of Ian Young and Martin Ehrensvärd. As argued above in chapter 1, Young, Rezetko, and Ehrensvärd have, in my opinion, successfully undermined the consensus understanding of linguistic development for Biblical Hebrew and have, therefore, provided implicit support for Auld's Shared Text thesis by countering this challenge from his critics.

Second, Auld's thesis received criticism that portions of his Shared Text required knowledge of material that, according to the consensus model, the Chronicler omitted when copying from his *Vorlage*. This line of criticism was made especially by Steven McKenzie, Ralph Klein, Gary Knoppers, and Zipora Talshir. For example, Talshir analyzed the references to Solomon's marriage to

---

1. Auld, *Kings without Privilege*, 9–10.

Pharaoh's daughter (1 Kgs 3:1b; 9:24//2 Chr 8:11).[2] Since the Chronicler later referred to this marriage in material Auld included in his Shared Text (1 Kgs 9:24//2 Chr 8:11), then, in her opinion, the earlier reference to the actual marriage was necessarily in the *Vorlage* but was omitted by the Chronicler (1 Kgs 3:1b). As discussed above in chapters 4 and 5, this type of criticism of Auld's thesis is based on a valid observation, but at the same time it makes an unnecessary assumption. While it is true that Chronicles assumes that its audience has additional background information about people and events briefly mentioned—for example, Solomon's marriage to Pharaoh's daughter—this observation is not peculiar to Chronicles but applies to all literature, including the Deuteronomic History. For example, the references to Abraham in the Deuteronomic History require its audience to know more about the Abraham tradition. The unnecessary assumption is that this background knowledge could come only from one specific literary work—that is, the audience of Chronicles necessarily must be familiar with Samuel–Kings in order to understand fully Chronicles, including especially what the Chronicler omitted of his *Vorlage*. As argued above in chapters 4 and 5, this background information may have come from the broader tradition in which the interpretation of written texts (including both the Deuteronomic History and Chronicles) occurred in an interaction with oral tradition that provided much of this additional background material. Thus, for example, knowledge about Solomon's marriage to Pharaoh's daughter did not necessarily come from 1 Kgs 3:1b alone but could come from the broader tradition of which 1 Kgs 3:1b is but one instantiation.

Although I have rejected these two primary criticisms of Auld's Shared Text thesis, I have not wholly accepted his thesis. Auld argued that his Shared Text was not Deuteronomistic; in fact, he argued that the Former Prophets in any version were not Deuteronomistic. With some of Auld's critics, I maintain not only that the thesis of a Deuteronom(ist)ic History remains valid but that the *Vorlage* of Chronicles is also Deuteronom(ist)ic. Where I differ with Auld's critics is that this *Vorlage* was also the *Vorlage* of MT Samuel–Kings—that is, MT Samuel–Kings and Chronicles are both descended from a common source of earlier Deuteronomic versions of Samuel–Kings.

I have also criticized Auld for at times not following his own stated criteria for reconstructing his Shared Text. Auld stated that a different arrangement of texts strongly suggests that those passages were later additions. In some cases, however, Auld nevertheless included these passages without explanation. For example, Auld included the reference to Solomon's marriage to Pharaoh's daughter in 1 Kgs 9:24//2 Chr 8:11 in his Shared Text, even though 1 Kgs 9:24

---

2. Talshir, "Reign of Solomon," 236–38. Talshir also based her criticism on the consensus model of historical linguistics (248 n. 31).

occurs in different locations in MT Kings and LXX Kings. Thus, Julio Trebolle suggested the possibility that 1 Kgs 9:24//2 Chr 8:11 is a later addition to the written text. In fact, if we accept Trebolle's argument combining the evidence of MT Samuel–Kings, LXX Samuel–Kings, and MT Chronicles, a reconstructed common text becomes smaller by considering the following as secondary, all of which Auld included in his Shared Text: 2 Sam 23:8–39//1 Chr 11:10–47; 2 Sam 6:1–11//1 Chr 13:5–14; 2 Sam 12:26–31//1 Chr 20:1b–3; 2 Sam 21:18–22//1 Chr 20:4–8; 2 Sam 24:1–25//1 Chr 21:1–27; and 1 Kgs 2:10–12//1 Chr 29:20–30.[3] However, Trebolle has correctly cautioned us on the basis of his understanding of the plurality of the ancient textual traditions against the tendency to assume that one original text existed. Rather, he stated that we should accept "the co-existence of parallel editions."[4] Thus, Auld's thesis requires another revision. Whereas Auld imagined a single Shared Text that to some degree may be reconstructed, I imagine, like Trebolle, a common source that from the beginning allowed for a multiformity of texts that necessarily complicates any attempt to reconstruct the *Vorlagen* in any meaningful way. Therefore, the earliest version of Samuel–Kings was not one authoritative text but a family of texts, each one of which was considered to be an instantiation of Samuel–Kings that existed in its multiformity.

Given the criticism Auld's thesis has received, in some ways his critics may justifiably think that I have exacerbated the problem. Whereas he has been criticized for eliminating what has been understood as necessary background information omitted by the Chronicler for the audience's understanding of material the Chronicler included, I have argued that Auld actually should have omitted even more from his Shared Text, if he consistently applied his methodology. In other words, from the perspective of Auld's critics I may have multiplied the number of passages in which the Chronicler "presupposes knowledge of passages in the books of Samuel [and Kings] that he did not include in his own narration of history."[5] Even though I may have increased the number of these passages, this apparent problem is based on an unnecessary assumption about the source for the background information. Such background information did not necessarily come from only one written source but could have come from a variety of written sources as well as the continuing oral tradition itself.

Auld has also been criticized for not identifying his Shared Text more precisely. For example, Steven McKenzie wrote that "it is not unfair now to request a tighter definition of this document [Auld's Shared Text], especially

---

3. Trebolle, "Samuel/Kings and Chronicles." See my revision of this work by Trebolle above, pp. 89–94. Auld, *Kings without Privilege*, 51, 44, 50, 50–51, 52–53, 54–55.

4. Trebolle, "Samuel/Kings and Chronicles," 98.

5. Klein, *1 Chronicles*, 31.

in form-critical terms. If it was a history of the Judahite monarchy, when was it written and for what purpose? In particular, where did it begin?"[6] I have argued against the attempt to reconstruct a singular common source text; therefore, to some extent McKenzie's request of Auld for a tighter definition of the document of the common source does not apply to my thesis. Without some type of more objective controls for the reconstruction of sources and redactional layers (for example, text-critical variants) I hesitate to make such reconstructions. At the same time, I do not imagine my common source to differ so much from the consensus model's understanding that these questions are insurmountable. The common source was a collection of earlier, no longer extant versions of Samuel–Kings that were produced by the Deuteronomic school in the exile by drawing from preexilic sources, both written and oral. Thus, the common source shares features with the later extant versions of Samuel–Kings, even though the extant versions are all expansions of this common source. Others may then reasonably ask the question of why the Chronistic school did not use other books in the Deuteronomic History in much the same way, but of course the consensus model has faced the same question.[7] Various possible answers obtain. Perhaps the book of Judges, for example, was a later addition to the Deuteronomic History, such that it was not considered part of the common tradition by the Chronistic school. Perhaps the Chronistic school simply did not have access to all of the written scrolls of what constituted the Deuteronomic History after the Deuteronomic school returned to Jerusalem.[8]

Despite my thesis that the Deuteronomic History and Chronicles were competing contemporary historiographies, I do not assume that their basic theological messages differed significantly. Furthermore, even though I argue that the Chronistic school eclipsed the Deuteronomic school after Ezra and his scribes took control of the Jerusalem bureacracy, this conflict was not necessarily motivated by theological differences. In fact, the Chronistic school would most likely depend on the cooperation of at least some of the lower-level Deuteronomic scribes. Thus, although I conclude that the Chronistic school supplanted the Deuteronomic school, I understand this primarily

---

6. McKenzie, "Chronicler as Redactor," 81.

7. The consensus model's general response is that the Chronicler was theologically motivated to omit much of the Deuteronomistic History and to add new material in order to emphasize the all-Israel theme and to give a more idealized portrayal of David. However, above I have argued that the consensus model lacks an adequate understanding of the role of multiformity and how it allows for what from our modern perspective we may consider theologically significant variants.

8. Some of Trebolle's work points to the fruitfulness of this line of thought. For example, see his discussion of the *kaige-* and non-*kaige* recensions as one possible means of determining scroll divisions in Trebolle, "Samuel/Kings and Chronicles."

in terms of institutional support. Theological differences may have played a somewhat insignificant role. Here my argument is similar to those recently made by Ehud Ben Zvi. Concerning their supposed theological differences, Ben Zvi concluded the following:

> particularly at the level of ground ideas, core ideological concepts, and basic communicative (rhetorical) grammar as well as general historiographical tendencies, the gap between Chronicles and the Deuteronomistic History (in its present form) was not as large as often claimed. [9]

Had he considered the important role of multiformity in the tradition rather than focusing on his notion of a text-centered community, Ben Zvi might have concluded that the gap is narrowed even further. He also noted that the Pentateuch, the Deuteronomic History, and the Latter Prophets—what he called his literary "triad"—are all written in EBH rather than LBH, even though there are good arguments that the final forms of these literary works are postexilic.[10] Moreover, after surveying later Second Temple literature including the apocrypha, pseudepigrapha, Qumran, Philo, Josephus, and Eupolemus, Ben Zvi concluded that "in general, the deuteronomistic account of the monarchic history received more attention" than Chronicles.[11] As Ben Zvi has so aptly demonstrated, the Deuteronomic History as literature continued its place of honor in the tradition relative to Chronicles. Despite the continuing influence of Deuteronomic literature, at some point new Deuteronomic texts and redactions ceased to be produced. The demise of the Deuteronomic school as a result of the Chronistic school's institutional ascent can, on the one hand, explain the eventual end of the production of Deuteronomic literature but, on the other hand, also explain how Deuteronomic literature continued to have a significant influence. The Chronistic school was not necessarily motivated theologically to displace the Deuteronomic school's literature; in fact, the two scribal groups shared a common history and a common source for their historiographies. Therefore, the Chronistic school displaced the Deuteronomic school institutionally but not necessarily theologically or in terms of what was considered the most authoritative literature. Because the tradition allowed for multiformity, the Chronistic school had no reason to reject the Deuteronomic History as authoritative, and the broader tradition had no reason to dismiss Chronicles. Both could continue as authoritative literature, even though the Deuteronomic History continued as its primary place of honor in the tradition. Chronicles's place as authoritative literature was strengthened also by its

---

9. Ben Zvi, "Are There Any Bridges Out There?" 85.
10. Ben Zvi, "Communicative Message," 270.
11. Ben Zvi, *History, Literature and Theology*, 259.

connection to the later Chronistic work Ezra–Nehemiah; however, the Chronistic school's influence also must have also waned, since other Chronistic works were not produced.

ORAL TRADITION AND THE ROLE OF MULTIFORMITY

An important element of my argument for the Deuteronomic History and Chronicles as competing contemporary historiographies has been the role of multiformity in the broader tradition. Such multiformity is a characteristic of both the Deuteronomic History and Chronicles as well as of their intertextual relationship. The consensus model acknowledges the role of multivocality within these texts, especially when scholars reconstruct different sources and redactional layers within these works on the basis of this multivocality (for example, pro-monarchical versus anti-monarchical). Nevertheless, in my judgment, the consensus model downplays the role of multiformity concerning the text-critical evidence but then overemphasizes apparent differences concerning the relationship of Samuel–Kings to Chronicles. The text-critical evidence demonstrates a multiplicity of extant text-types. Although this is less the case with Chronicles, the multiplicity of textual forms for Samuel and Kings is significant. When one takes seriously this multiformity, Trebolle's conclusion of coexisting parallel editions of Samuel–Kings, none of which may have been considered superior by the ancient tradents, seems obviously valid. Thus, an argument for the Chronistic school using a text-type essentially the same as MT Samuel–Kings, LXX Samuel–MT Kings, or LXX Samuel–Kings is problematic. This is especially the case when, with David Carr, we understand that there was a trend toward expansion as the broader tradition preserved more and more of the oral tradition in written texts. If so, then it is unlikely that any of the extant texts preserve the earlier shorter forms, especially given the amount of unique material in both Samuel–Kings and Chronicles. Therefore, careful attention to the variety of parallel texts may serve as a text-critical control for imagining what these shorter texts may have looked like in their multiformity.

Trebolle's thesis of coexisting parallel editions is based on his analysis of text-critical evidence. Like Carr, I have drawn substantially from the study of oral traditions to understand multiformity in greater depth. When we understand how important a characteristic multiformity is in oral traditions and in literature from primarily oral societies, the notion of an original text becomes far more problematic. Although some portion of the tradition was recorded for the first time in writing in a very specific time and place, that first text did not necessarily become determinant for all future texts that recorded that portion of the tradition. In an oral tradition, no single performance can be understood as the primary authoritative performance that must be replicated verbatim. All performances are simply one instantiation of the tradition, such that past and future performances may represent more or less of the tradition but none of them can alone represent the tradition in its fullness. Likewise, no single text in a primarily oral society can fully represent the broader tradition in its fullness. Therefore, no single text is determinant for future texts. In a primarily oral society a constant interplay between literary texts and the broader oral tradition preserved in the community's memory occurs. Thus, coexisting parallel editions of texts, despite their apparent differences, can nevertheless equally re-present the tradition, and the broader tradition is best understood by the collective re-presentation of the texts in all of their multiformity. We must, therefore, practice great caution when reconstructing theological differences on the basis of what from our modern perspective are variant readings but what may be from the ancient perspective a faithful representation of the tradition.

Applying this insight from oral traditions to the relationship between the Deuteronomic History and Chronicles is actually independent of my thesis of a common source. Even if the Chronicler or the Chronistic school used a form of Samuel–Kings closely related to the extant texts, an understanding of the role of multiformity would caution us against too easily assuming that the so-called omissions, additions, and substitutions to the *Vorlage* were necessarily theologically motivated. Chronicles can simply be understood as one more representation of the broader tradition in its mutiformity. However, given the text-critical evidence of the plurality of texts for Samuel–Kings, each of the extant texts of Samuel–Kings can also be understood as just one more representation of the broader tradition. If MT Samuel–Kings thus loses the place of superiority in representing the broader tradition, then the thesis of a common source for Samuel–Kings and Chronicles gains support. Hence, the Deuteronomic History and Chronicles were, in the words of Ben Zvi, "co-existing communal tools for imagining and re-imagining the past" in the Persian period.[12]

IMPLICATIONS

THE INTERPLAY OF THE ORAL AND WRITTEN IN THE DEVELOPMENT OF BIBLICAL LITERATURE

The conclusions reached in this study have broader implications for the study of the Hebrew Bible. Others such as Tov, Auld, Trebolle, and Rezetko have advocated for the close interaction of the methods of text criticism and source/

---

12. Ehud Ben Zvi, "Late Historical Books and Rewritten History," in *The Cambridge Companion to the Hebrew Bible—Old Testament* (ed. Stephen B. Chapman and Marvin A. Sweeney; Cambridge: Cambridge University Press, forthcoming), 15.

redaction criticism; however, the inclusion of the study of oral traditions and orally derived literature, especially concerning the role of multiformity, requires us to reimagine the processes that produced the literature of ancient Israel. We especially need to reimagine the work of ancient scribes as authors/ redactors in relation to multiformity. Too often we assume that even minor differences in wording between texts is evidence of authorial intention. Because of the plurality of text-critical variants, some commentators have already discussed this danger. For example, Gary Knoppers wrote the following:

> Some modern treatments of Chronicles have been indiscriminate in detecting ideological nuances whenever the text of Chronicles differed even slightly from that of Genesis, Samuel, or Kings. In light of studies on the LXX and the Qumran literature, a more complicated picture emerges. . . . On the one hand, caution is dictated in attributing tendentious intention to a Chronicles text whenever it differs from Genesis or Samuel, as the alleged change may be due either to the textual tradition represented by the Chronicler's *Vorlage* or to textual corruption. On the other hand, when neither of these two options seems likely, especially in dealing with the text of Kings, one can with confidence more clearly recognize those instances in which the Chronicler consciously made a change in his text.[13]

Knoppers's nuanced critique of some contemporary treatments of Chronicles moves in the right direction; however, he still maintained that, whenever one can rule out text-critical variants as the explanation for a difference, the remaining explanation is a conscious decision by the Chronicler that helps us understand his "ideological nuances." Knoppers and most others do not even consider the possibility that such differences would not necessarily be considered differences by the ancients—that is, the ancients may have concluded that these apparent variations simply fall within the realm of the accepted multiformity in the tradition. In fact, the multiformity expressed in the multiplicity of text-critical variants that Knoppers acknowledges as complicating the picture points us in this direction, since the tradition obviously valued the text-critical multiformity.

The consensus model assumes a linear process of textual development. Admittedly, later texts may influence each other in ways that complicate the linear development of texts, but the model nevertheless assumes an original text from which all other texts descended. In the case of the discussion concerning Samuel–Kings and Chronicles, this assumption is found equally in the work of Knoppers, McKenzie, and others in the consensus model as well as in the work of Auld. A new model of the development of literary texts in the ancient world is now necessary. This model should take seriously both the

---

13. Knoppers, *I Chronicles 1–9*, 70–71. See similarly Kalimi, *Reshaping of Ancient Israelite History*, 12.

reality of textual plurality and the significant role of multiformity in primarily oral societies. Rather than envisioning one original, authoritative, determinant text, we should envision a collection of coexisting parallel editions, none of which preserves the tradition in its entirety and, therefore, none of which can be authoritative alone. Whenever a scribe copied a particular text, the scribe was not simply copying that one text. Since that text represented the broader tradition and did so only selectively, the scribe may have, from our modern perspective, significantly revised the *Vorlage* with additions, omissions, and substitutions; however, from the perspective of the scribe and the other ancients, both the *Vorlage* and the new copy may equally have represented the broader tradition, although imperfectly, so that in one sense nothing was changed in the process of copying. If this is the case, then we can explain how a multiplicity of textual forms came to be and why the tradition preserves parallel texts, not only Samuel–Kings//Chronicles but others such as 2 Kgs 18–20// Isa 36–39 and 2 Kgs 24:18–25:30//Jer 52.

Text critics have long argued that over time texts are more likely to expand as scribes add material to them. Building on this argument, Carr has argued that there is a trend toward expansion as the tradition as primarily preserved in the community's memory became recorded more often in written texts. As the tradition increasingly valued the preservation of verbal art in written texts, literary texts expanded in order to preserve more of the broader tradition. If so, this helps to explain why texts increased over time in their multiformity. For example, MT 1 Sam 16–18 preserved not only the tradition as contained in the earlier written version behind LXX 1 Sam 16–18 but another version as well. This type of the conflation of traditions seems to be a later attempt to preserve more of the multiformity of the tradition in written form.

Critics of the Parry-Lord-Foley study of oral traditions and orally derived literature have often used the complexity of literary structures as an argument against the role of orality in the production of literature. Structures such as Wiederaufnahme and ring composition have been identified as organizing devices unlikely to occur in the messiness of oral discourse. Although this criticism requires a much more detailed response, I offer here a preliminary consideration.[14] This criticism is based on an inaccurate notion of how simple conversational structures are in comparison to the complexity of literary discourse. The field of conversation analysis has clearly demonstrated the complexity and intricacy of the structures in face-to-face conversation, involving not only those lexical items found in standard dictionaries but also prosody, body movement, and nonlexical items (for example, "mm hm"). In *Structure*

---

14. My fuller response to this criticism will appear in a forthcoming monograph tentatively entitled *From Conversation to Oral Tradition*.

and Meaning in Conversation and Literature, I drew significantly from conversation analysis to show that this complexity in talk-in-interaction can be represented in modern English literary narratives, including nonlexical items, prosody, and body movement.[15] Thus, oral discourse is not as simple as linguists once thought, and the complexity of oral discourse is somewhat analogous to that of literary discourse. In "A Reassessment of Wiederaufnahme from the Perspective of Conversation Analysis," I illustrated how literary structures, such as the ancient so-called scribal technique of Wiederaufnahme or resumptive repetition, are adaptations of structures found in everyday conversation, in this case a structure called restarts.[16]

In light of my argument of the influence of oral tradition on Chronicles, Isaac Kalimi's comprehensive study of the literary techniques found in Chronicles requires further attention. Kalimi discussed various "literary" techniques such as Wiederaufnahme, chiasmus, inclusio, and simile and concluded the following:

> I consider the Chronicler to be a creative artist, a *historian* who selected the material he desired out of his sources and edited it in the order, the context, and the form he found fitting, thus creating a literary composition comprising part of late biblical historiography. [17]

I suspect that some readers, like Kalimi, may conclude that such literary creativity in Chronicles requires an author in a text-centered society, thereby downplaying the role of oral tradition in ancient Israel.[18] However, as I suggested in the preceding paragraph, I think that such "literary" devices are not exclusive to written literature in that they are found also in oral traditions and that, furthermore, these "literary" structures are actually adaptations of conversational structures.

---

15. Raymond F. Person Jr., *Structure and Meaning in Conversation and Literature* (Lanham, Md.: University Press of America, 1999).

16. Raymond F. Person Jr., "A Reassessment of Wiederaufnahme from the Perspective of Conversation Analysis," *BZ* 43 (1999): 241–48.

17. Kalimi, *Reshaping of Ancient Israelite History*, 7. See similarly Kalimi, *Ancient Israelite Historian*, 10.

18. At least this criticism would be consistent with arguments already published by, for example, Schniedewind ("Chronicler as an Interpreter of Scripture") and John Van Seters ("Problems in the Literary Analysis of the Court History of King David," *JSOT* 1 [1976]: 22–29; and idem, *The Edited Bible: The Curious History of the "Editor" in Biblical Criticism* [Winona Lake, Ind.: Eisenbrauns, 2006]).

The Relationship between the Deuteronomic School and the Chronistic School

This work has focused on the relationship between Samuel–Kings and Chronicles as a way of understanding the relationship between the Deuteronomic school and the Chronistic school; however, the book's thesis has implications for the study of Ezra–Nehemiah in relationship to the Deuteronomic History and to the book of Chronicles. Therefore, I will conclude with some brief remarks about these possible implications.

I have argued that the Deuteronomic school lost its institutional support when it was displaced by the Chronistic school as a part of Ezra's mission; however, this displacement does not necessarily require significant theological conflict. Therefore, the Deuteronomic History could continue its place of honor within the literary tradition relative to Chronicles, especially since these two historiographies do not necessarily represent the generally assumed theological conflict between the tradents (as individuals or as schools). Furthermore, the Chronistic school could continue its literary work in Chronicles and later in the early Hellenistic period with its production of Ezra–Nehemiah.

This historical reconstruction has implications for the literary relationships between the literature of the Deuteronomic school and that of the Chronistic school. Some related questions that should be explored further are as follows. What influence might the Deuteronomic literature have had on the later Chronistic work of Ezra–Nehemiah? What subtle differences are there between Chronicles and Ezra–Nehemiah that might reflect their literary history relative to my reconstruction?[19] Some recent work on Ezra–Nehemiah points in the direction of some possible answers to these questions. For example, Tamara Cohn Eskenazi and Mark Brett have both discussed the influence of Deuteronomy on Ezra–Nehemiah, and Christine Mitchell has contrasted the lack of language concerning the Other in Chronicles with an emphasis on the Other in Ezra–Nehemiah.[20]

---

19. For my preliminary answers to these questions, see my response to recent essays on the Deuteronomistic History, Chronicles, and Ezra–Nehemiah (Person, "Identity (Re)formation as the Historical Circumstances Required").

20. Tamara Cohn Eskenazi, "Missions of Ezra and Nehemiah," 509; Mark G. Brett, "National Identity as Commentary and as Metacommentary," in *Historiography and Identity: (Re)formulation in Second Temple Historiographical Literature* (ed. Louis C. Jonker; Library of Hebrew Bible/Old Testament Studies 534; London: T&T Clark, 2010), 32–33; and in the same volume Mitchell, "Otherness and Historiography in Chronicles."

BIBLIOGRAPHY

Abadie, Philippe. "From the Impious Manasseh (2 Kings 21) to the Convert Manasseh (2 Chronicles 33): Theological Rewriting by the Chronicler." Pages 89–104 in *The Chronicler as Theologian: Essays in Honor of Ralph W. Klein.* Edited by M. Patrick Graham, Steven L. McKenzie, and Gary N. Knoppers. JSOTSup 371. London: T&T Clark, 2003.

Albertz, Rainer. "The Canonical Alignment of the Book of Joshua." Pages 287–303 in *Judah and the Judeans in the Fourth Century B.C.E.* Edited by Oded Lipschits, Gary N. Knoppers, and Rainer Albertz. Winona Lake, Ind.: Eisenbrauns, 2007.

————. *A History of Israelite Religion in the Old Testament Period.* Translated by John Bowden. 2 vols. OTL. Louisville: John Knox, 1994.

Amit, Yairah. "The Saul Polemic in the Persian Period." Pages 647–61 in *Judah and the Judeans in the Persian Period.* Edited by Oded Lipschits and Manfred Oeming. Winona Lake, Ind.: Eisenbrauns, 2006.

Auld, A. Graeme. "The Deuteronomists and the Former Prophets, Or What Makes the Former Prophets Deuteronomistic?" Pages 116–26 in *Those Elusive Deuteronomists: The Phenomenon of Pan-Deuteronomism.* Edited by Linda S. Schearing and Steven L. McKenzie. JSOTSup 268. Sheffield: Sheffield Academic Press, 1999.

————. "The Deuteronomists between History and Theology." Pages 353–67 in *Congress Volume: Oslo 1998.* Edited by A. Lemaire and M. Sæbø. VTSup 80. Leiden: Brill, 2000.

————. *Joshua, Judges, and Ruth.* Daily Study Bible. Philadelphia: Westminster Press, 1984.

————. "Judges 1 and History: A Reconsideration." *VT* 25 (1975): 261–85.

————. *Kings without Privilege: David and Moses in the Story of the Bible's Kings.* Edinburgh: T&T Clark, 1994.

————. "The 'Levitical Cities': Text and History." *ZAW* 91 (1979): 194–206.

————. "Prophets Shared—But Recycled." Pages 19–28 in *The Future of the Deuteronomistic History.* Edited by Thomas Römer. BETL 147. Leuven: Leuven University Press, 2000.

————. "Prophets through the Looking Glass: A Response to Robert Carroll and Hugh Williamson." *JSOT* 27 (1983): 41–44.

————. "Prophets through the Looking Glass: Between Writings and Moses." *JSOT* 27 (1983): 3–23.

————. "Reading Joshua after Kings." Pages 167–81 in *Words Remembered, Texts Renewed: Essays in Honour of John F. A. Sawyer*. Edited by J. Davies, G. Harvey, and W. G. E. Watson. JSOTSup 195. Sheffield: Sheffield Academic Press, 1995.

————. "What If the Chronicler Did Use the Deuteronomistic History?" *BibInt* 8 (2000): 137–50.

————. "What Was the Main Source of the Books of Chronicles?" Pages 91–99 in *The Chronicler as Author: Studies in Text and Texture*. Edited by M. Patrick Graham and Steven L. McKenzie. JSOTSup 263. Sheffield: Sheffield Academic Press, 1999.

Barthélemy, Dominique, David W. Gooding, Johan Lust, and Emanuel Tov, eds. *The Story of David and Goliath: Textual and Literary Criticism*. OBO 73. Fribourg: Éditions Universitaires Fribourg; Göttingen: Vandenhoeck & Ruprecht, 1986.

Becking, Bob. "'We All Returned as One!': Critical Notes on the Myth of the Mass Return." Pages 3–18 in *Judah and the Judeans in the Persian Period*. Edited by Oded Lipschits and Manfred Oeming. Winona Lake, Ind.: Eisenbrauns, 2006.

Ben Zvi, Ehud. "Are There Any Bridges Out There? How Wide Was the Conceptual Gap between the Deuteronomistic History and Chronicles?" Pages 59–86 in *Community Identity in Judean Historiography: Biblical and Comparative Perspectives*. Edited by Gary N. Knoppers and Kenneth A. Ristau. Winona Lake, Ind.: Eisenbrauns, 2009.

————. "The Communicative Message of Some Linguistic Choices." Pages 269–90 in *A Palimpsest: Rhetoric, Ideology, Stylistics and Language Relating to Persian Israel*. Edited by Ehud Ben Zvi, Diana V. Edelman, and Frank Polak. Perspectives on Hebrew Scriptures and Its Contexts 5. Piscataway, N.J.: Gorgias Press, 2009.

————. "A Deuteronomistic Redaction in/among 'The Twelve'? A Contribution from the Standpoint of the Books of Micah, Zephaniah, and Obadiah." Pages 232–61 in *Those Elusive Deuteronomists: The Phenomenon of Pan-Deuteronomism*. Edited by Linda S. Schearing and Steven L. McKenzie. JSOTSup 268. Sheffield: Sheffield Academic Press, 1999.

————. *History, Literature and Theology in the Book of Chronicles*. London/ Oakville, Conn.: Equinox, 2006.

————. "Imagining Josiah's Book and the Implications of Imagining It in Early Persian Yehud." Pages 193–212 in *Berührungspunkte: Studien zur Sozial- und Religionsgeschichte Israels und seiner Umwelt: Festschrift für Rainer Albertz zu seinem 65. Geburtstag*. Edited by Ingo Kottsieper, Rüdiger Schmitt, and Jakob Wöhrle. AOAT 350. Münster: Ugarit-Verlag, 2008.

————. "Late Historical Books and Rewritten History." In *The Cambridge Companion to the Hebrew Bible—Old Testament*. Edited by Stephen B. Chapman and Marvin A. Sweeney. Cambridge: Cambridge University Press, forthcoming.

————. "Looking at the Primary (Hi)Story and the Prophetic Books as Literary/ Theological Units within the Frame of the Early Second Temple: Some Considerations." *JSOT* 12 (1998): 26–43.

————. "Observations on Josiah's Account in Chronicles and Implications for Reconstructing the Worldview of the Chronicler." Pages 89–106 in *Essays on Ancient Israel in Its Near Eastern Context: A Tribute to Nadav Na'aman*. Edited by Yairah Amit, Ehud Ben Zvi, Israel Finkelstein, and Oded Lipschits. Winona Lake, Ind.: Eisenbrauns, 2006.

————. "The Secession of the Northern Kingdom in Chronicles: Accepted 'Facts' and New Meanings." Pages 61–88 in *The Chronicler as Theologian: Essays in Honor of Ralph W. Klein*. Edited by M. Patrick Graham, Steven L. McKenzie, and Gary N. Knoppers. JSOTSup 371. London: T&T Clark, 2003.

————. "The Urban Center of Jerusalem and the Development of the Literature of the Hebrew Bible." Pages 194–209 in *Urbanism in Antiquity*. Sheffield: Sheffield Academic Press, 1997.

————. "Who Knew What? The Construction of the Monarchic Past in Chronicles and Implications for the Intellectual Setting of Chronicles." Pages 349–60 in *Judah and the Judeans in the Fourth Century B.C.E.* Edited by Oded Lipschits, Gary N. Knoppers, and Rainer Albertz. Winona Lake, Ind.: Eisenbrauns, 2007.

Berquist, Jon L. "Identities and Empire: Historiographical Questions for the Deuteronomistic History in the Persian Period." Pages 3–13 in *Historiography and Identity: (Re)formulation in Second Temple Historiographical Literature*. Edited by Louis C. Jonker. Library of Hebrew Bible/Old Testament Studies 534. London: T&T Clark, 2010.

Blenkinsopp, Joseph. "The Sage, the Scribe, and Scribalism in the Chronicler's Work." Pages 307–15 in *The Sage in Israel and the Ancient Near East*. Edited by John G. Gammie and Leo G. Perdue. Winona Lake, Ind.: Eisenbrauns, 1990.

————. "Was the Pentateuch the Civic and Religious Constitution of the Jewish Ethnos in the Persian Period?" Pages 41–62 in *Persia and Torah: The Theory of Imperial Authorization of the Pentateuch*. Edited by James W. Watts. Symposium 17. Atlanta: Society of Biblical Literature, 2001.

Blount, Ben G. "Agreeing to Agree on Genealogy: A Luo Sociology of Knowledge." Pages 117–35 in *Sociocultural Dimensions of Language Use*. Edited by Mary Sanches and Ben G. Blount. New York: Academic Press, 1975.

Boda, Mark J. "Identity and Empire, Reality and Hope in the Chronicler's Perspective." Pages 249–72 in *Community Identity in Judean Historiography: Biblical and Comparative Perspectives*. Edited by Gary N. Knoppers and Kenneth A. Ristau. Winona Lake, Ind.: Eisenbrauns, 2009.

Boda, Mark J., and Paul L. Redditt, eds. *Unity and Disunity in Ezra–Nehemiah: Redaction, Rhetoric, and Reader.* Sheffield: Sheffield Phoenix, 2008.

Brett, Mark G. "National Identity as Commentary and as Metacommentary." Pages 29–40 in *Historiography and Identity: (Re)formulation in Second Temple Historiographical Literature.* Edited by Louis C. Jonker. Library of Hebrew Bible/Old Testament Studies 534. London: T&T Clark, 2010.

Brooke, George J. "The Books of Chronicles and the Scrolls from Qumran." Pages 35–48 in *Reflection and Refraction: Studies in Biblical Historiography in Honour of A. Graeme Auld.* Edited by Robert Rezetko, Timothy H. Lim, and W. Brian Aucker. VTSup 113. Leiden: Brill, 2007.

Carr, David M. "'Empirical' Comparison and the Analysis of the Relationship of the Pentateuch and the Former Prophets." In *Pentateuch, Hexateuch, or Enneateuch: Identifying Literary Works in Genesis through Kings.* Edited by Konrad Schmid and Thomas Dozeman. Ancient Israel and Its Literature. Atlanta: Society of Biblical Literature, forthcoming in 2011.

———. "Empirische Perspektiven auf das Deuteronomistische Geschichtswerk." Pages 1–17 in *Die deuteronomistischen Geschichtswerke. Redaktions- und religionsgeschichtliche Perspektiven zur "Deuteronomismus"-Diskussion in Tora und Vorderen Propheten.* Edited by Markus Witte et al. BZAW 365. Berlin: Walter de Gruyter, 2006.

———. "Response to W. M. Schniedewind, *How the Bible Became a Book: The Textualization of Ancient Israel,*" in "In Conversation with W. M. Schniedewind, *How the Bible Became a Book: The Textualization of Ancient Israel.*" *Journal of Hebrew Scriptures* 5 (2004–5): Article 18, 1–19.

———. *Writing on the Tablet of the Heart: Origins of Scripture and Literature.* Oxford: Oxford University Press, 2005.

Carroll, Robert P. *Jeremiah: A Commentary.* OTL Philadelphia: Westminster, 1986.

Carter, Charles E. *Emergence of Yehud in the Persian Period: A Social and Demographic Study.* JSOTSup 294. Sheffield: Sheffield Academic Press, 1999.

———. "The Province of Yehud in the Post-Exilic Period: Soundings in Site Distribution and Demography [graphs, maps, tables]." Pages 106–45 in *Second Temple Studies,* vol. 2, *Temple and Community in the Persian Period.* Edited by Tamara Cohn Eskenazi and Kent H. Richards. JSOTSup 175. Sheffield: JSOT Press, 1994.

Christian, Mark A. "Priestly Power That Empowers: Michel Foucault, Middle-tier Levites, and the Sociology of 'Popular Religious Groups' in Israel." *Journal of Hebrew Scriptures* 9 (2009): Article 1.

Clanchy, M. T. *From Memory to Written Record: England, 1066–1307.* Cambridge, Mass.: Harvard University Press, 1979.

Cogan, Mordechai. *1 Kings: A New Translation with Introduction and Commentary.* AB 10. New York: Doubleday, 2001.

Coggins, Richard. "What Does 'Deuteronomistic' Mean?" Pages 135–48 in *Words Remembered, Texts Renewed: Essays in Honour of John F. A. Sawyer.*

Edited by J. Davies, G. Harvey, and W. G. E. Watson. JSOTSup 195. Sheffield: Sheffield Academic Press, 1995.

Crawford, Sidnie White. *Rewriting Scripture in Second Temple Times.* Studies in the Dead Sea Scrolls and Related Literature. Grand Rapids: Eerdmans, 2008.

Crenshaw, James L. "Education in Ancient Israel." *JBL* 104 (1985): 601–15.

———. *Education in Ancient Israel: Across the Deadening Silence.* Anchor Bible Reference Library. New York: Doubleday, 1998.

Cross, Frank Moore. "A New Reconstruction of 4QSamuel^a 24:16–22." Pages 77–83 in *Studies in the Hebrew Bible, Qumran, and the Septuagint Presented to Eugene Ulrich.* Edited by Peter W. Flint, Emanuel Tov, and James C. VanderKam. VTSup 101. Leiden: Brill, 2006.

Culley, Robert C. *Oral Formulaic Language in the Biblical Psalms.* Toronto: University of Toronto Press, 1967.

———. "Oral Tradition and Biblical Studies." *Oral Tradition* 1 (1986): 30–65.

———, ed. *Oral Tradition and Biblical Studies.* Semeia 5. Missoula, Mont.: Scholars Press, 1976.

———. *Studies in the Structure of Hebrew Narrative.* Philadelphia: Fortress, 1976.

———. *Themes and Variations: A Study of Action in Biblical Narrative.* Semeia. St. Atlanta: Scholars Press, 1992.

Davies, Graham. "Some Uses of Writing in Ancient Israel in the Light of Recently Published Inscriptions." Pages 155–74 in *Writing and Ancient Near Eastern Society: Papers in Honor of Alan R. Millard.* Edited by Piotr Bienkowski, Christopher Mee, and Elizabeth Slater. Library of Hebrew Bible/Old Testament Studies 426. London: T&T Clark, 2005.

———. "Were There Schools in Ancient Israel?" Pages 199–211 in *Wisdom in Ancient Israel: Essays in Honor of J. A. Emerton.* Edited by John Day, Robert P. Gordon, and H. G. M. Williamson. Cambridge: Cambridge University Press, 1995.

Davies, Philip R. *Scribes and Schools: The Canonization of the Hebrew Scriptures.* Louisville: Westminster John Knox, 1998.

Dell, Katherine. "Scribes, Sages, and Seers in the First Temple," Pages 125–44 in *Scribes, Sages, and Seers: The Sage in the Eastern Mediterranean World.* Edited by Leo G. Perdue. FRLANT 219. Göttingen: Vandenhoeck & Ruprecht, 2008.

Dirksen, Peter B. *1 Chronicles.* Translated by Antony P. Runia. Historical Commentary on the Old Testament. Leuven/Dudley, Mass.: Peeters, 2005.

Doane, Alger N. "The Ethnography of Scribal Writing and Anglo-Saxon Poetry: Scribe as Performer." *Oral Tradition* 9 (1994): 420–39.

Duke, Rodney K. *The Persuasive Appeal of the Chronicler.* JSOTSup 88. Sheffield: Almond, 1990.

———. "Recent Research in Chronicles." *Currents in Biblical Research* 8 (2009): 10–50.

Edelman, Diana V. "The Deuteronomist's David and the Chronicler's David: Competing or Contrasting Ideologies." Pages 67–83 in *The Future of the*

Deuteronomistic History. Edited by Thomas Römer. BETL 147. Leuven: Leuven University Press, 2000.

Ehrensvärd, Martin. "Linguistic Dating of Biblical Texts." Pages 164–88 in *Biblical Hebrew: Studies in Chronology and Typology.* Edited by Ian Young. JSOTSup 369. London: T&T Clark, 2003.

———. "Why Biblical Texts Cannot Be Dated Linguistically." *HS* 47 (2006): 177–89.

Endres, John C., et al. *Chronicles and Its Synoptic Parallels in Samuel, Kings, and Related Biblical Texts.* Collegeville, Minn.: Liturgical Press, 1998.

Eskenazi, Tamara Cohn. *In an Age of Prose: A Literary Approach to Ezra–Nehemiah.* SBLMS 36. Atlanta: Scholars Press, 1988.

———. "The Missions of Ezra and Nehemiah." Pages 509–29 in *Judah and the Judeans in the Persian Period.* Edited by Oded Lipschits and Manfred Oeming. Winona Lake, Ind.: Eisenbrauns, 2006.

Fishbane, Michael. *Biblical Interpretation in Ancient Israel.* Oxford: Oxford University Press, 1985.

Floyd, Michael H. Review of *Second Zechariah and the Deuteronomic School,* by Raymond F. Person Jr. *JBL* 114 (1995): 726.

Foley, John Miles. "Analogues: Modern Oral Epic." Pages 196–212 in *A Companion to Ancient Epic.* Edited by John Miles Foley. Oxford: Blackwell, 2005.

———, ed. *A Companion to Ancient Epic.* Oxford: Blackwell, 2005.

———. "Comparative Oral Traditions." Pages 65–81 in *Voicing the Moment: Improvised Oral Poetry and Basque Tradition.* Edited by Samuel G. Armistead and Joseba Zulaika. Center for Basque Studies Conference Papers 3. Reno: University of Nevada at Reno, 2005.

———. "Editing Oral Epic Texts: Theory and Practice." *Text* 1 (1981): 77–78.

———. *Homer's Traditional Art.* University Park: Pennsylvania State University Press, 1999.

———. *Immanent Art: From Structure to Meaning in Traditional Oral Epic.* Bloomington: Indiana University Press, 1991.

———. "Memory in Oral Tradition." Pages 83–96 in *Performing the Gospel: Orality, Memory, and Mark: Essays Dedicated to Werner Kelber.* Edited by Richard A. Horsley, Jonathan A. Draper, and John Miles Foley. Minneapolis: Fortress, 2006.

———. "Oral Theory in Context." Pages 27–122 in *Oral Traditional Literature: A Festschrift for Albert Bates Lord.* Edited by John Miles Foley. Columbus: Slavica, 1981.

———, ed. *Oral Traditional Literature: A Festschrift for Albert Bates Lord.* Columbus: Slavica, 1981.

———. *The Singer of Tales in Performance.* Bloomington: Indiana University Press, 1995.

————. *The Theory of Oral Composition: History and Methodology*. Folkloristics. Bloomington: Indiana University Press, 1988.

————. *Traditional Oral Epic: The Odyssey, Beowulf, and the Serbo-Croatian Return Song*. Berkeley: University of Californa Press, 1990.

Fried, Lisbeth S. "The '*am ha'ares* in Ezra 4:4 and Persian Imperial Administration." Pages 123–45 in *Judah and the Judeans in the Persian Period*. Edited by Oded Lipschits and Manfred Oeming. Winona Lake, Ind.: Eisenbrauns, 2006.

————. "Who Wrote Ezra–Nehemiah—and Why Did They?" Pages 75–97 in *Unity and Disunity in Ezra–Nehemiah: Redaction, Rhetoric, and Reader*. Edited by Mark J. Boda and Paul L. Redditt. Sheffield: Sheffield Phoenix, 2008.

Fritz, Volkmar. *1 & 2 Kings: A Continental Commentary*. Translated by Anselm Hagedorn. Minneapolis: Fortress, 2003.

Gammie, John G. and Leo G. Perdue, eds. *The Sage in Israel and the Ancient Near East*. Winona Lake, Ind.: Eisenbrauns, 1990.

Gray, John. *I & II Kings: A Commentary*. OTL. Philadelphia: Westminster, 1963.

Halpern, Baruch. "Sacred History and Ideology: Chronicles' Thematic Structure—Indications of an Earlier Source." Pages 35–54 in *The Creation of Sacred Literature: Composition and Redaction of the Biblical Text*. Edited by Richard Elliott Friedman. Near Eastern Studies 22. Berkeley: University of California Press, 1981.

Heaton, Eric. *The School Tradition of the Old Testament*. Oxford: Clarendon, 1994.

Ho, Craig Y. S. "Conjectures and Refutations: Is 1 Samuel XXXI 1–13 Really the Source of 1 Chronicles X 1–12?" *VT* 45 (1995): 82–106.

Hoglund, Kenneth G. "The Chronicler as Historian: A Comparativist Perspective." Pages 19–29 in *The Chronicler as Historian*. Edited by M. Patrick Graham, Kenneth G. Hoglund, and Steven L. McKenzie. JSOTSup 238. Sheffield: Sheffield Academic Press, 1997.

Horsley, Richard A. *Scribes, Visionaries, and the Politics of Second Temple Judea*. Louisville: Westminster John Knox, 2007.

Hurvitz, Avi. "The Recent Debate on Late Biblical Hebrew: Solid Data, Experts' Opinions, and Inconclusive Arguments." *HS* 47 (2006): 191–210.

Isser, Stanley. *The Sword of Goliath: David in Heroic Literature*. Studies in Biblical Literature 6. Atlanta: Society of Biblical Literature, 2003.

Jamieson-Drake, David W. *Scribes and Schools in Monarchic Judah: A Socio-Archeological Approach*. JSOTSup 109. Sheffield: Almond, 1991.

Janzen, David. "The 'Mission' of Ezra and the Persian-Period Temple Community." *JBL* 119 (2000): 619–43.

Japhet, Sara. *I & II Chronicles: A Commentary*. OTL. Louisville: Westminster John Knox, 1993.

———. *The Ideology of the Book of Chronicles and Its Place in Biblical Thought.* BEATAJ 9. Frankfurt: Peter Lang, 1989.

———. "Periodization between History and Ideology II: Chronology and Ideology in Ezra–Nehemiah." Pages 491–508 in *Judah and the Judeans in the Persian Period.* Edited by Oded Lipschits and Manfred Oeming. Winona Lake, Ind.: Eisenbrauns, 2006.

———. "Postexilic Historiography: How and Why?" Pages 144–73 in *Israel Constructs Its History: Deuteronomistic Historiography in Recent Research.* Edited by Albert de Pury, Thomas Römer, and Jean-Daniel Macchi. JSOTSup 306. Sheffield: Sheffield Academic Press, 2000.

———. "The Wall of Jerusalem from a Double Perspective: Kings versus Chronicles." Pages 205–19 in *Essays on Ancient Israel in Its Near Eastern Context: A Tribute to Nadav Na'aman.* Edited by Yairah Amit, Ehud Ben Zvi, Israel Finkelstein, and Oded Lipschits. Winona Lake, Ind.: Eisenbrauns, 2006.

Jonker, Louis C. "David's Officials according to the Chronicler." Pages 65-91-15 in *Historiography and Identity: (Re)formulation in Second Temple Historiographical Literature.* Library of Hebrew Bible/Old Testament Studies 534. London: T&T Clark, 2010.

———, ed. *Historiography and Identity: (Re)formulation in Second Temple Historiographical Literature.* Library of Hebrew Bible/Old Testament Studies 534. London: T&T Clark, 2010.

———. *Reflections of King Josiah in Chronicles: Late Stages of the Josiah Reception in II Chr. 34f.* Textpragmatische Studien zur Literatur- und Kulturgeschichte der Hebräischen Bibel 2. Gütersloh: Gütersloher Verlagshaus, 2003.

Kalimi, Isaac. *An Ancient Israelite Historian: Studies in the Chronicler, His Time, Place, and Writing.* SSN 46. Assen: Van Gorcum, 2005.

———. *The Reshaping of Ancient Israelite History in Chronicles.* Winona Lake, Ind.: Eisenbrauns, 2005.

Kelber, Werner. "Orality and Biblical Studies: A Review Essay." *Review of Biblical Literature* 12 (2007), http://www.bookreviews.org/pdf/2107_6748.pdf.

———. "Scripture and Logos. The Hermeneutics of Communication." Paper presented at the annual meeting of the Society of Biblical Literature, Kansas City, November 1991.

Kessler, John. "Reconstructing Haggai's Jerusalem: Demographic and Sociological Considerations and the Quest for an Adequate Methodological Point of Departure." Pages 137–58 in *Every City Shall Be Forsaken: Urbanism and Prophecy in Ancient Israel and the Near East.* Edited by L. Grabbe and R. Haak. JSOTSup 330. Sheffield: Sheffield Academic Press, 2001.

Keulen, Percy S. F. van. *Two Versions of the Solomon Narrative: An Inquiry into the Relationship between MT 1 Kgs. 2–11 and LXX 3 Reg. 2–11.* VTSup 104. Leiden: Brill, 2005.

Klein, Ralph W. *1 Chronicles: A Commentary.* Hermeneia. Minneapolis: Fortress Press, 2006.

————. "Chronicles, Books of 1–2." *ABD* 1:992-1002.

————. "Reflections on Historiography in the Account of Jehoshaphat." Pages 643–57 in *Pomegranates and Golden Bells: Studies in Biblical, Jewish, and Near Eastern Ritual, Law, and Literature in Honor of Jacob Milgrom*. Edited by David P. Wright, David Noel Freedman, and Avi Hurvitz. Winona Lake, Ind.: Eisenbrauns, 1995.

Knauf, Ernst Axel. "Does 'Deuteronomistic Historiography' (DH) Exist?" Pages 388–98 in *Israel Constructs Its History: Deuteronomistic Historiography in Recent Research*. Edited by Albert de Pury, Thomas Römer, and Jean-Daniel Macchi. JSOTSup 306. Sheffield: Sheffield Academic Press, 2000.

Knoppers, Gary N. *I Chronicles 1–9: A New Translation with Introduction and Commentary*. AB 12. New York: Doubleday, 2003.

————. *1 Chronicles 10–29: A New Translation with Introduction and Commentary*. AB 12A. New York: Doubleday, 2004.

————. "Greek Historiography and the Chronicler's History: A Reexamination." *JBL* 122 (2003): 627–50.

————. "Hierodules, Priests, or Janitors? The Levites in Chronicles and the History of the Israelite Priesthood." *JBL* 118 (1999): 49–72.

————. "History and Historiography: The Royal Reforms." Pages 178–203 in *The Chronicler as Historian*. Edited by M. Patrick Graham, Kenneth G. Hoglund, and Steven L. McKenzie. JSOTSup 238. Sheffield: Sheffield Academic Press, 1997.

————, ed. "In Conversation with W. M. Schniedewind, *How the Bible Became a Book: The Textualization of Ancient Israel*." *Journal of Hebrew Scriptures* 5 (2004–5): Article 18.

————. "Treasures Won and Lost: Royal (Mis)appropriations in Kings and Chronicles." Pages 181–208 in *The Chronicler as Author: Studies in Text and Texture*. Edited by M. Patrick Graham and Steven L. McKenzie. JSOTSup 263. Sheffield: Sheffield Academic Press, 1999.

————. *Two Nations under God: The Deuteronomistic History of Solomon and the Dual Monarchies*. Vol. 2, *The Reign of Jeroboam, the Fall of Israel, and the Reign of Josiah*. HSM 53. Atlanta: Scholars Press, 1994.

————. "'Yhwh Is Not with Israel': Alliances as a *Topos* in Chronicles." *CBQ* 58 (1996): 601–26.

Koch, Klaus. "Weltordnung und Reichsidee im alten Iran und ihre Auswirkungen auf die Province Jehud," Pages 133–337 in *Reichsidee und Reichsorganisation im Perserreich*. Edited by Peter Frei and Klaus Koch. OBO 55. Göttingen: Vandenhoeck & Ruprecht, 1996.

Kottsieper, Ingo. "'And They Did Not Care to Speak Yehudit': On Linguistic Change in Judah during the Late Persian Era." Pages 95–124 in *Judah and the Judeans in the Fourth Century B.C.E.* Edited by Oded Lipschits, Gary N. Knoppers, and Rainer Albertz. Winona Lake, Ind.: Eisenbrauns, 2007.

Kratz, Reinhard G. "Ezra—Priest and Scribe. Pages 163–88 in *Scribes, Sages, and Seers: The Sage in the Eastern Mediterranean World*. Edited by Leo G. Perdue. FRLANT 219. Göttingen: Vandenhoeck & Ruprecht, 2008.

Lemaire, André. "The Sage in School and Temple." Pages 165–81 in *The Sage in Israel and the Ancient Near East*. Edited by John G. Gammie and Leo G. Perdue. Winona Lake, Ind.: Eisenbrauns, 1990.

Lemke, Werner E. "The Synoptic Problem in the Chronicler's History." *HTR* 58 (1965): 349–63.

Leuchter, Mark, ed. "Scribes before and after 587 BCE: A Conversation," *Journal of Hebrew Scriptures* 7 (2007): Article 10.

Levin, Yigal. "Who Was the Chronicler's Audience? A Hint from His Genealogies." *JBL* 122 (2003): 229–45.

Lohfink, Norbert, "Gab es eine deuteronomistische Bewegung?" Pages 313–82 in *Jeremia und die "deuteronomistische Bewegung."* Edited by Walter Groß. Bonner Biblische Beiträge 98. Weinheim: BELTZ Athenäum, 1995.

Lord, Albert B. *The Singer of Tales*. Harvard Studies in Comparative Literature 24. Cambridge, Mass.: Harvard University Press, 1960.

McCarter, P. Kyle, Jr. *I Samuel: A New Translation with Introduction, Notes, and Commentary*. AB 8. Garden City, N.Y.: Doubleday, 1980.

———. *II Samuel: A New Translation with Introduction, Notes, and Commentary*. AB 9. New York: Doubleday, 1984.

———. "The Sage in the Deuteronomistic History." Pages 289–93 in *The Sage in Israel and the Ancient Near East*. Edited by John G. Gammie and Leo G. Perdue. Winona Lake, Ind.: Eisenbrauns, 1990.

McDonald, M. C. A. "Literacy in an Oral Environment." Pages 49–118 in *Writing and Ancient Near Eastern Society: Papers in Honor of Alan R. Millard*. Edited by Piotr Bienkowski, Christopher Mee, and Elizabeth Slater. Library of Hebrew Bible/Old Testament Studies 426. London: T&T Clark, 2005.

McKenzie, Steven L. *1–2 Chronicles*. Abingdon Old Testament Commentaries. Nashville: Abingdon, 2004.

———. "1 Kings 8: A Sample Study into the Texts of Kings Used by the Chronicler and Translated by the Old Greek." *BIOSCS* 19 (1986): 15–34.

———. "The Chronicler as Redactor." Pages 70–90 in *The Chronicler as Author: Studies in Text and Texture*. Edited by M. Patrick Graham and Steven L. McKenzie. JSOTSup 263. Sheffield: Sheffield Academic Press, 1999.

———. *The Chronicler's Use of the Deuteronomistic History*. HSM 33. Atlanta: Scholars Press, 1985.

———. "The Prophetic History and the Redaction of Kings." *HAR* 9 (1985): 203–20.

———. "A Response to Thomas Römer, *The So-Called Deuteronomistic History*." Pages 15–21 in "In Conversation with Thomas Römer, *The So-Called Deuteronomistic History: A Sociological, Historical, and Literary Introduction*." *Journal of Hebrew Scriptures* 9 (2009): Article 17.

————. "The Trouble with King Jehoshaphat." Pages 299–314 in *Reflection and Refraction: Studies in Biblical Historiography in Honour of A. Graeme Auld.* Edited by Robert Rezetko, Timothy H. Lim, and W. Brian Aucker. VTSup 113. Leiden: Brill, 2007.

————. *The Trouble with Kings: The Composition of the Book of Kings in the Deuteronomistic History.* VTSup 42. Leiden: Brill, 1991.

————. "Trouble with Kingship." Pages 286–314 in *Israel Constructs Its History: Deuteronomistic Historiography in Recent Research.* Edited by Albert de Pury, Thomas Römer, and Jean-Daniel Macchi. JSOTSup 306. Sheffield: Sheffield Academic Press, 2000.

McKenzie, Steven L., and M. Patrick Graham, eds. *The History of Israel's Traditions: The Heritage of Martin Noth.* JSOTSup 182. Sheffield: Sheffield Academic Press, 1994.

McKenzie, Steven L., and Linda S. Schearing, eds. *Those Elusive Deuteronomists: The Phenomenon of Pan-Deuteronomism.* JSOTSup 268. Sheffield: Sheffield Academic Press, 1996.

Meyers, Carol L., and Eric M. Meyers. *Haggai–Zechariah 1–8: A New Translation with Introduction and Commentary.* AB 25B. Garden City, N.Y.: Doubleday, 1987.

Miller, J. Maxwell. "The Elisha Cycle and the Accounts of the Omride Wars." *JBL* 85 (1966): 441–54.

Mitchell, Christine. "The Dialogism of Chronicles." Pages 311–26 in *The Chronicler as Author: Studies in Text and Texture.* Edited by M. Patrick Graham and Steven L. McKenzie. JSOTSup 263. Sheffield: Sheffield Academic Press, 1999.

————. "Otherness and Historiography in Chronicles." Pages 93–109 in *Historiography and Identity: (Re)formulation in Second Temple Historiographical Literature.* Edited by Louis C. Jonker. Library of Hebrew Bible/Old Testament Studies 534. London: T&T Clark, 2010.

Niditch, Susan. *Oral World and Written Word: Ancient Israelite Literature.* Louisville: Westminster John Knox, 1996.

Noth, Martin. *The Chronicler's History.* Translated by H. G. M. Williamson. JSOTSup 50. Sheffield: Sheffield Academic Press, 2001.

————. *The Deuteronomistic History.* Translated by E. W. Nicholson. JSOTSup 15. Sheffield: JSOT Press, 1981.

————. *Überlieferungsgeschichtliche Studien.* Tübingen: Niemeyer, 1943.

Oeming, Manfred. "'See, We Are Serving Today' (Nehemiah 9:36): Nehemiah 9 as a Theological Interpretation of the Persian Period." Pages 571–88 in *Judah and the Judeans in the Persian Period.* Edited by Oded Lipschits and Manfred Oeming. Winona Lake, Ind.: Eisenbrauns, 2006.

O'Keefe, Katherine O. *Visible Song: Transitional Literacy in Old English Verse.* Cambridge: Cambridge University Press, 1990.

Orlinsky, Harry M. "The Kings-Isaiah Recensions of the Hezekiah Story." *JQR* 30 (1939/40): 33–49.

Parry, Milman. "A Comparative Study of Diction as One of the Elements of Style in Early Greek Epic Poetry." Pages 421–36 in *The Making of Homeric Verse: The Collected Papers of Milman Parry.* Edited by A. Parry. Oxford: Oxford University Press, 1971.

Peltonen, Kai "Function, Explanation and Literary Phenomena: Aspects of Source Criticism as Theory and Method in the History of Chronicles Research." Pages 18–69 in *The Chronicler as Author: Studies in Text and Texture.* Edited by M. Patrick Graham and Steven L. McKenzie. JSOTSup 263. Sheffield: Sheffield Academic Press, 1999.

―――. "A Jigsaw with a Model? The Date of Chronicles." Pages 225–71 in *Did Moses Speak Attic? Jewish Historiography and Scripture in the Hellenistic Period.* Edited by Lester L. Grabbe. JSOTSup 317. Sheffield: Sheffield Academic Press, 2001.

Perdue, Leo G. "Sages, Scribes, and Seers in Israel and the Ancient Near East: An Introduction," Pages 1–34 in *Scribes, Sages, and Seers: The Sage in the Eastern Mediterranean World.* Edited by Leo G. Perdue. FRLANT 219. Göttingen: Vandenhoeck & Ruprecht, 2008.

Person, Raymond F., Jr. "II Kings 24, 18–25, 30 and Jeremiah 52: A Text-Critical Case Study in the Redaction History of the Deuteronomistic History." *ZAW* 105 (1993): 174–205.

―――."The Ancient Israelite Scribe as Performer." *JBL* 117 (1998): 601–9.

―――. "The Deuteronomic History and the Book of Chronicles: Scribal Works in an Oral World." In *Raising Up a Faithful Exegete: Essays in Honor of Richard D. Nelson.* Edited by Kurt L. Noll and Brooks Schramm. Winona Lake, Ind.: Eisenbrauns, 2010.

―――. "The Deuteronomic History and the Books of Chronicles: Contemporary Competing Historiographies." Pages 315–36 in *Reflection and Refraction: Studies in Biblical Historiography in Honour of A. Graeme Auld.* Edited by Robert Rezetko, Timothy H. Lim, and W. Brian Aucker. VTSup 113. Leiden: Brill, 2006.

―――. *The Deuteronomic School: History, Social Setting, and Literature.* Studies in Biblical Literature 2. Atlanta: Society of Biblical Literature, 2002.

―――, ed. "In Conversation with Thomas Römer, *The So-Called Deuteronomistic History: A Sociological, Historical, and Literary Introduction.*" *Journal of Hebrew Scriptures* 9 (2009): Article 17.

―――. "Identity (Re)Formation as the Historical Circumstances Required." Pages 113–21 in *Historiography and Identity: (Re)formulation in Second Temple Historiographical Literature.* Edited by Louis C. Jonker. Library of Hebrew Bible/Old Testament Studies 534. London: T&T Clark, 2010.

―――. *The Kings–Isaiah and Kings–Jeremiah Recensions.* BZAW 252. Berlin: Walter de Gruyter, 1997.

―――. "A Rolling Corpus and Oral Tradition: A Not-So-Literate Solution to a Highly Literate Problem." Pages 263–71 in *Troubling Jeremiah.* Edited by

A. R. P. Diamond, K. M. O'Connor, and L. Stulman. JSOTSup 260. Sheffield: Sheffield Academic Press, 1999.

———. "A Reassessment of Wiederaufnahme from the Perspective of Conversation Analysis." *BZ* 43 (1999): 241–48.

———. Review of *The So-Called Deuteronomistic History*, by Thomas Römer. *CBQ* 69 (2007): 561–62.

———. *Second Zechariah and the Deuteronomic School*. JSOTSup 167. Sheffield: Sheffield Academic Press, 1993.

———. "The Story of David and Goliath from the Perspective of the Study of Oral Traditions." In *Celebrate Her for the Fruit of Her Hands: Studies in Honor of Carol L. Meyers*. Edited by Charles C. Carter and Karla G. Bolmbach. Winona Lake, Ind.: Eisenbrauns, forthcoming.

———. *Structure and Meaning in Conversation and Literature*. Lanham, Md.: University Press of America, 1999.

Person, Raymond F., Jr., and Konrad Schmid, eds. *Deuteronomy in the Pentateuch, Hexateuch, and the Deuteronomistic History*. FAT. Stuttgart: Mohr Siebeck, forthcoming in 2012.

Pietersma, Albert, and Benjamin G. Wright. *A New English Translation of the Septuagint*. Oxford: Oxford University Press, 2009. Also at http://ccat.sas.upenn.edu/nets/edition/.

Polak, Frank H. "The Septuagint Account of Solomon's Reign: Revision and Ancient Recension." Pages 139–64 in *X Congress of the International Organization for Septuagint and Cognate Studies, Oslo 1998*. Edited by Bernard A. Taylor. SBLSCS 51. Atlanta: Society of Biblical Literature, 2001.

Polaski, Donald C. "What Mean These Stones? Inscriptions, Textuality and Power in Persia and Yehud." Pages 37–48 in *Approaching Yehud: New Approaches to the Study of the Persian Period*. Edited by Jon L. Berquist. SemeiaSt 50. Atlanta: Society of Biblical Literature, 2007.

Polzin, Robert. *Late Biblical Hebrew: Toward a Historical Typology of Biblical Hebrew Prose*. HSM 12. Missoula, Mont.: Scholars Press, 1976.

Puech, Émile "Les écoles dans l'Israël preexilique: données épigraphiques." Pages 189–203 in *Congress Volume: Jerusalem 1986*. Edited by J. A. Emerton. VTSup 40. Leiden: Brill, 1988.

Redditt, Paul L. "The Dependence of Ezra–Nehemiah on 1 and 2 Chronicles." Pages 216–40 in *Unity and Disunity in Ezra–Nehemiah: Redaction, Rhetoric, and Reader*. Edited by Mark J. Boda and Paul L. Redditt. Sheffield: Sheffield Phoenix, 2008.

Rendsburg, Gary A. "Hurvitz Redux: On the Continued Scholarly Inattention to a Simple Principle of Hebrew Philology." Pages 104–28 in *Biblical Hebrew: Studies in Chronology and Typology*. Edited by Ian Young. JSOTSup 369. London: T&T Clark, 2003.

Rendtorff, Rolf. "Chronicles and the Priestly Torah." Pages 259–66 in *Text, Temples, and Traditions: A Tribute to Menahem Haran*. Edited by Michael V. Fox et al. Winona Lake, Ind.: Eisenbrauns, 1996.

Rezetko, Robert. "Dating Biblical Hebrew: Evidence from Samuel-Kings and Chronicles." Pages 215–50 in *Biblical Hebrew: Studies in Chronology and Typology*. Edited by Ian Young. JSOTSup 369. London: T&T Clark, 2003.

———. "'Late' Common Nouns in the Book of Chronicles." Pages 379–417 in *Reflection and Refraction: Studies in Biblical Historiography in Honour of A. Graeme Auld*. Edited by Robert Rezetko, Timothy H. Lim, and W. Brian Aucker. VTSup 113. Leiden: Brill, 2007.

———. *Source and Revision in the Narratives of David's Transfer of the Ark: Text, Language, and Story in 2 Samuel 6 and 1 Chronicles 13; 15–16*. Library of Biblical Studies 470. London: T&T Clark, 2007.

———. "The Spelling of 'Damascus' and the Linguistic Dating of Biblical Texts." *SJOT* 24 (2010): 119-37.

———. "What Happened to the Book of Samuel in the Persian Period and Beyond?" Pages 237-52 in *A Palimpsest: Rhetoric, Ideology, Stylistics and Language Relating to Persian Israel*. Edited by Ehud Ben Zvi, Diana V. Edelman, and Frank Polak. Perspectives on Hebrew Scriptures and Its Contexts 5. Piscataway, N.J.: Gorgias Press, 2009.

Ristau, Kenneth A. "Reading and Rereading Josiah: The Chronicler's Representation of Josiah for the Postexilic Community." Pages 219–47 in *Community Identity in Judean Historiography: Biblical and Comparative Perspectives*. Edited by Gary N. Knoppers and Kenneth A. Ristau. Winona Lake, Ind.: Eisenbrauns, 2009.

Rofé, Alexander. "The Battle of David and Goliath: Folklore, Theology, Eschatology." Pages 117–51 in *Judaic Perspectives on Ancient Israel*. Edited by J. Neusner, A. Levine, and E. S. Frerichs. Philadelphia: Fortress, 1987.

Römer, Thomas. "Response to Richard Nelson, Steven McKenzie, Eckart Otto, and Yairah Amit." Pages 36–49 in "In Conversation with Thomas Römer, *The So-Called Deuteronomistic History: A Sociological, Historical, and Literary Introduction*." *Journal of Hebrew Scriptures* 9 (2009): Article 17.

———. *The So-Called Deuteronomistic History: A Sociological, Historical and Literary Introduction*. London: T&T Clark, 2007.

Schams, Christine. *Jewish Scribes in the Second Temple Period*. JSOTSup 291. Sheffield: Sheffield Academic Press, 1998.

Schaper, Joachim. "The Living Word Engraved in Stone: The Interrelationship of the Oral and the Written and the Culture of Memory in the Books of Deuteronomy and Joshua." Pages 9–23 in *Memory in the Bible and Antiquity: The Fifth Durham-Tübingen Research Symposium (Durham, September 2004)*. Edited by Stephen C. Barton, Loren T. Stuckenbruck, and Benjamin G. Wold. WUNT 212. Tübingen: Mohr Siebeck, 2007.

———. "A Theology of Writing: The Oral and the Written, God as Scribe, and the Book of Deuteronomy." Pages 97–119 in *Anthropology and Biblical Studies: Avenues of Approach*. Edited by Louise J. Lawrence and Mario I. Aguilar. Leiden: Deo, 2004.

Schenker, Adrian. *Älteste Textgeschichte der Königsbücher: Die hebräischen Vorlage der ursprunglichen Septuaginta als älteste Textform der Königsbucher.* OBO 199. Fribourg: Academic Press, 2004.

—————, ed. *The Earliest Text of the Hebrew Bible: The Relationship between the Masoretic Text and the Hebrew Base of the Septuagint Reconsidered.* SBLSCS 52. Atlanta: Society of Biblical Literature, 2003.

—————. "Jeroboam and the Division of the Kingdom in the Ancient Septuagint: LXX 3 Kingdoms 12:24a–z, MT 1 Kings 11–12; 14 and the Deuteronomistic History." Pages 214–57 in *Israel Constructs Its History: Deuteronomistic Historiography in Recent Research.* Edited by Albert de Pury, Thomas Römer, and Jean-Daniel Macchi. JSOTSup 306. Sheffield: Sheffield Academic Press, 2000.

—————. "Junge Garden oder akrobatische Tänzer? Das Verhältnis zwischen 1 Kön 20 MT und 2 Regn 21 LXX." Pages 17–34 in *The Earliest Text of the Hebrew Bible: The Relationship between the Masoretic Text and the Hebrew Base of the Septuagint Reconsidered.* Edited by Adrian Schenker. SBLSCS 52. Atlanta: Society of Biblical Literature, 2003.

—————. *Septante et texte massorétique dans l'histoire la plus ancienne du texts de 1 Rois 2–14.* CahRB 48. Paris: J. Gabalda, 2000.

—————. "Die Textgeschichte der Königsbücher und ihre Konsequenzen für die Textgeschichte der hebräischen Bibel, illustriert am Beispiel von 2 Kön 23:1–3." Pages 65–79 in *Congress Volume: Leiden 2004.* Edited by André Lemaire. VTSup 109. Leiden: Brill, 2006.

Schniedewind, William M. "The Chronicler as an Interpreter of Scripture." Pages 158–80 in *The Chronicler as Author: Studies in Text and Texture.* Edited by M. Patrick Graham and Steven L. McKenzie. JSOTSup 263. Sheffield: Sheffield Academic Press, 1999.

—————. "The Evolution of Name Theology." Pages 228–39 in *The Chronicler as Theologian: Essays in Honor of Ralph W. Klein.* Edited by M. Patrick Graham, Steven L. McKenzie, and Gary N. Knoppers. JSOTSup 371. London: T&T Clark, 2003.

—————. *How the Bible Became a Book: The Textualization of Ancient Israel.* Cambridge: Cambridge University Press, 2003.

Shenkel, James Donald. *Chronology and Recensional Development in the Greek Text of Kings.* HSM 1. Cambridge, Mass.: Harvard University Press, 1968.

Snyman, Gerrie. "A Possible World of Text Production for the Genealogy in 1 Chronicles 2.3–4.23." Pages 32–60 in *The Chronicler as Theologian: Essays in Honor of Ralph W. Klein.* Edited by M. Patrick Graham, Steven L. McKenzie, and Gary N. Knoppers. JSOTSup 371. London: T&T Clark, 2003.

Sonnet, Jean-Pierre. *The Book within the Book: Writing in Deuteronomy.* Biblical Interpretation Series 14. Leiden: Brill, 1997.

Sparks, James T. *The Chronicler's Genealogies: Towards an Understanding of 1 Chronicles 1–9.* Academia Biblica 28. Atlanta: Society of Biblical Literature, 2008.

Stock, Brian. *The Implications of Literacy: Written Language and Models of Inter-pretation in the Eleventh and Twelfth Centuries*. Princeton: Princeton University Press, 1983.

———. *Listening for the Text: On the Uses of the Past*. Parallax. Baltimore: John Hopkins University Press, 1990.

Stott, Katherine M. *Why Did They Write This Way? Reflections on References to Written Documents in the Hebrew Bible and Ancient Literature*. Library of Hebrew Bible/Old Testament Studies 492. New York: T&T Clark, 2008.

Talmon, Shemaryahu. "Conflate Readings (OT)." *IDBSup*, 170–73.

Talshir, Zipora. *The Alternative Story of the Division of the Kingdom. 2 Kingdoms 12:24a–z*. Jerusalem Biblical Studies 6. Jerusalem: Simor, 1993.

———. "The Contribution of Diverging Traditions Preserved in the Septuagint to Literary Criticism of the Bible." Pages 21–41 in *VIII Congress of the International Organization for Septuagint and Cognate Studies*. Edited by Leonard Greenspoon and Olivier Munnich. SBLSCS 41. Atlanta: Scholars Press, 1995.

———. "Is the Alternate Tradition of the Division of the Kingdom (3 Kgdms 12:24a–z) Non-Deuteronomistic?" Pages 599–621 in *Septuagint, Scrolls and Cognate Writings*. Edited by George J. Brooke and Barnabas Lindars. SBLSCS 33. Atlanta: Scholars Press, 1992.

———. "The Reign of Solomon in the Making: Pseudo-Connections between 3 Kingdoms and Chronicles." *VT* 50 (2000): 233–49.

Thomas, Rosalind. *Oral Tradition and Written Record in Classical Athens*. Cambridge Studies in Oral and Literate Culture 18. Cambridge: Cambridge University Press, 1989.

Throntveit, Mark A. "The Relationship of Hezekiah to David and Solomon in the Books of Chronicles." Pages 105–21 in *The Chronicler as Theologian: Essays in Honor of Ralph W. Klein*. Edited by M. Patrick Graham, Steven L. McKenzie, and Gary N. Knoppers. JSOTSup 371. London: T&T Clark, 2003.

Toorn, Karel van der. *Scribal Culture and the Making of the Hebrew Bible*. Cambridge, Mass.: Harvard University Press, 2007.

Tov, Emanuel. "The Composition of I Samuel 16–18 in the Light of the Septuagint Version." Pages 97–130 in *Empirical Models for Biblical Criticism*. Edited by Jeffrey H. Tigay. Philadelphia: University of Pennsylvania Press, 1985.

———. "Some Sequence Differences between the MT and LXX and Their Ramifications for the Literary Criticism of the Bible." *JNSL* 13 (1987): 151–60.

———. *Textual Criticism of the Hebrew Bible*. Minneapolis: Fortress, 1992.

Trebolle, Julio C. "Conflate Readings in the Old Testament." *ABD* 1:1125–28.

———. "The Different Textual Forms of MT and LXX in Kings and the History of the Deuteronomistic Composition and Redaction of These Books." Paper presented at the annual meeting of the Society of Biblical Literature, New Orleans, November 2009.

———. "From the 'Old Latin' through the 'Old Greek' to the 'Old Hebrew' (2 Kings 10:23–25)." *Textus* 11 (1984): 17–36.

————. "Kings (MT/LXX) and Chronicles: The Double and Triple Textual Tradition." Pages 483–501 in *Reflection and Refraction: Studies in Biblical Historiography in Honour of A. Graeme Auld.* Edited by Robert Rezetko, Timothy H. Lim, and W. Brian Aucker. VTSup 113. Leiden: Brill, 2007.

————. "Light from 4QJudgᵃ and 4QKgs on the Text of Judges and Kings." Pages 315–24 in *The Dead Sea Scrolls: Forty Years of Research.* Edited by Devorah Dimant and Uriel Rappaport. STDJ 10. Leiden: Brill, 1992.

————. "Old Latin, Old Greek and Old Hebrew in the Book of Kings (1 Ki. 18:25 and 2 Ki. 20:11)." *Textus* 13 (1986): 85–94.

————. "Redaction, Recension, and Midrash in the Books of Kings." *BIOSCS* 15 (1982): 12–35.

————. *Salomón y Jeroboán: Historia de la recensión y redacción de 1 Reyes, 2–12, 14.* Bibliotheca Salmanticensis: Dissertationes 3. Salamanca: Universidad Pontificia, 1980.

————. "Samuel/Kings and Chronicles: Book Divisions and Textual Composition." Pages 96–108 in *Studies in the Hebrew Bible, Qumran, and the Septuagint Presented to Eugene Ulrich.* Edited by Peter W. Flint, Emanuel Tov, and James C. VanderKam. VTSup 101. Leiden: Brill, 2006.

————. "The Story of David and Goliath (1 Sam 17–18): Textual Variants and Literary Composition." *BIOSCS* 23 (1990): 16–30.

————. "The Text-Critical Use of the Septuagint in the Books of Kings." Pages 285–99 in *VII Congress of the International Organization for Septuagint and Cognate Studies, Leuven, 1989.* Edited by Claude E. Cox. SBLSCS 31. Atlanta: Scholars Press, 1991.

Ulrich, Eugene C. *The Qumran Text of Samuel and Josephus.* HSM 19. Missoula, Mont.: Scholars Press, 1978.

VanderKam, James C. "Ezra–Nehemiah or Ezra and Nehemiah?" Pages 55–75 in *Priests, Prophets and Scribes: Essays on the Formation and Heritage of Second Temple Judaism in Honour of Joseph Blenkinsopp.* Edited by Eugene Ulrich et al. JSOTSup 149. Sheffield: Sheffield Academic Press, 1992.

Van Seters, John. "The Chronicler's Account of Solomon's Temple-Building: A Continuity Theme." Pages 283–300 in *The Chronicler as Historian.* Edited by M. Patrick Graham, Kenneth G. Hoglund, and Steven L. McKenzie. JSOTSup 238. Sheffield: Sheffield Academic Press, 1997.

————. *The Edited Bible: The Curious History of the "Editor" in Biblical Criticism.* Winona Lake, Ind.: Eisenbrauns, 2006.

————. "Problems in the Literary Analysis of the Court History of King David," *JSOT* 1 (1976): 22–29.

————. "The 'Shared Text' of Samuel–Kings and Chronicles Re-examined." Pages 503–15 in *Reflection and Refraction: Studies in Biblical Historiography in Honour of A. Graeme Auld.* Edited by Robert Rezetko, Timothy H. Lim, and W. Brian Aucker. VTSup 113. Leiden: Brill, 2007.

Weinfeld, Moshe. *Deuteronomy and the Deuteronomic School.* Oxford: Clarendon, 1972.

Westermann, Claus. *Die Geschichtsbücher des Alten Testaments: Gab es ein deuteronomistisches Geschichtswerk?* Theologische Bücherei 87. Gütersloh: Chr. Kaiser, 1994.

Whybray, R. N. "The Sage in the Israelite Royal Court." Pages 133–39 in *The Sage in Israel and the Ancient Near East.* Edited by John G. Gammie and Leo G. Perdue. Winona Lake, Ind.: Eisenbrauns, 1990.

Williamson, H. G. M. *1 and 2 Chronicles.* NCB. Grand Rapids: Eerdmans, 1982.

———. "The Death of Josiah and the Continuing Development of the Deuteronomic History." *VT* 32 (1982): 242–48.

———. *Israel in the Books of Chronicles.* Cambridge/New York: Cambridge University Press, 1977.

———. "Reliving the Death of Josiah: A Reply to C. T. Begg." *VT* 37 (1987): 9–15.

Wright, Jacob L. "A New Model for the Composition of Ezra–Nehemiah." Pages 333–48 in *Judah and the Judeans in the Fourth Century B.C.E.* Edited by Oded Lipschits, Gary N. Knoppers, and Rainer Albertz. Winona Lake, Ind.: Eisenbrauns, 2007.

———. "Seeking, Finding and Writing in Ezra–Nehemiah." Pages 277–304 in *Unity and Disunity in Ezra–Nehemiah: Redaction, Rhetoric, and Reader.* Edited by Mark J. Boda and Paul L. Redditt. Sheffield: Sheffield Phoenix, 2008.

———. "Writing the Restoration: Compositional Agenda and the Role of Ezra in Nehemiah 8," Pages 19–29 in "Scribes Before and After 587 BCE: A Conversation," *Journal of Hebrew Scriptures* 7 (2007): Article 10.

Wright, John W. "The Fabula of the Book of Chronicles." Pages 136–55 in *The Chronicler as Author: Studies in Text and Texture.* Edited by M. Patrick Graham and Steven L. McKenzie. JSOTSup 263. Sheffield: Sheffield Academic Press, 1999.

———. "Remapping Yehud: The Borders of Yehud and the Genealogies of Chronicles." Pages 67–89 in *Judah and the Judeans in the Persian Period.* Edited by Oded Lipschits and Manfred Oeming. Winona Lake, Ind.: Eisenbrauns, 2006.

Würthwein, Ernst. "Erwägungen zum sog. Deuteronomistischen Geschichtswerk: Eine Skizze." Pages 1–11 in *Studien zum Deuteronomistischen Geschichtswerk.* BZAW 227. Berlin: Walter de Gruyter, 1994.

Young, Ian, ed. *Biblical Hebrew: Studies in Chronology and Typology.* JSOTSup 369. London: T&T Clark, 2003.

———. "Introduction: The Origin of the Problem." Pages 1–6 in *Biblical Hebrew: Studies in Chronology and Typology.* Edited by Ian Young. JSOTSup 369. London: T&T Clark, 2003.

———. "Late Biblical Hebrew and Hebrew Inscriptions." Pages 276–311 in *Biblical Hebrew: Studies in Chronology and Typology.* Edited by Ian Young. JSOTSup 369. London: T&T Clark, 2003.

————. "Late Biblical Hebrew and the Qumran Pesher Habakkuk," *Journal of Hebrew Scriptures* 8 (2008): Article 25.

————. "What Is 'Late Biblical Hebrew'?" Pages 253–68 in *A Palimpsest: Rhetoric, Ideology, Stylistics and Language Relating to Persian Israel.* Edited by Ehud Ben Zvi, Diana V. Edelman, and Frank Polak. Perspectives on Hebrew Scriptures and Its Contexts 5. Piscataway, N.J.: Gorgias Press, 2009.

Young, Ian, Robert Rezetko, and Martin Ehrensvärd. *Linguistic Dating of Biblical Texts.* 2 vols. London/Oakville, Conn.: Equinox, 2008.

Zevit, Ziony. Review of *Biblical Hebrew: Studies in Typology and Chronology,* edited by Ian Young. *Review of Biblical Literature* 8 (2004), http://www.bookreviews.org/pdf/4084_3967.pdf.

Index of Authors

Abadie, Philippe, 175
Aguilar, Mario I., 54n.43, 188
Albertz, Rainer, 14, 175, 192
Amit, Yairah, 9n.17, 57n.53, 133n.2, 175, 177, 182, 188
Armistead, Samuel G., 46n.14, 180
Aucker, W. Brian, ix n.3, xii, 17n.45, 26n.11, 116n.87, 178, 185, 186, 188, 191
Auld, A. Graeme, ix, 5, 6–9, 10, 16–17, 19, 25, 27–28, 88–89, 95, 97, 101n.41, 102n.43, 104, 105, 108, 109, 110–11, 114–15, 116, 118, 120, 125–27, 129, 134n.7, 135, 137, 163, 164–67, 170, 171, 175–76

Barthélemy, Dominique, 176
Barton, Stephen C., 54n.43, 188
Becking, Bob, 176
Ben Zvi, Ehud, xi, 12n.25, 32n.30, 35n.45, 37n.52, 39n.57, 57n.53, 82n.28, 116–17, 121n.102, 123, 125, 129n.120, 137n.20, 148nn.54–55, 149–50, 156–57, 158n.90, 168, 170, 176–77, 182, 188, 193
Berquist, Jon L., 12–13, 54n.45, 159n.91, 177, 187
Bienkowski, Piotr, 45n.13, 52n.36, 179, 184
Blenkinsopp, Joseph, 19n.55, 51n.31, 52n.38, 64n.62, 177
Blount, Ben G., 72–74, 80, 85, 177
Boda, Mark J., 14nn.33–34, 35n.45, 64n.62, 157–59, 161, 177–78, 181, 187, 192
Bolmbach, Karla G., xii, 187

Brett, Mark G., 174, 178
Brooke, George J., 17, 178, 190

Carr, David M., xi, 45, 49–50, 51nn.31–32, 51nn.35–36, 52n.38, 54, 56, 84, 88, 100, 109–10, 128, 159, 169, 172, 178
Carroll, Robert P., 10, 178
Carter, Charles C., xii, 178, 187
Chapman, Stephen B., 170n.12, 176
Christian, Mark A., 12n.25, 66n.65, 178
Clanchy, M. T., 46n.15, 178
Cogan, Mordechai, 111n.76, 178
Coggins, Richard, 7n.15, 178–79
Cox, Claude E., 107n.53, 191
Crawford, Sidnie White, 93n.23, 179
Crenshaw, James L., 52, 179
Crim, Keith, vii
Cross, Frank Moore, 3, 17n.47, 179
Culley, Robert C., 45, 179

Davies, Graham, 52n.36, 179
Davies, Jon, 7n.15, 176, 179
Davies, Philip R., 51n.32, 51nn.34–36, 179
Day, John, 52n.36, 179
de Pury, Albert, 6n.12, 10n.19, 141n.32, 149n.59, 182, 183, 185, 189
Dell, Katherine, 51n.34, 179
Diamond, A. R. P., 187
Dimant, Devorah, 106n.53, 191
Dozeman, Thomas, 88n.7, 178
Draper, Jonathan A., 49n.26, 180
Duke, Rodney K., 13n.30, 127n.117, 179

INDEX OF SCRIPTURE CITATIONS

CPSIA information can be obtained at www.ICGtesting.com
Printed in the USA
BVOW04s0107230614

356988BV00001B/34/P